Evans, Christopher R.
Cults of unreason

DATE DUE		
Ret FEB 18	MAR 14 1989 RET	FEB 12 1997
JUL 17 Ret	APR 19 1989 RET	MAR 15 1999
FEB 3 Ret	NOV 22 1989 RET	FEB 18 2005
APR 25 ref	FEB 19 1990	APR 22 2014
JUL 13 Ret	APR 27 1990 RET	[redacted] 1995
OCT 4 Ret	NOV 28 1990 RET	MAR 16
JUL 17 RET	.1994	
DEC 02 1988 RET		
FEB 28 1999 RET		

A FINE WILL BE CHARGED FOR EACH OVERDUE BOOK

Cults of Unreason

Cults of Unreason

DR CHRISTOPHER EVANS

Farrar, Straus and Giroux
New York

First American edition, 1974
Library of Congress catalog card number: 73–87694

ISBN 0–374–13324–7

Printed in the United States of America

Contents

Introduction

We live in a world in which change has become the norm. The mountains, rivers, seas and continents may preserve an appearance of immutability, seeming as fixed and as stable to us as they ever seemed to our ancestors, but the fabric of our society, the pattern of rules which governs the complex interrelationships of human beings, is tearing and changing as never before in history. Two centuries ago it was possible for a man to live his life through in an environment devoid of change, with technology static and social laws and philosophical beliefs rigid and unquestionable. Neighbours would remain neighbours, houses rarely changed owners, and the tools which a young man might start work with would be passed on with his death to a new generation. Attitudes to life and death were governed by the religious dogma of the time and were generally held without question and even without much consideration. For most people, apart from those caught up in the convulsion of some war or insurrection, the time course of significant social and political change was such that it could barely be detected within any one lifetime. Society must have seemed as stable as any mountain, as predictable as the procession of the seasons.

The Industrial Revolution wrecked all this. Hillsides which had produced grass and trees for a hundred thousand years were suddenly torn apart and blackened in the hunt for coal. Villages which had maintained social and agricultural dominance of a region since Roman times dwindled into insignificance in comparison with the new industrial cities, populated by migrant workers who have travelled distances which their fathers would have been unable to contemplate. Communications networks of road and rail sprang up, linking all urban and rural communities irrevocably, and human beings began in earnest that restless shuffling from place to place which is the lot of nearly all of us today.

Other data communication networks—cheap books and newspapers, telephones, radio and television—all combined to totter the happy complacency of the old societies. Men could impose their personality and their philosophy on other men by the astute use of such networks infinitely more rapidly, and with far greater effectiveness, than could the conquering generals of the past.

At this time the frenetic rush continues, with technological development hurtling ahead of the conceptual and ideological advances which should ideally match its pace. The tremendous successes of the American and Russian space programmes, which have considerably exceeded even the most optimistic predictions of the science fiction of the 1940s, should warn us of what we are about to face in the future. Even more significant, and yet almost totally unappreciated by the ordinary man or woman, is the really remarkable growth of computer technology which will impact in its most spectacular and far-reaching form in the 1980s to make the upheavals of the Industrial Revolution look tranquil and insignificant.

Faced with these facts, and with the inescapable signs of the impact of science and technology on the world's social organization, one sees some critical questions that need to be answered. The first is probably simply whether Man can survive changes of this kind without some vast neurotic upheaval manifesting either in a major move towards what might be called 'drop-out anarchy', or in a manic swing into nuclear war. To date, no psychologist, anthropologist or sociologist seems to have been able to confront this question adequately—we have no way of knowing whether the human species has the inherent or potential capability to handle the technology it can create, and at the same time preserve identity at both the personal and social level. For this we will have to wait and see, and those of us who are optimists are the fortunate ones. The second major question, which embraces the subject matter of this book, concerns the apparently widening gap between Man's ability to manipulate his environment—as with engineering, physics, astronautics, etc.—and his capacity to comprehend the implications of his technological success and to become a part of the much wider world that has opened up to him. It is in this area—the system of beliefs by which Man relates himself to the unknown forces of the Universe and the great mysteries of space and time, of beginnings, middles and ends—that what we know generally as Religion has lately failed in its ancient role. This failure has become more obvious and dramatic in the the last decade, though the rot set in at the time of Copernicus and the first overt signs of decay did not appear until a century ago.

In fact, until somewhere around the beginning of the nineteenth century—probably there is an association with the disquiet accompanying the Industrial Revolution—the average individual looked to the Bible and to orthodox religious teaching for answers to what he considered to be the important questions about the Universe. At the time these were such natural ones as, 'What is Man?', 'How did he come into existence?', 'Where does God live?', 'What happens after death?', etc., etc. If studied assiduously, the Bible in fact gives fairly straightforward and quite categoric answers to all such questions, and with a little imagination can produce reasonable answers to a good many others of a less religious kind. At the time of Galileo, for example, a flat quotation from Joshua 13 '. . . and the sun stood still . . . and hasted not to go down about a whole day' was counted as being a most suitable refutation for the theories of Copernicus which were based on painstaking scientific observation, but only a few gallant diehards would take this line today. In the past hundred years in particular, what we might term the 'religious answer' has progressively lost its punch, with more and more people turning to the textbooks of science in an attempt at understanding the strange physical and mental environment we live in. The galloping decline of the authority of the Church—particularly in liberal societies such as England, and, to a lesser extent, in the USA—is evident in the shrunken congregations at Anglican churches, and in the decaying brick buildings, proudly erected as Baptist churches a century ago, which now spend their last days ignominiously as cut-price carpet centres, or temporary warehouses. And this decline, despite all the best efforts of media-conscious Bishops on motorcycles, shows no sign of being arrested. For who in this day and age, now that astronauts have waddled around the moon, can really feel that the Archbishop of Canterbury has anything important to say on celestial matters?

Unfortunately where the answers provided by religious

dogma fail to satisfy, there is frequently, as we have pointed out above, no suitable alternative answer provided by science. Science in general refuses to speculate, proffering to its adherents only those facts it considers to be established by virtue of the inductive experimental method. It is useless to ask a scientist—in his working role—such questions as 'Why are we here?', or 'How could the Universe come into being?', for he will merely say that he does not know. Answers are, of course, available from religious teaching, but they are answers which to most people simply don't gel and are really no better than no answer at all. The gap between the discoveries at the frontiers of science and their assimilation into some useful cosmological theory is already immense, and there is a danger that it may grow wider still. To the working scientist this is not necessarily alarming. He realizes that his technology can easily outstrip his philosophy, and holding himself to be a technologist he is content to leave it to the philosopher to make sense of it all. To the vast majority of mankind, however, who are still not yet scientists by any stretch of the imagination, but who are acquiring a more articulate curiosity which modern telecommunications only serve to titillate, this attitude is basically unsatisfying. In their heart of hearts most people still want some fairly simple, reasonably logical answers to the questions that human beings have always asked—answers which will ease the chill which we have all felt when, in the small hours of the morning, we wonder about life and death, time and space, creation and destruction.

These gaps, we will have to agree, need plugging. And if science and present-day philosophy—currently obsessed with semantics and linguistics—are unprepared to offer help, while the great world religions offer only outdated, timeworn and implausible concepts, then the field is ripe as never before for stop-gap systems, pseudo-scientific philosophies, quasi-technological cults and new Messiahs to emerge. They are, in fact, already here, and there is evidence that their strength is growing. We shall examine some of them in this book, and when gazed at with a clinical eye they amuse rather than alarm. Yet they beg for careful study for they are sociological phenomena of great interest and significance. Perhaps more important, they give one a taste of things to come, for if the decline of the old-established religions continues at its present pace, and if technology continues to outstrip advances in the philosophy of science, the need for such cults will increase so that not only will they proliferate but some of the existing ones will rise to real power.

What form do these surrogate belief-systems take? To some extent this depends upon their antiquity, for a full-fledged cult requires some time to mature. Scientology, for example, which is perhaps the most important and in some ways the most disturbing, has now got a measurable history behind it and an international organization with considerable financial resources to support it. It also has a leader who is of the greatest possible significance to the movement, and an organized dogma with means for distributing it. On the other hand, there are more nebulous cults—such as that surrounding a belief in flying saucers—not crystallized into any single organized body, but with considerable intellectual and emotional support in all parts of the world. Yet again there are relatively tiny cults, run by minor eccentric individuals and commanding limited support, though always with the potential for rapid expansion. Some are intellectually naive, others sophisticated to the point of semantic complexity. All are equatable in that, when looked at in close-up, they serve to fill a need which science and technology have created by cutting away the power of the old established religions.

In this book, in the interests of keeping it down to reasonable size, I have concentrated on a cross-section of cults and fads. The best documented and the most immediately significant—that of Scientology—I have tackled at some length for its origins, history and evolution are immensely revealing and of the greatest interest to anyone interested in psychology and sociology. I have also gone into the topic of flying saucers at some length, for, while there is no single dominant cult connected with this, the belief in flying saucers—as Jung pointed out a decade ago—is another important sociological phenomena of our time.

The third segment of the book is devoted to an examination of an interesting, but I hope allowable, diversion from the main theme—the various devices grouped under the generic heading of 'Black Boxes'. Time and again I have found that individuals interested in one or other of today's cults have been peripherally fascinated by mysterious gadgetry of one kind or another, varying from devices such as pendulums used for detecting hidden gold or oil to elaborate boxes with valves, coloured lights and intriguing rotating parts. These devices, I believe, play a very significant role in providing quasi-scientific backing for many cultish beliefs, and are treated—as is the case with the Scientologists' E-meter—with considerable reverence by adherents. They serve to demonstrate (to believers) what is after all the fundamental thesis lying behind all cults—that the mind or soul of Man is a real thing, not a mere epiphenomenon of the brain, and as such is measurable to some degree. They are an attempt to provide tangible proof of the existence of the spirit or life force that motivates our actions, and that survives the disintegration of our puny physical bodies.

Finally I have included a section on a number of the strange varieties of Eastern religious beliefs which are currently flourishing and which have attracted such excitement in the media. If I appear to have spent so little time on such significant figures as the Maharishi Yogi, and concentrated on such lesser characters as Mr Tuesday Lobsang Rampa, it is because in a curious way the latter seems to be exhibiting more staying power. Perhaps the Maharishi's message was really too ascetic for most people's tastes—or maybe Mr Rampa simply tells a better story!

I have deliberately refrained from a detailed analysis of the rather well-known variants of religious belief such as Christian Science, Theosophy, Spiritualism, etc., since these are well-documented elsewhere. Christian Science is a world religion of minority status which sprang up in the nineteenth century as the result of the teachings of Mary Baker Eddy, a curious and dominant personality whose principal belief was that all sickness was illusion—essentially the product of inadequate mental or spiritual outlook. Faith in the fact of the illusory nature of illness is sufficient in itself to ensure total restoration to health. Like Spiritualism, another vigorous minority religion which preaches the possibility of communication with the spirits of dead people, Christian Science is essentially an attempt at a practical expression of basic Christian belief—in one case the power of Faith to heal and in the other the survival of the soul after death. Both these tenets are implicit in orthodox Christian belief (and in most major religious systems even of a non-Christian nature) but are supposed only to have been demonstrated practically in the past by great spiritual figures such as Jesus Christ, certain saints, and so on. The upsurge of both these important variants of Christianity in the nineteenth century is a significant comment on the growing feeling that the orthodox lure was weak in some important aspects. Only now, after decades of formal opposition either to spiritual healing or psychic manifestations, are certain sections of the Established Church beginning to see in these outcrops of orthodoxy their one possible hope for the salvation of a fading cause, and it is no coincidence that a good number of Bishops are members of the Church's Fellowship for Psychical Study and that the Archbishop of Canterbury thought it worthwhile only a decade or so ago to set up a Commission to investigate divine or supernormal healing. However, the rush to incorporate the alleged findings of psychical research to bolster religious dogma appears to have come too late, as these findings are now themselves viewed with the utmost scepticism by most scientists, unlike their eminent Victorian predecessors who treated them with grave sympathy.

They are also not truly contemporary cults, arising to fill gaps in cosmology caused by the onslaught of science, but rather attempts at practical application of one or other aspect of Christian thought. (Nowadays both varieties have almost totally dissociated themselves from the Christian Church, many Spiritualists in fact refusing to accept the divine origin of Christ.) The cults and fads that follow are, as the reader will soon see, products not of the nineteenth century, but very much of the second half of the twentieth century. They draw their logic, their language and their philosophy more from the raw material of science, of psychoanalysis and of the existentialist philosophers than from the traditional sources of religion. The mixture is often a bizarre one, but it is evidently potent enough to capture the minds of hundreds of thousands, even millions, of 'sane men and women on earth today. The students of society among us will watch their evolution with care, and contemporary religious leaders may look to them for possible practical truths, and perhaps even for some useful lessons to be learned.

Cults of Unreason

PART I: THE SCIENCE FICTION RELIGION

In the Beginning . . .

IN THE EARLY summer of 1968 newspapers in England began carrying stories of strange doings in the town of East Grinstead in Sussex. On the outskirts of this well-heeled and slightly snooty community, a commuter suburb for the better type of London advertising executive, an odd cult had set up its headquarters—rather improperly it was felt—in the Maharajah of Jaipur's former abode, Saint Hill Manor. From this elegant Georgian mansion emanated the policies and propaganda of one of the most curious, disturbing and, occasionally, highly entertaining quasi-religious cults of this century, Scientology. Here too, until his exile to a yacht in the Mediterranean, lived the cult's flamboyant founder, one Lafayette Ronald Hubbard, an American science fiction writer, explorer, philosopher *manqué*, mystic and Messiah. In that year of 1968 Scientology and L. Ron Hubbard were to make big news, and people in Britain, and most other parts of the world for that matter, were suddenly to become aware of the name of the cult and to get a taste of its largely unwanted flair for making headlines. Few were to understand what it was all about, and most took it as another passing phase, a nine-day wonder geared to the 'silly season' of the newspaper year. For others, who had looked at it more closely, slightly edgy questions concerning religious tolerance and freedom were raised when the Home Office began to harass the organization on a limited scale, and these issues are not entirely resolved to date. The press turned out to be almost universally hostile, subjecting the Scientologists to a series of flaying and often ill-judged assaults. The police and forces of law and order, provoked by complaints from public and press, reacted uncertainly. Were Scientologists breaking the law? If so, how? Their activities might seem odd, but that was their affair. Still the headlines appeared, first in the local press (SCIENTOLOGY GIRLS IN COURT; ESTATE AGENT HITS BACK AT SCIENTOLOGISTS; CULT BANS 25 BUSINESSES IN GRINSTEAD; etc.) and then in the national papers (MIND BENDERS PESTERED MAN BY POST; CULT CUTS SON OFF FROM FAMILY; SCIENTOLOGY INQUIRY BY THE YARD; etc.) increasing in frequency until a climax was reached in July 1968 when, in a blaze of publicity, Hubbard himself was banned from re-entering the country by order of the Home Secretary.

Of the millions who sampled the delights of this flap in the papers and on TV, few realized that Scientology had had such heady moments before; far from being a mushroom cult destined for a few months of spongy glory, it had been founded with, if possible, even more publicity way back in the early fifties when Hubbard and his activities had leapt into prominence in the United States following the publication of a best-selling book, *Dianetics: The Modern Science of Mental Health.* This is still, incidentally, Hubbard's most famous work and the Scientologists' basic text.

With only the current newspapers to go on the average person can be forgiven for feeling unable to plumb the mysteries of the cult, or to understand the motivation of its founder or, even more, its capacity for attracting enthusiastic and passionate devotees. Scientologists, of course, argue that no one can really understand their movement unless they become part of it themselves—a familiar strategy advanced by almost all other similar organizations. In fact, thanks to the frequently huge press coverage, to the loquacious ranks of its former adherents and, in particular, to Hubbard's own pacy and voluminous writings, a fairly comprehensive history of the movement can be put together, and some clear idea of its principal thesis, its origins and its aims can be grasped. It turns out to be a fascinating story, a sociological legend of our time and, as I have suggested in the introduction, an index of the shape of things to come.

Hubbard claims that the genesis of his ideas lay back in the pre-war years when, as a young man, he trotted around the world with his father, a naval officer, and was able to sample the numerous exotic religious systems that the world enjoys. In a number of his written or spoken statements he makes out that long periods of 'intensive study and research' in far-flung parts of the globe convinced him that the world was in a pretty awful mess and that it ought to be possible for someone, or some new philosophy, to straighten it out. Never unduly modest, he makes it fairly clear that he, Lafayette Ronald Hubbard, and his brainchild, Scientology, ought between them to be able to do the trick.

One of the prime problems in researching the background to Scientology is not that there is any shortage of material, for details are supplied quite lavishly by Hubbard and his aides, but rather the contradictory nature of the details, which are often disconcertingly at odds with the facts that can be gleaned from non-Scientological sources. Nevertheless, Hubbard and Scientology are pretty well inseparable and no history of the cult makes sense without a close inspection of his own background. We must do what we can, therefore, to sort the wheat out from the chaff.

The early years of his life are not particularly well documented and information about his forbears is sparse and confusing. He was born in Tilden, Nebraska, in 1911. In an interview he granted the Sussex *Evening Argus* on 30th April 1959 (just about the time of his move to East Grinstead), he is stated to have claimed that his grandfather was one of the racy pioneers of the far West and 'owned a quarter of Montana'. Hubbard's firstborn son, who also bears the name of Lafayette Ronald Hubbard but is better known by his nick-name, 'Nibs', contradicts this grandiose suggestion. According to him none of his father's family had much in the way of money or property, most of them being small farmers of one kind or another in the American North West and certainly not owning a quarter of the State of Montana. The founder of Scientology's father, who at the time of writing this book, is nearly ninety and still alive and well in the State of Washing-ton, joined the US Navy straight from the farm in 1902 and was an ordinary seaman when Teddy Roosevelt sent the great white fleet around the world. After a year or so he left the navy and worked for a short while as a newspaper reporter but, after being awarded a commission in the Supply Corps, rejoined the navy in 1908. From then until his retirement in later years he toured the world with long spells of duty in China and Japan, and took his wife and young son along with him. No doubt this Asiatic backcloth to his boyhood served to inject into L. Ron's philosophies that unmistakable flavour of the Mystic East which can be detected in them. He has stated that he began formulating the principles of Dianetics and Scientology in 1923 which is not bad for a lad of twelve and suggests that he was a thoughtful, intellectually inclined child.

Occasionally there are references in his writings and lectures to a 'Commander Thompson USN' who had 'studied with Freud in Vienna' and who was to teach Hubbard all he knew about psychoanalysis and Freudian psychology. Thompson, who laboured under the unfortunate nickname of 'Snake', was in fact a navy doctor who was a great chum of L. Ron's father and certainly exerted a good deal of influence over the boy. 'Stimulated by Freud's investigatory spirit and by the encouragement of the late Commander Thompson', the blurb to a recent Scientology publication reads, 'and equipped with personal experience in the Orient with phenomena not generally known in the Western world, Dr Hubbard bent the exactitudes of Occidental engineering to the investigation and practical application of such data to the human mind.'

This, a typical Scientology puff, is the sort of eulogistic waffle that anyone attempting a history of the movement has to contend with. What the phenomena 'not generally known' to the West consists of is impossible to establish, and what the exactitudes of occidental engineering are is never made clear. Commander Thompson, incidentally, is by no means the only intellectual character whose assistance and inspiration Hubbard acknowledges. In the preface to his weird book, *Scientology 8-8008*, he admits to having drawn a few ideas from such other great thinkers as Aristotle, Euclid, Newton, Jesus of Nazareth and Voltaire, to name but five.

The reference to 'Dr' Hubbard in the blurb above is no misprint. In the same piece he is referred to as a 'nuclear physicist' and an engineer and credited with the degree of Ph.D. These claims wilt somewhat under close investigation, but they are of interest and relevance here because they serve to warn one that much of the data on Hubbard or Scientology which appears in its official publications needs to be inspected with a critical eye. What exactly are the facts about Hubbard's professional and academic background?

In the early 1930s a student named Lafayette Ronald

Hubbard was certainly enrolled in the Engineering School of the George Washington University in Washington DC, but evidently something (perhaps it was the occidental engineering) got in the way and he is not recorded as having graduated with even the American Bachelor's degree—something corresponding to a good set of 'A' levels in England. In fact it appears that he did not even see the course through. Despite the fact that there is no record of him having studied nuclear physics, or any other branch of physics for that matter, to degree level the myth has long persisted in Scientology circles that he has a profound knowledge of such matters.

For example, it evidently seemed in no way incongruous to Scientologists that at the height of the radiation scare in the 1950s he could write, as a 'nuclear physicist', a book entitled *All About Radiation*, which is described in the blurb as a book 'vital to the survival of your possessions, your family and the future of this planet'. In this unscholarly work Hubbard, who seems to consider himself an expert on vitamins too, publishes the formula for a mixture supposed to lower one's susceptibility to radiation damage. Called 'Dianazene' and consisting of:

nicotinic acid	*200 mg*
iron ferrous gluconate	*10 gr*
vitamin B1	*25 mg*
vitamin B2 (riboflavin)	*50 mg*
vitamin C (ascorbic acid)	*200–500 mg*
dicalcium phosphate	*23–35 gr*

it is a harmless mixture of vitamins which Hubbard recommends should be 'taken daily, all at the same time, with milk and chocolate'. Its role as an effective barrier to high energy radiation would, one feels, be a difficult scientific and medical case to argue. The interest of Hubbard in vitamins goes back further than this, for in the early days of Dianetics the movement's eccentric medical director, Joseph Winter M.D., fell out with him over another vitamin brew he was urging followers to take. It was assumed greatly to assist Dianetic techniques and was picturesquely known as 'GUK'. His latest achievement, according to *Certainty*, Volume 18, Number 7, is to discover the secret of how aspirin works. Pharmacologists the world over have been toiling away for decades in an attempt to solve the mystery of how acetylsalicylic acid (aspirin's main constituent) exercises its remarkable anti-inflammatory, antipyretic and analgesic properties, and have as yet got next to nowhere. Whether they will put away their test-tubes and microscopes on hearing L. Ron's solution is another matter. It seems the action of aspirin is to 'inhibit the ability of the thetan to create and to impede the electrical conductivity of nerve channels'. Hubbard himself is in no doubt whatsoever about the merits of his achievement which he states 'could be the medical bio-chemical discovery of the century'. He expects no thanks from the scientific community, however, and declares that he is content to 'let the Nobel prizes continue to go to the inventors of nose drops and new ways to kill'.

As for Hubbard's doctorate, it was awarded, one learns, from the magnificently styled 'Sequoia University of California'—an establishment which you will search for endlessly in the standard list of American universities, but which used to be well known to quacks on the West Coast as a degree mill where 'qualifications' could be bought for suitable sums. There is some evidence, as it happens, that L. Ron has had occasion to regret his involvement with the diminutive faculty of the Sequoia University, for his bogus Ph.D. has been frequently brought up by unkind critics as a stick to beat him with—and one for which he can find no ready defence. On 8th March 1966, possibly tiring of suffering on behalf of this valueless embarrassment, but with a typically flamboyant gesture, he took an advertisement in the personal column of *The Times*, 'resigning' his degree in the following words:

> I, L. Ron Hubbard of Saint Hill Manor, East Grinstead, having reviewed the damage being done in our society with nuclear physics and psychiatry by persons calling themselves 'Doctor', do hereby resign in protest my university degree as a doctor of philosophy (Ph.D.), anticipating an early public outcry against anyone called 'Doctor'; and although not in any way connected with bombs or 'psychiatric treatment' or treatment of the sick, and interested only and always in philosophy and the total freedom of the human spirit, I wish no association of any kind with these persons and do so publicly declare, and request my friends and the public not to refer to me in any way with this title.

With this characteristic piece, which it is impossible not to admire, he partly sealed a crack in his armour, at the same time cleverly taking the opportunity to pound psychiatrists, his perpetual antagonists. Having considered the Founder of Scientology's scanty academic background we now pass on to inspect other interesting claims which have helped to bolster his image as a man of wild and far-reaching talents. The claims are many and apart from the obvious, and quite unchallengable, one that he is a writer, he is also often referred to as an explorer, a naval war hero, a philosopher, a master mariner and, most extraordinary of all, 'one of the prime movers in the US effort of getting man into space'.

As far as exploring is concerned there is not much doubt that Hubbard has roamed the world quite a bit. Quite apart from his roving childhood, he is a member in good standing (No. 99) of the exclusive Explorers Club in New York and in the American *Who's Who in the South and West,* he is listed as having commanded the 'Caribbean Motion Picture Expedition and WI Minerals Expedition, 1935'. He is also stated to have led the '1940 Alaskan Radio Expedition' and is a fellow of the International Oceanographic Foundation. According to the Explorers Club he conducted 'the first complete mineralogical survey of Puerto Rico in 1932 and 1933' and the 'Caribbean Expedition resulting in valued data for the Hydrographic Office and the University of Michigan'. In February 1970 the Explorers Club stated that Hubbard was 'conducting archaeological research' in the Mediterranean.

On sailing, navigation and various other nautical topics L. Ron is an unquestioned expert. The sea has always held a deep fascination for him and in times less affluent than the present he told a close friend that one of the greatest desires of his life was to own a large personal yacht and that if ever he acquired a fortune the first thing he would do would be to buy one. This possibly underlies his present preoccupation, and that of the Scientologists as a whole, with their aquatic headquarters known as the 'Sea Orgs' about which we shall be hearing more later. During the war he served as a lieutenant in the navy and at one stage commanded a corvette which did some sub-chasing in the Pacific. He also worked for a short time in naval intelligence, during which period he took a four-week course in military government at Princeton.

One aspect of his war record particularly confused, and again typical of the mixture of glamour and obscurantism which surrounds Hubbard and his past, is the matter of wounds or injuries suffered on active service. It is frequently implied in the Scientology literature and also in tape recordings of his public lectures that he was severely wounded during his spell of duty with the navy. One official account (i.e., published by a Scientology organization) states that he was ordered to the Philippines on the entry of the US into the war and 'flown home in the late Spring of 1942 in the Secretary of the Navy's private plane as the first US returned casualty from the Far East'. The same account states that at the end of the war 'because of his physical condition Hubbard was relegated to the amphibious forces in the Pacific'. In other Scientology publications he is quoted as having been 'crippled and blind at the end of the war'. Despite these handicaps he 'resumed his studies of Philosophy and by his discoveries recovered so fully that he was reclassified in 1949 for full combat duty'. It is a 'matter of medical record', the same publication adds, 'that he has twice been pronounced dead'. Hubbard himself, in the now rare early publication, *Dianetics: Axioms*, first published in 1951, states that he spent a year (1945) in a naval hospital which he 'utilized in the study of endocrine substances and protein'.

Faced with this impressive, if annoyingly undetailed, record, it is hard to assess the nature or extent of Hubbard's battle scars in the service of his country. Many Scientologists believe that Hubbard was indeed severely wounded in action and it is certainly true that the Veterans Administration have confirmed that he receives $160 a month in compensation for disablities incurred during the Second World War. However the conditions listed as being '40% disabling' are: duodenal ulcer, bursitis (right shoulder), arthritis, and blepharo-conjunctivitis. It is possible that some of these conditions could have arisen as the result of some wound or wounds, though no mention of them as such seems to be given in the VA records. It is probably also relevant to point out that a Navy Department spokesman has stated that 'an examination of Mr Hubbard's record does not reveal any evidence of injuries suffered while in the service of the United States Navy'.

As for the alleged contribution to the United States' space

effort, there doesn't seem to be much to back this up either. NASA could trace no recorded contribution to their own extra-terrestrial excursions, but among his followers Ron is often accredited with achievements in this sphere. For example, in a sycophantic piece in the Scientology journal *Certainty*, published shortly after the first successful satellites were launched, a Mr Tom Esterbrook wrote: 'Ron spent five hours the other night trying to convince us that he had no hand in artificial moons. But you know who the favourite science fiction authors are in Russia? Jack London, H. G. Wells and L. Ron Hubbard.' Particularly popular in Russia, Esterbrook claimed, was Ron's nine-thousand-word article on 'Moons' in the American magazine *Air Trails* published in 1946. 'The Russkis could research it because they had read about it', he added, presumably implying that Hubbard's feature had triggered off the Soviet interest in Sputniks.

If this failed to convince fellow Scientologists of Hubbard's great (though modestly denied) contributions to astronautics, Esterbrook had more revelations up his sleeve. Why, he asks rhetorically, only '48 hours before the Russians launched the moon, 24 hours before the US stock markets crashed for guided missile companies', had Ron 'unloaded a huge number of guided missile shares he owned?'. 'Ron told people a week before the flying moon was launched', Esterbrook concludes. ' "There's more than one way to shock US science into action".'

Hubbard, of course, is no more responsible for the fatuous adulation of his followers than is any other Messiah-figure. But there is a curious sidelight to all this which helps to put the whole discussion above in weird perspective. Who, you may ask, is the uncritical Mr Esterbrook who writes in such glowing terms about the Founder of Scientology's contribution to the US and Russian space efforts? The answer turns out to be rather complicated. According to a Scientology spokesman, the name Tom Esterbrook served as a blanket pen-name for various staff writers in *The Auditor* and *Certainty*. As he claims that 'at least 10 people' had written under that pseudonym we will probably never be able to identify the author of the piece linking Hubbard with sputniks. Incidentally, one of the major users of the Esterbrook *nom-de-plume* was L. Ron Hubbard himself, as some senior members of the Scientology organization in those days knew quite well.

The plain fact is that for all Scientologists 'L. Ron' is a legendary figure, a man endowed with talents and qualities above those of normal men. To them he is a philosopher of the first magnitude, a literary, artistic and scientific genius all in one. Most of all, he is a brave pioneer in the exploration of that great uncharted area of the universe, the human mind. He undoubtedly has charisma, a magnetic lure of an indefinable kind which makes him the centre of attraction in any kind of gathering. He is also a compulsive talker and pontificator—a conversation with Hubbard is anything but the two-way process so fundamental to Scientology. His restless energy keeps him on the go throughout a long day—he is a poor sleeper and rises very early—and provides part of the drive which has allowed him to found and propagate a major international organization. He smokes heavily and has had pneumonia twice which leads him to seek the sun wherever and whenever he can. Hubbard is also reported to suffer, or to have suffered, from exceedingly bad teeth and this, coupled with an apparent reluctance to spend much time in the dentist's chair, has plagued him with dental abscesses. Whether the infected teeth have anything to do with an ulcer condition mentioned in his US Naval Record file is open to question.

Even today, in his early sixties and a portly version of his former self, he is still equipped with the sustained dynamism that so many people find attractive in men and—quite reasonably—he enjoys the company of attractive women. He has had three wives, and a stormy relationship with at least two of these. His first wife, Margaret Louise Grubb, was born in Beltsville, Maryland, on 22nd September 1907 and bore him two children—the boy 'Nibs' and a girl, Katherine May. Nibs, who was once one of the leading figures in the world of Scientology[1] but has long since severed connections with the movement, recalls that his parents' domestic life was turbulent and unhappy. His father's Bohemian ways and fluctuating professional success led to long absences from hearth and home, and the family finances seesawed wildly from peaks of

[1] Scientologists claim that, despite the close family relationship, Nibs has never been a 'leading figure' in the movement. They also point out that his statements on Scientology matters have been occasionally contradictory.

brief but considerable affluence to troughs of near poverty. On one occasion, typical of their slap-happy life, Nibs recalls that after a lengthy period when his father was almost totally broke and the family had been 'living on beans' for weeks, he received a cheque from a publisher for 2,800 dollars. With the envelope still freshly opened, L. Ron went straight to the local boatyard and purchased a yacht on which he and his wife promptly set sail for Alaska. As the years passed, Hubbard spent longer and longer periods away from home—they lived near Seattle in the State of Washington—and relations with his wife steadily deteriorated. By 1947 a divorce was proposed and in due course Hubbard was remarried to Sarah Northrup, whose name figures prominently in the early Dianetics literature. By all accounts this marriage was a total disaster and his second wife was suing him for divorce in May 1951. She also claimed that Hubbard had attempted to abduct their thirteen-month-old baby girl, Alexis, and West Coast newspapers of the time are filled with sensational headlines such as 'CULT FOUNDER ACCUSED OF TOT KIDNAP', and 'HIDING OF BABY CHARGED TO DIANETICS AUTHOR'. So painful do the memories of these incidents appear to be that L. Ron has more than once denied that he was ever married to Sarah Northrup at all. For example in *Dianetics: Axioms* there is a curious reference to a woman who had 'represented herself' as his wife and who had been 'cured of a severe psychosis by Dianetics' but who, because of structural brain damage, would evidently 'never be entirely sane'. Later in the book he refers to her again, but this time describes her as 'the woman who had been my wife'.

A more recent example of this apparent erasure of Sarah Northrup from his mind was revealed in a television interview for the Granada news feature *World in Action.* The *World in Action* team, in September 1968, pulled off a fine scoop by getting cameras aboard Hubbard's big boat in the Mediterranean and conducting a three-hour-long filmed interview with the man himself. Amazingly—or is it really surprising?—they left with thousands of feet of film but little extra information about Scientology or its founder. They did, however, record him denying that he had a second wife in between his first, who died, and the present one, Mary Sue.

In the same programme the Granada interviewer questioned an ex-Scientologist about how Hubbard's flock reacted when such evidence of error, if not of downright dishonesty, on his part was pointed out to them. It depended, came the answer, on how high up in the movement the people were and how recently recruited. Anyone who had been in Scientology for a long time, however, simply wouldn't dare to think in any terms other than those which fitted in with Hubbard's statements.

For them Scientology was the *real* universe, and Hubbard's statements were facts whether or not they conflicted with material in the 'outside' world. In any language, in any part of the world, or in any part of history for that matter, such attitudes are tragic.

It is true that some of his statements would only be questioned by specialists. One good example is the claim that in 1938 the Soviet government—knowing that he was working on research of some significance—offered him the opportunity to take over the laboratories of Academician Ivan Pavlov, the great physiologist and discoverer of the conditioned reflex, with massive financial backing to complete his work under their auspices. This would seem an astonishing offer to say the least, though Hubbard refers to it in a letter he wrote to the late President Kennedy in 1962. However, few Scientologists would question it and most will presumably accept it at face value.

But what of the even more fantastic statements, some so ludicrous that one doubts one's eyes when reading them? There is no scarcity of raw material here, but one can hardly quote a better example than the famous visit to Heaven, an event described by L. Ron in a bulletin issued on 11th May 1963. Here he tells his readers that he has twice visited Heaven, once '43,891,832,611,177 years, 344 days, 10 hours, 20 minutes and 40 seconds from 10.02½ p.m., Daylight Greenwich Time, 9th May 1963'. He found 'the gates . . . well done, well built. An avenue of statues of saints leads up to them. The gate pillars are surmounted by marble angels. The entering grounds are very well kept, laid out like the Bush Gardens in Pasadena, so often seen in movies.'

It seems to have been an insipid scene. On a second visit, eons later, the place had gone to seed: 'The place is shabby', he tells us, 'the vegetation is gone. The pillars are scruffy. The saints have vanished. So have the angels. A sign on one (the left as you enter) says: *This is Heaven*. The right has the sign *Hell*.'

Hubbard, as should by now be coming clear, is a highly

skilled professional writer, capable of turning his hand to quite a range of topics and styles. His successes in the literary field, long before Dianetics was launched on an unsuspecting world, began in the 1930s when he began to churn out a vast series of pulp magazine fiction including Westerns (using the rather unsubtle pen-name of Winchester Remington Colt), adventure tales of one kind or another, and even romances of the True Love variety. He also had numerous stints in the movie script-writing mill of Hollywood when, at one stage, he was making 500 dollars a week helping to feed the public's ravenous appetite for the cinema. In the late thirties, when Hubbard was known as a minor literary figure in the Greenwich Village area of New York—somewhat given to wearing flowing cloaks and other strange attire according to acquaintances of the time—he began to generate under his own name, and also under the pseudonyms Kurt von Rachen and René Lafayette, a series of pacy science fiction stories which were to earn him an international reputation as one of the leading writers in this expanding field. The first of these was a short story called *The Dangerous Dimension*, which was followed by a novel, *The Tramp*. Both these stories were built around themes of paranormal human powers such as teleportation and the capacity of the mind to act on other human beings at a distance, which, as we shall see, are ideas inherent in the philosophy of Scientology itself. Another strain of Hubbard's science fiction consists of stories which are frequently classed by fans today under the heading 'Sword and Sorcery', in which handsome, muscular and intelligent men incongruously armed with swords and magic powers, shoot round in space rescuing beautiful damsels in the teeth of opposition from pirate spaceships, dragons and wizard-scientists. In many of these—*Kingslayer* is a good example—one feels that one discerns in the hero Hubbard himself, complete with red hair and a strong line of blarney. Other stories are more traditional SF of the period—such as *Beyond the Black Nebula* with a miniaturized army fighting a colossal battle against phagocytes in the stomach of a worm.

His prodigious output, according to his son 'Nibs', was the envy of his fellow professionals for his technique was to lock himself away with a typewriter—he could type with two fingers at ninety words a minute—for a day or so and emerge with a complete, saleable manuscript on its very first draft! In such a fashion did he generate not only the novel, *Fear*, first published in 1943 which many critics consider to be his fictional masterpiece, but also the manuscript of *Dianetics: The Modern Science of Mental Health* which was to launch him into a fame extending far beyond the parochial boundaries of the world of science fiction. Significantly, however, Dianetics found its first platform in the pages of the leading science fiction journal of the day, *Astounding Science Fiction.* For some idea as to why this turned out to be such an effective platform we need to consider the role of science fiction at the time as a purveyor and percolator of uninhibited intellectual speculation.

To a large number of people, who have never taken it too seriously, science fiction conjures up visions of stories of the Flash Gordon kind—rockets engaged in orbital dogfights over the Martian moons with sinister bearded space tyrants, with names like Krang or Vargon, etc. In point of fact this kind of twenty-first century Western has not been the meat and drink of serious science fiction fans since the 1930s and is only to be met nowadays in books written for the most juvenile end of the scale.

From around about 1940, SF magazines fed their growing army of fans an increasingly sophisticated diet, their authors—many of whom were working scientists—cleverly playing with the technological developments of the time and extrapolating into the future. Their predictions on occasions could be too successful. A story published in *Astounding Science Fiction* in 1943 so clearly anticipated the development of a nuclear fission weapon that its author received a visit from Federal Security forces suspicious that this might constitute a leak from the top secret Manhattan project. By the end of the war, when the average individual was only superficially aware of what had happened at Hiroshima and Peenemünde, science fiction fans were gaily devouring stories about the social problems of a world shattered by a nuclear war or reading learned articles about the payloads that could be landed on the moon with developments of the existing V2. The concept of a talking, thinking, dying computer—which seems to have rocked everyone so much in Kubrick's recent space opera *2001*—was old hat to fantasy fiction readers twenty years ago, and words like 'psychokinesis', 'artificial gravity', 'analogue' and 'digital' were part of their breakfast vocabulary.

Of all the magazines published in those halcyon days, there was none to match *Astounding Science Fiction* for the depth and quality of its material, and pace and sophistication of its writing. At one time its readership ran into the hundreds of thousands and it was known to be read by some of the leading scientists of the day. The man responsible for its success, and one of the most influential figures in the field, was the editor John Campbell Jnr. He was also the man who gave Hubbard his big break, and as such may be thought of as having quite a bit to answer for.

Campbell, who died in 1971, was originally a fantasy writer himself. He was also a competent and persuasive editor with a tolerance for the off-beat and the suspected crank, which led him to pull off some spectacular scoops and at the same time to sanction a good deal of nonsense. Traditionally the opening feature of the magazine was his leading article and for most readers this was the highspot of the journal. In these leaders Campbell would argue a controversial scientific, philosophical or even political point, cleverly tapping ideas and trains of thought which had hitherto lain dormant in his readers' minds. The issues raised might vary from scientific prejudice against ESP, to the possibilities of submarine farming.

To many of the young SF fans of the time, Campbell was the most important writer on earth, fertilizer of the intellect, liberator of the mind and father-figure all in one. His scientific training, though not exceptional was sound—he studied engineering at MIT and graduated at Duke University, later working for a brief period in the laboratories of Mack Trucks Inc.—and he numbered among his friends some of the best-known working scientists in the States.

For years Campbell had been an acquaintance of Hubbard's and had published some of the latter's excellent science fiction. Some time in 1949 he became sufficiently interested in the new philosophical and psychological ideas that Hubbard was kicking around to experiment with them, and was one of the first to learn that they were gravid with a dramatic new system of psychotherapy. He was also one of the first to benefit from this, for that same year he underwent a course in Dianetic processing, as it was then known, and found to his utter amazement that he had been apparently completely cured of the chronic sinusitis which had plagued him for years.[1]

In Christmas of that year the tom-toms were beating out the message that Hubbard was about to come out with something sensational and in April of 1950 first details were given with an announcement in that month's issue of *Astounding Science Fiction*. In an enthusiastic preview Campbell wrote:

> Next month's issue will, I believe, cause one full-scale explosion across the country. We are carrying a sixteen-thousand word article entitled 'Dianetics . . . An Introduction to a New Science', by L. Ron Hubbard. It will, I believe, be the first publication of the material. It is, I assure you, in full and absolute sincerity, one of the most important articles ever published. In this article, reporting on Hubbard's own research into the engineering question of how the human mind operates, immensely important basic discoveries are related.

In the same eulogistic vein Campbell continued:

> This is no wild theory. It is not mysticism. It is a coldly precise engineering description of how the human mind operates, and how to go about restoring correct operation tested and used on some two hundred fifty cases. And it makes only one overall claim: the methods logically developed from that description *work*. The memory stimulation technique is so powerful that, within thirty minutes of entering therapy, most people will recall in full detail their own birth. I have observed it in action, and used the techniques myself.

After such a build-up it was no wonder that the May issue of *ASF* practically sold out on publication day. The article itself is a strange piece of work, rattled off in a series of gasping phrases and peppered with exclamation marks, 'like', as a contemporary critic remarked, 'the commentary on a football match'. Its message, however, was unequivocal and simple. A dramatic breakthrough had occurred in psychotherapy. As the result of years of research and a number of important in-

1 When the author met Campbell in New York in 1969 he complained of his sinusitis and from time to time took penetrating sniffs at a pocket inhaler. The 'cure' had evidently only been transient.

sights, new techniques had been discovered which sensationally struck at the roots of psychosomatic illnesses—and even some physical ones too. So effective were these techniques, all of which were bundled under the term Dianetics, that individuals could with a few hours of 'auditing' (the name for the actual running of the treatment, which was later also given the somewhat unfortunate title of 'processing') be rid of illnesses which had steadfastly resisted years and years of orthodox medical or psychiatric treatment.

Furthermore—and here the bait was offered at its most tempting—these techniques were simple, easily describable and easily taught. They were available to any more or less normal individual after a minimal amount of instruction. The article claimed (over and over again) that they worked, as doubters could demonstrate for themselves.

No more fertile ground could have been picked for the publication of such a piece. Telephone calls and mail flooded the offices of the publisher (2,000 letters in the first two weeks) and when Hubbard's book—*Dianetics: The Modern Science of Mental Health*—was published by Hermitage House shortly afterwards, it moved into the best-seller list overnight. In essence it is a greatly expanded version of the original *ASF* article, somewhat, though not much more, cogently argued and enlivened by a number of 'case histories'. It also included enough information to allow readers to practise the principles of Dianetics on each other and enough details of the philosophy of the system to titillate the curiosity of the tens of thousands of amateur psychologists who are traditionally among the ranks of science fiction fans.

For such individuals, eager for marvels and in many cases desperately interested in abnormal psychology, yet lacking the academic training to practise it, the advent of Dianetics signalled the onset of the Golden Era. *Anyone* could now practise psychotherapy with a skill and facility far superior to that of the blundering psychologists who had ruled the roost in the past. Even more convenient was the fact that one didn't have to spend tedious years at university or medical school, listening to dull lectures and swotting up stuffy tomes. A few hours of Dianetics and one was a working Dianeticist who could get results!

Such was unquestionably the image created by Hubbard's

enormously successful book, and within weeks a Dianetic fad was sweeping the United States. In August Hermitage House reported that the book, at four dollars a copy, was still selling at the rate of a thousand copies a day, and even the leather-bound limited edition at twenty-five dollars a shot was sold out. How much of this, one wonders, could the author and originator have predicted as he battered away at his electric typewriter—a special one equipped with individual keys for 'the', 'and', etc., writing the book which was to sweep him to fame? He claims the manuscript was completed in three weeks, and its breathless style suggests that this could well be true. But what were the actual revelations which set the whole circus in motion and which still give it impetus today?

As it happens, the principles of Dianetics are disarmingly simple and economic, and they have a naive precision which, when backed by the hyper-confident pronouncements of the originator, make the newcomer fleetingly wonder where they can be wrong. A closer examination soon shows the precision to be superficial and the logic either incomplete or contradictory. Furthermore, in a number of cases, one sees that what are offered up as important new discoveries or major philosophical advances are merely props of psychological and psychoanalytic theory renamed in tempting new jargon.

The old Cartesian dichotomy of the distinction between mind and body is retained, and argued with great firmness. The mind controls the brain, in the manner of a signalman in a signal box, and this in turn controls the body. The mind itself is divided into two distinct entities, the analytic and the reactive. The former corresponds to the conscious mind of Freudian terminology and is likened by Hubbard, with his brushing acquaintance with electronic engineering, to a computer. This analytic mind works with great precision according to the data fed into it, and in a normal individual this will lead to a speedy and appropriate response to events in the external environment. Unfortunately the reactive mind—which bears some relationship to the Freudian unconscious—frequently intervenes to upset the apple cart, causing an individual to make a totally unsuitable response to a given set of circumstances. These Hubbard calls 'aberrations' and they correspond in lots of ways to the neuroses and psychoses of orthodox psychopathology.

Now the cause of the aberrations is interesting. In normal circumstances, when the analytic mind is fully operational, it stores and computes all sensory input and reacts appropriately. But in moments of unconsciousness or great emotional distraction, the analytic mind ceases to function properly and the reactive mind, which has been brooding away cloddishly without much to do, momentarily comes into play. It immediately begins to record details of the experiences—generally alarming—which have caused the analytic mind's loss of consciousness, and stores them in the form of some unspecified kind of traces which are called 'engrams'. With the return of consciousness and of 'normal' functioning the analytic mind gets under way again, having 'forgotten' its recent traumatic experience which is, however, firmly stored in the data banks of the reactive mind.

These engrams (this is not Hubbard jargon but a useful word culled from neurophysiology where it is used to denote the memory trace) are often very complex things consisting not only of the actual traumatic experience which caused unconsciousness—such as a punch in the teeth or a general anaesthetic—but also of all the sense data associated with it at the time it took place. For example, if someone is knocked down by a car the engram stored in the reactive mind will include the screech of brakes, the sound of the horn, the chatter of passers-by, the clang of the ambulance bell and even the feel of the pavement under the unconscious person's body.

The reactive mind then becomes a special kind of lumber room filled with unpleasant junk (again notice the similarities to Freudian views of the unconscious) and, what is worse, it is junk which has some definite power. For throughout one's life the engrams remain, exerting their baleful influence when the environmental conditions replicate one or more of the original conditions of the trauma. A person might be constantly handicapped by some odd experience stored in the reactive mind which manifested itself in a neurotic or even physical complaint. In fact, it was one of the earliest claims of Dianetics that all neuroses, psychoses and possibly even major physical illnesses, such as cancer, were caused by engrams.

To this point one might feel that Hubbard's theory took matters little further than the idea of psychosomatic illnesses caused by repressed memories of physical or psychical trauma which Freud began to kick around nearly a century previously. But there is more to Dianetics than this, as the notion of the pre-natal engram demonstrates. Here again the idea is simple, if fantastic.

According to his 'researches' Hubbard became convinced that engrams were laid down not only in the individual's childhood and adult life, but also in the period when the foetus was developing in the womb. At this time, while the analytic mind was still in the early stages of development, the reactive mind could register traumatic experiences. These might be beatings by the husband of his pregnant wife, or violent rows in which the threatening or cruel phrases uttered by either of the parties would be rigidly impressed in the data banks, to pop up with tiresome frequency during the individual's subsequent lifetime.

The peace which we normally feel is associated with foetal development turns out, according to the practitioners of Dianetics, to be a pretty illusory one. The wretched baby, it seems, is more or less continually being knocked unconscious, either by thumps, kicks, violent sexual intercourse or the mother bumping against furniture—all these incidents of course storing engrams in the receptive mind. The blandly literal way in which the reactive mind stores this material, later to reproduce it with crippling force, is illustrated by one case history involving the processing of a kleptomaniac. Routine hunting through the reactive data banks revealed a memory of the father beating the mother during pregnancy, shouting as he did so, 'Take that! Take it, I tell you! You've got to take it!', thus inevitably storing these commands with the foetus for future reference in adult life.

The technique of the therapy is simple beyond all measure—or was in its early days. The patient simply lay on a couch in a relaxed state, prattling on with any fantasies that came to his mind as the result of the probing of the therapist, who in Dianetic and Scientological terms is known as the auditor. By suitable guiding the auditor would soon begin to pick up areas on which it seemed worth concentrating, and when the patient began to look or act disturbed—feeling weird pains in different parts of the body, sweating, moaning and groaning, or hysterically laughing—the auditor knew an engram was near. The confrontation of the patient with the memory has the effect of pushing it out of the reactive banks, whence it is erased to free the individual of this particular aberration. This is the point at which the sinusitis disappears, the mysterious backache vanishes, the acne of twenty-five years' standing fades away, or the stutter miraculously improves.

By many contemporary accounts—such as the case of Campbell himself—these manifestations of past traumas did yield dramatically to Dianetic therapy. Unfortunately after a variable period of time, which could be as short as a day but might be as long as a year or two, the symptoms, which should in theory have gone for ever, would often return in their former glory, and it became obvious that some model, a little less simple and all-embracing, would have to be dreamt up. Amazingly it took a long time for this realization to dent the Dianetic fad, and when it did Hubbard had other material to exhibit. But so rapidly did it get under way, and such was the immense aura of confidence given off by its founder and his converts, that literally hundreds of thousands of people—many of them the intelligent and well educated—were drawn into the movement.

Lives Past, Lives Remembered

IN 1950 L. R. HUBBARD found himself a figure of national prominence. He rose to the occasion splendidly, happily enjoying the publicity, dashing off new tracts to supplement the original thesis and at the same time attempting to seal up the cracks which were beginning to appear in its logic. The success of his book (it sold over a million) had put large sums of money into his hands and these he decided to reinvest rapidly in establishing Dianetic Research Centres across America. The first, and in the early days the most famous, was established at Elizabeth, New Jersey and here, auditing each other like mad and listening to *ad hoc* lectures of incredible length, were to be found an amazing collection of individuals. Some were lonely neurotics for whom the techniques had struck a spark, some science fiction writers such as the brilliant A. E. Van Vogt, some figures such as John Campbell himself—who must have been beginning to wonder what it was he had started —and some academics such as the political scientist from Massachusetts, Professor F. L. Schuman (who risked the ridicule of his university colleagues in order to champion Dianetics in the weekly *New Republic*). There was even a sprinkling of scientists and mathematicians who were at least intrigued at the song and dance that Hubbard was making.

Businessmen too found Dianetics of compelling interest. It wasn't long before at least two millionaires had enthusiastically involved themselves in the movement, one of whom was the oil king, Don Purcell, who considerably expanded Hubbard's empire by building a spanking new headquarters for him in Wichita, Kansas, Here, in expensively furnished offices, secretaries clacked away at typewriters, telephones rang nonstop and all the signs were evidence of a business going into boom. In a specially constructed lecture theatre, for a fee of a hundred dollars a time, Ron Hubbard (paid by Purcell) lectured daily to full houses.

In other parts of the country eager audiences awaited the words of the master who flew back and forth from coast to coast, addressing enthusiastic groups and gathering around him the collection of sensation seekers, sycophants, fanatics, fortune hunters and considerable numbers of honest individuals who believed that Hubbard had really got hold of something of significance. For, despite the aura of razzamatazz which had swiftly surrounded the topic and its originator, there was at this time a brief but measurable period when the world of psychology quaked. Was it possible, was it just conceivable, that this fantastic, academically unqualified extrovert had developed techniques which worked, and had really pulled something out of the bag?

Hubbard himself evidently had no doubt, for the opening lines of the synopsis to his first book describe Dianetics as 'a milestone for Man comparable to his discovery of fire and superior to his inventions of the wheel and arch'. But he must have realized also that this was no time to rest on his laurels.

Thanks to intensive research, the frontiers of Dianetics were being steadily advanced, and the concept of a 'Clear' became particularly important. This is a word which appears in Scientology literature today *ad nauseam* and it continually mystifies ordinary people not conversant with the cult's elaborate jargon. It is also a concept which has changed quite considerably as the years have passed.

It will be recalled that in therapy the auditor undertook a quest for his patient's engrams and, by causing him to confront them or 'run them through', erased them from the reactive memory banks. As each engram slid away in limbo, so the patient gradually rid himself of the tedious physical and psychological afflictions which they had caused, gradually becoming a healthier and happier person. Now obviously, if these engrams were, as Hubbard claimed, the source of practically all human ills, then one should be able to produce a physically and psychologically perfect individual if only they could all be cleared away. Any such individual would then become a 'Clear', all others being *ipso facto* 'preclear—the name used to denote the rank and file of Dianetics, and later Scientology.

Clears, as you may imagine, would be very superior people indeed, and Hubbard spelt out the fact in no uncertain terms. They would, he claimed, not only be totally without neuroses, etc., but their bodies would cease to be a prey to the minor tribulations of life. Clears would not get colds for example. Their eyesight would improve to the point where they would not need glasses. If wounded they would heal abnormally quickly. Even their IQ would be raised.

To many, Clear sounded a tempting state of being and a goal to be vigorously pursued. Unfortunately, Dianetic processing was not cheap. In 1951 the Wichita Foundation was charging over five hundred dollars for thirty-six hours' processing, and personal attention at the hands of Hubbard was even costlier. Thirty-six hours, however, never seemed to be quite enough to produce any Clears, and no one seemed sure, since there were no comparison samples around, just how long it would take to reach the final state. But it was obvious to all that at nearly fourteen dollars an hour clearing could be quite expensive if it turned out to take, say, a year. There didn't seem much point in going to Hubbard himself about this either, for he was uncharacteristically coy on the matter of whether he was Clear himself. He did, however, promise that the state was attainable, and so the processing continued.

In the meanwhile more exciting new facts emerged. Behind every reactive and analytic mind, it appeared, lay an entity known as the 'Thetan'. Thetans are the really important part of the human being—the part that is 'aware of being aware', as Hubbard put it nicely. They are entirely non-physical and also quite immortal. They inhabit bodies, moving them around like someone operating a puppet, but have for the most part *forgotten* that they are immortal. They have, in principle, complete and absolute power over their bodies. Most of them, Hubbard sorrowfully points out, even think they *are* bodies! The reasons for this unaccountable error we will go into later, merely noting at this time that since they are immortal, on the death of their puppet body they must presumably go elsewhere. Where? Well you guessed right if you say to yet another body—taking it over at the point of conception and sticking with it, for better or for worse, until it dies of old age or whatever.

And now we come to another revelation, and this is the point at which many people feel that Dianetics began the long and slippery descent into occultism. When the Thetan enters this new body it comes not, as one might hope, fresh and clean, but equipped with the accumulated detritus of its *previous* lives, all the engrams which have piled up in its apparently limitless backlog of existence. Fortunately Ron Hubbard soon found it was quite possible, though arduous and expensive, to clear even *these* ancient engrams, some of which had been thwarting their Thetans for millions of years. Thus encouraged, the faithful plunged back into battle, and in houses and apartments, in Dianetic Centres, in colleges and even army camps across America the fans of Dianetics began the exploration of their many, many past lives. In countless sessions, in countless houses, auditors watched as their preclears ran through the traumatic engrams of the past, re-dying dramatic deaths in blazing zeppelins, in sinking ocean liners, in the retreat from Moscow, beneath the guillotine, during the Black Death, leaping from the Wooden Horse of Troy, etc., etc. The cheery swopping of past lives and deaths became a feature of sophisticated conversation at many parties, anticipating the Bridey Murphy 'reincarnation' vogue by several years.

Obviously it now became necessary to reconsider the concept of Clear, for the techniques of Dianetics, potent though they might be, could hardly be expected to whisk away the engrams of a million previous lifetimes in the twinkling of an eye. Most people would have to rest content with the prospect of one day becoming a MEST-Clear (these being the initials for the universe of Matter, Energy, Space and Time) when they would find themselves with only the limited rewards of perfect health, boundless energy, a photographic memory, a vastly increased IQ and some measure of telepathic ability. For the real achievers, assuming some speeding up of the Dianetic technique, the next step would be the clearing of past life engrams, and then the state of 'Operating Thetan'—i.e., the state in which an individual becomes capable of exercising literally miraculous powers and being pretty well independent of the shackles of the MEST-universe—would be attained.

Like that of Clear, the concept of Operating Thetan has today been considerably watered down, and at the time of writing the latter state has not yet been fully achieved. There is, however, a suggestion that in 1952 or thereabouts Hubbard must have felt that there were some OTs in existence for in an extraordinary passage in one of his more extraordinary books (*History of Man*) he urges such beings to preserve their anonymity and:

> . . . not go upsetting governments and putting on a show to prove anything to homo sapiens for a while; its a horrible temptation to knock off hats at 50 yards and read books a couple of countries away . . . but you'll just make it tough on somebody else who's trying to get across this bridge.

Compared with such nonsense Hubbard's earlier words, on the potential of Clear, seem like crystal sanity, though they do have slightly unpleasant overtones:

> One sees with some sadness that more than three quarters of the world's population will become subject to the remaining quarter as a natural consequence about which we can do exactly nothing.

In these days Hubbard was still able to talk about Clears without actually having to produce one. It was a sunny period free of carping criticism or childish backsliding, and he was able, with a few choice friends, to engage in some peaceful research in the friendly surroundings of the Wichita Foundation. It was at this point that a young mathematician appeared on the scene and, impressed by Hubbard's platform manner and convinced for various reasons of the workability of at least some of the Dianetic's methods, offered his services in the cause. His name was Perry Chapdelaine, and today he is a distinguished computer scientist who looks back wryly on his youthful love-affair with the cult. He was, somewhat to his surprise, to play a significant role in its further evolution and became a close associate of Hubbard. He also served as his personal auditor and soon found, even in his own first flush of enthusiasm, that the Master's research methods did not match the vigour of even the most rudimentary scientific study.

The actual procedure, Chapdelaine reports, was for Hubbard to settle himself on a couch with a tape recorder handy and an 'auditor' who would be expected to provide appropriate feedback. In no time a flow of introspection—like the free association characteristic of a psychoanalytic session—would begin. But, unlike an orthodox session in analysis where the material is treated with the suspicion that all ramblings from the unconscious deserve, in Hubbard's research periods all was apparently accepted with solemn deliberation—the most *outré* fantasies, the most oddball ideas being treated as unshakable fact. Much of the text of *History of Man*, which is quite one of Hubbard's odder works, emerged from these Wichita sessions, and knowing this one can see why it reads so peculiarly. Candidly, the more one inspects its text, the more one begins to wonder whether he ever meant it to be taken seriously. It is, one feels, not particularly rich in literary merit, but because it marks a transition point at which the technically oriented Dianetics became the philosophically oriented Scientology we will need to take a rather close look at it. Fortunately it has the saving grace of being exceedingly funny, so the process of inspection is less painful than one might fear.

History of Man begins soberly enough with the following remark: 'This is a cold-blooded and factual account of your last sixty trillion years', and after tossing off a few remarks about making the blind see and the lame walk, it gets down to real business. The message is simple. Dianetics, which deals largely with the technique of clearing engrams, is a relatively slow and temporary measure. Scientology, its bouncing progeny, takes up where Dianetics leaves off and provides techniques which allow one to tackle the problem of past lives with relative ease and pave the way to achieving the states of Clear and Operating Thetan. Furthermore, it is no longer just a technique in isolation, but has a philosophy with it.

For those interested, the *real* secret of the universe is as follows. In the beginning are the Thetans. These are omnipotent, indestructible beings who suffer from being immortal. The reason they suffer is because immortality, when one has nothing to do, becomes intolerably boring. There are, it is true, other Thetans about, but since they too do nothing it's just as boring as if there were only one. Now in order to help while away eternity they decided to play some games. These consist, in the first instance, of creating universes of one kind and another, and playing with them. The games could be of any kind. They might create a world, for example, where pigs fly and centipedes wear green socks, or a world, like the one in *Alice in*

Wonderland, entirely made of treacle. You name it, the Thetans can make it.

After a while this too becomes boring, and the Thetans begin to realize that their omnipotence and omniscience is the real trouble. So with a master-stroke typical of their genius they decide voluntarily to handicap themselves, limiting their powers and cutting down the range of their knowledge. Now the game becomes more interesting, and the Thetans enter into it with greater enthusiasm. Then, imperceptibly, something begins to happen.

Slowly but surely, as the countless millions of years pass by, the lures of the universe they have created out of matter, energy, space and time (MEST) begin to snare them. They become more and more immersed in the game, less and less concerned about their true status as Thetans. Slowly, like flies sinking into honey, they become more hopelessly trapped in the material universe, reaching their present state (almost total ensnarement) many millions of years ago. And the path has been steadily downward. Nowadays the Thetans have *forgotten what they really are,* and go around thinking they are bodies. They have even forgotten that they are playing a game at all!

But something has happened. One man, Lafayette Ronald Hubbard, has stumbled on the secret, has remembered what it's all about and will lead us back until we cease to be pawns and return to our heritage as players. Such is the grand design behind all our lives as revealed by Scientology. It is imaginative, if nothing else, and smacks from top to bottom of the very best science fiction. If this seems unfair, then a closer look at the contents of *History of Man* is prescribed.

Much of the book is devoted to details of past lives and intensely traumatic encounters in the Thetan's catastrophic past. In the long haul of evolution the Thetan has struggled up through a number of life forms, all of which have left their mark on poor twentieth-century homo sapiens. For several million years, for example, the principal form of life was THE CLAM, the normal type of bivalve, one supposes, tossed about on beaches and subject to the whim of wind and wave. You can soon tell, advises Hubbard, whether a preclear is really hung up on incidents from his past as a clam by saying to him, 'Can you imagine a clam sitting on the beach, opening and closing its shell very rapidly?'. At the same time you make a motion with your thumb and forefinger as of rapid opening and closing. This gesture will suffice to upset large numbers of people, causing a clam-type to 'grip his jaws with his hand and feel quite upset. He may even have to have a few teeth pulled . . . and he will feel quite sad emotionally.' 'You will be amazed', Hubbard adds later, 'to find the clam sufficiently advanced as a cellular-somatic mind to have postulates, to think thoughts'.

After the clam comes THE WEEPER, a mollusc which also lay around on beaches for vast tracts of evolutionary history. We have all been through this too, as the Thetans, and our memory banks bear the scars. It must have been a tedious period for the plights of the weeper were 'many and pathetic. Still obtaining its food from the waves, it had yet to breathe. Waves are impetuous and often irregular. The WEEPER [the capitals are Hubbard's] would often open up to get food from the water and get a wave in the shell. It would vigorously pump out the water and try to get some air and then, before it could gulp atmosphere, be hit by another wave. Here was anxiety.' Indeed. But worse was to follow, for the creature had two respiratory tubes which continually had 'very rough treatment, getting full of sand, being battered by surf'.

The inability of the preclear to cry, we are informed, is a particularly good sign that he is hung up on his past lives as a weeper for he is afraid of getting sand in his eyes. The weeper, Hubbard informs us, was originally called the 'Grim Weeper' or the 'Boohoo', and it had 'trillions of misadventures'.

Other ghastly incidents in the past include a period on earth when volcanoes abounded. Smoking tobacco, Hubbard hints, might well be a 'dramatization of volcanoes'.

Skipping past THE SLOTH, which 'had bad times falling out of trees' and being attacked by baboons, and THE APE, which is usually 'an area of overt acts against animals and incidents of protecting young', we pass on to THE PILTDOWN MAN, an area rich in engrams containing 'freakish acts of strange logic, of demonstrating dangerous [*sic*] on one's fellows, of eating one's wife and other somewhat illogical activities'. The Piltdown teeth, we read, were 'ENORMOUS and he was quite careless as to whom and what he bit'. Piltdown's successor, THE CAVEMAN, was a more complicated individual, being concerned with 'keeping women at home for men and keeping a man from keeping one at home for women'.

If you feel here that your own personal hold on sanity is beginning to slip, then Hubbard's amazing book is not for you. Just be glad that Scientology is around to unburden you of all the trauma of your past lives as CLAM, WEEPER, and SLOTH, to say nothing of PILTDOWN with his ENORMOUS teeth.

Anyone who has wondered at what happens, if anything, after death will be relieved to hear that a good deal of information is now available, thanks to the work Hubbard undertook at Wichita. 'At death', we learn, 'the theta being leaves the body and goes to the between-lives area. Here he "reports in", is given a strong forgetter implant and is then shot down to a body just before it is born'.

The forgetter implant sounds very unpleasant. 'The preclear is seated before a wheel which contains numbers of pictures. As the wheel turns the pictures go away from him. . . . A force screen hits him through these pictures. . . . The whole effect is to give him the impression that he has no past life, that he is no longer the same identity, that his memory has been erased'. Some individuals do not always report—small wonder—but we are not told what happens to them. Presumably they hang around in limbo putting off the inevitable as one postpones dental appointments on earth. Hubbard reveals that a good deal is known about the location of the report areas. 'The report area for most', he declared, 'has been Mars. Some women report to stations elsewhere in the solar system. There are occasional incidents about Earth report stations. These are protected by screens. The last Martian report station on earth was established in the Pyrenees.'

This rather extensive coverage of what must be, intentionally or unintentionally, one of the most absurd books ever written, would not of course be justifiable if it were an obscure cranky work, read at the most by a few hundreds of people. The real oddity—and it is a slightly frightening one—is that *History of Man* (which was first published in 1951) has not sold hundreds, but probably hundreds of thousands of copies and is devoured with great eagerness and diligence by Scientologists young and old in all parts of the world.

The rest of the book concerns the kind of engrams which are implanted as the result of various wars and conflicts between

Thetans which have occurred on and off in the past '60 trillion years' and, if anything, it is even sillier than the first part. A large number of devices were employed to trap Thetans, who when caught were subjected to various weird punishments, all of which get soaked into the eternal memory and which manifest themselves during auditing.

Among the traps were the 'Jack-in-the-Box', a curious contrivance which operated like a booby-trap, exploding when touched by a nosey Thetan and 'filling his beingness full of pictures which are extremely confusing, being pictures of boxes of pictures'. Human beings who are particularly hung up on this episode reveal themselves by being 'very curious about cereal boxes which have pictures of boxes of cereal which have pictures of boxes of cereal'. If you can wade your way through that one you might stand a chance of making sense of the 'Coffee Grinder'—one of my own personal favourites. This episode goes back to a time when Thetans brainwashed each other with a 'two-handled portable machine which, when turned, emits a heavy push-pull electronic wave in a series of stuttering "baps" '.

People are attracted to the job of operating pneumatic drills not, as we all thought in our ignorance, because they could find nothing better to do but because they had, a trillion years ago, been 'bapped' by a coffee grinder. These devices, it happens were operated by Thetans wearing hoods and goggles, rather like asbestos fire-fighting suits, and this provided added trauma to the victim. The operators, no doubt aware of their odd appearance, concealed themselves behind a black gauze curtain while operating the machine, but the victims nevertheless generally caught a glimpse of them at least once.

If you are wondering what mark this vision leaves on Thetans when they assume human forms eons later, you will be interested to know that they show an intense dislike of people who wear horn-rimmed glasses. And what type of people tend to wear horn-rimmed glasses? Correct! The former operators of the coffee grinders.

Grow New Teeth

THE FRUITS OF Hubbard's Wichita research, which we have just been describing, were received with enthusiasm by his supporters, despite their mind-boggling contents, but things were not going as well as they might for Dianetics. All over the country relapses were beginning to occur, the original wild claims were not being met, and the peak of growth of the cult seemed to have been reached. Furthermore—and this to Hubbard was, as it always has been, anathema—some of his more level-headed adherents were beginning to dispute his judgement on points of technique as well as theory. Worst of all, from all sides rose a swelling chorus demanding to see a real honest-to-goodness Clear. If Clears were so easy to produce, well then let someone produce one!

From every point of view L. Ron was in a ticklish spot. He was in the very dangerous position of being expected to continually astound people, and there is no harder role to play. Moreover, he had been badly burnt once in the past when, not too long after the publication of *Dianetics,* he had exhibited in public someone supposed to be Clear. It had been a grave tactical error and Hubbard seems to have become justly cautious of committing himself as far as Clears were concerned. The circumstances were as follows:

In 1950 Dianetics was being taken up with great enthusiasm in San Francisco and Los Angeles, and it had become a fad among the well-to-do movie stars of the time. Gloria Swanson was one of the stars who received lengthy processing and the great jazz pianist, Dave Brubeck, made the claim that it had helped him in his musical career. A relation of Cecil B. de Mille even used his influence to get the phrase 'Dianetic processing' inserted into the scripts of a number of 'B' movies in place of the word 'psychoanalysis', and as a result uncomprehending movie audiences from Harwich to Hong

Kong heard a well-known actress announce in one film that she was late for a 'Dianetic session'.

The well-known film director, Cy Endfield—*Zulu*, *Hide and Seek* and, more recently, *de Sade* are some of his best known films—was at that time working in California. Like many others in the movie business he had been intrigued by the impact Dianetics was making in Hollywood, and was sufficiently curious to attend one or two meetings in Los Angeles where the well-known science fiction writer, A. E. Van Vogt, lectured warmly on the topic. Endfield found it all a bit unconvincing, but when it was announced that shortly the founder himself would be lecturing and *presenting the world's first Clear* to a public meeting he decided that this was too good an opportunity to miss.

The venue was the famous Shrine Auditorium in Los Angeles, a huge hall capable of accommodating six thousand. This was packed to capacity, for good—or at least interesting—news travels fast. Endfield recalls that a stir of excitement ran through the audience when Hubbard, after speaking at some length on various matters, called out on to the stage a pretty college student called Sonia Bianca, whom he introduced to the audience as the world's first Clear. Miss Bianca, who seemed somewhat overcome by it all, answered a few routine questions from Hubbard without revealing any spectacular powers, and it is possible that Hubbard thought that no more formal demonstration than this was necessary. But it was not to be, for Mr Endfield, remembering that Clears were currently supposed to have perfect recall of all sense perceptions and knowing Miss Bianca was a major in physics, decided to ask her some simple questions in her own topic. Amazingly she seemed unable to remember even rudimentary formulae, such as Boyle's Law, and fell down completely when asked to give the colour of Hubbard's tie when his back was turned. It was an awful moment. There was improper laughter and sections of the audience got up and left.

With this flop in mind it is no wonder that Hubbard showed no great enthusiasm when, in 1952, news came from an unexpected quarter that another Clear had been created. The story of this Clear, and the ones that followed, is revealing.

In 1951, it will be recalled, the mathematician Chapdelaine had been acting as an auditor for Hubbard during the so-called research period which gave the world the first news of the 'Clam' and the 'Weeper'. For various reasons Chapdelaine felt that Dianetics could achieve remarkable effects, and he was eager to do whatever he could to assist its progress, however unusual the tasks he might be called upon to do. And some of the tasks were very odd indeed. On one occasion Hubbard handed him a bundle of papers with some assorted rough notes on them, asking him to convert the data they contained into mathematical form. Chapdelaine strongly suspected that these notes were the famous 'original thesis' of Dianetics, and he burnt much midnight oil trying to get some way into what seemed an impossible task. He succeeded in part, and produced a set of semi-formalized statements which he handed to Hubbard telling him it was impossible to do any better with the material provided. It now seems likely that these efforts were later further adapted, probably by Hubbard himself, into what are now known as the *Logics, Pre-Logics and Axioms*, a set of numbered statements faintly reminiscent of Wittgenstein's *Tractatus*. From these appear to be derived the 'Factors'—30 numbered statements like 'And there are Universes' or 'The action of dimension point is reaching and withdrawing'. These have been set to music by Scientologist Bobby Richards and are sung rather like psalms at Scientology church meetings. Mr Richards presently holds the post of 'Master of the Commodore's Music'.

Another task given to the willing, but disconcerted mathematician, was to help Hubbard launch the ill-fated 'Allied Scientists of the World' organization. This, one of Ron's lesser-known enterprises, began with a direct-mail shot—six secretaries worked for weeks merely typing envelopes—to most of the working scientists in America and some other parts of the globe. They were invited, for a small fee, to enrol in a new organization which was to act as a clearing house for scientific literature, and was planning, among other schemes, to build an H-bomb-proof underground library. Chapdelaine was suddenly woken one night and dispatched peremptorily by Hubbard to Denver, Colorado to open the head office of the organization and to handle what was presumably expected to be a vast and enthusiastic rush to join. After a week or so, during which time only four out of the many thousands of scientists circulated showed any interest to the extent of sending in dollars, the 'Allied Scientists of the World' was rapidly wound up and Chapdelaine returned, penniless, to Wichita. Here he found the atmosphere distinctly unhappy, with Hubbard showing signs of quarrelling with his millionaire backer, and in a moment of decision he withdrew from the headquarters organization to practise Dianetics privately.

It was at this point he began auditing an individual named Ron Howes, and achieved such apparent success with him that in early 1952 he became convinced that he had in his hands a potential Clear. Howes was a physical chemist from Minneapolis who had recently undergone an operation for the removal of a kidney stone. His rapid return to health, accompanied by much auditing, and his abnormal visual memory led Chapdelaine to the view that the great breakthrough was imminent, and on 20th January 1952 Ron Howes was declared Clear.

If Chapdelaine was confident of this achievement, Howes was even more so. In an extraordinary interview which he gave a few days later, and which was published by the Psychological Research Foundation (a Scientology offshoot in Phoenix, Arizona), he reveals touches of megalomania and intellectual hyper-confidence which are characteristic of the manic state achieved with a religious conversion. The content of the dialogue turns out to be, unfortunately, middle-grade science fiction, spiced with some muddled philosophy. I am quoting now some extended passages below so that the reader may judge the flavour for himself.

Q: What do you intend to do with your new powers?

Howes: They are not new. All I have done is to recover the full use of my control centres. I am reintegrating all my purposes, goals, postulates, effects, causes, until I have rid myself of all my agreements to be modified cause.

Q: What is possible?

Howes: For me at the moment, anything and everything is possible. The only arbitrary is time. Now if I become other than what I am in the optimum state I may remove the arbitrary. Then everything, in an instant, is possible.

After a rather dull patch in which Howes delivers a homily

on creativity, and a point where he hints at telepathic powers he is asked a series of questions about his supposed supernormal abilities. The answers, which at the time were counted as being historic, are worth quoting verbatim to give some idea of what people were hoping for, for themselves and for others, from the achievement of the state of Clear:

Q: What is your reading speed compared to what it was?

Howes: It's mighty fast and improving steadily every day. I noticed, and my wife remarked upon it, that I seemed to be turning the pages about three times as fast. My comprehension of printed material has gone up enormously compared to the past. The more difficult paragraphs in technical reading are very easy now. No confusion, no identity, no failure. My ability to pick up errors in judgement of other people on paper is much higher.

Q: Can you be affected by bacteria?

Howes: I still believe that there are bacteria which I can't resist, but there must be many bacteria that I can resist now that I could never resist before.

Q: What do you contemplate as your duration of life?

Howes: In chronological years, if my anti-gravity plan works, I would assume approximately another four hundred years. Under present circumstances. one hundred and a quarter.

Q: What experiments have you performed on yourself?

Howes: One of them concerns such a simple little thing as sunburn. I had been sunburned approximately a full year, continuously, in my life. In the past had I taken even as much as fifty milligrams of niacin, I'd have burnt like a furnace for days. Now, after running out of sunburn, I can take niacin to my heart's content. No more sunburn. The other night I loaded myself with 400 milligrams of niacin—no blush, no heat, no pallor, no sunburn.

Another experiment concerns changing the total pH of the body. One very definitely affects ability by changing the balance between acidity and alkalinity. I'm attempting to find out just how alkaline I can get and still be maximum cause.

I've also tried to see if I can regenerate teeth. For the moment I've got some very sore gums but no teeth. Perry suggested to me, in a roundabout way, that I should regenerate teeth. Sunday, Monday, Tuesday, Wednesday I got extremely sore gums. Teeth were pulled out. I've regenerated tissue. To the maximum extent I can. The soreness is now disappearing. The gums are much more healthy. Next point is what constitutes a seed tooth? I think it's possible to construct them again. Incidentally, I haven't decided what I am going to look like yet.

Q: Have you made any experiment with sleep?

Howes: Yes. I went forty-eight hours without it. There was no diminution of my enthusiasm and my control, but there was a definite lag physically. The body requires rest. Rest permits muscles, blood, nerves to undergo certain readjustments. Without this rest one might continue for possibly two weeks without sleep.

Apart from the occasional word or phrase drawn from the jargon of Scientology, which may be unfamiliar to the general reader, there should be no difficulty in understanding the gist of this interview, nor its implications. It is quite evident that here were a number of intelligent human beings who, for a brief period of time, believed that one of their number had been created a superman—the first of a new species of man who would gradually replace the old as surely as homo sapiens replaced the Australopithecines and Neanderthal Man. In other contemporary literature the being which the techniques of Dianetics and Scientology were creating was even assigned a special name—*homo novus,* the New Man.

The creating of a superior race to replace our own seemed at the time to be an inevitable consequence of the arrival of Dianetics, and when the news of the 'clearing' of Ron Howes spread, a surge of new confidence ran through the movement. Only Hubbard, significantly, seemed sceptical, though he apparently became more interested when reports were circulated that Howes was developing unusual telepathic powers. The first specimen of *homo novus* certainly went through a period of hyperconfidence in his own powers and even began issuing a series of pretentious 'Bulletins' and 'Messages' to other Scientologists which must have considerably niggled Hubbard, who liked to reserve such *ex cathedra* statements for himself.

The first such Bulletin begins pompously: 'The following is addressed to all optimum and pre-optimum humans . . .', and then goes on to advise on the steps needed to develop the optimum race, using phrases such as 'tone-scale' (a Dianetics concept which allows one to assess the level of 'beingness', or super-power of the Thetan), 'life-cause', 'race intelligence' and other such mystic notions.

The reference to growing new teeth must have intrigued many readers. This, together with radical improvements in eyesight, increased muscle tone, etc., were counted at the time as being merely some of the inevitable concomitants of being a Clear, and would certainly seem to merit investigation. Howes, as we noted, felt that his new powers were beginning to make his gums itch—presumably a step in the right direction—but he seems not to have got much further than this. But before long a minor spate of new Clears arrived—none from Hubbard's stable, but rather from the hands of individual auditors in various parts of the country. These Clears, and their auditors, must have presented a ticklish dilemma to L. Ron, who could neither deny their genuineness, because they were merely following his gospel and producing the predicted miracles, nor publicly sponsor them in case—as he must certainly have expected—they were merely flashes in the pan. Instead he preserved a steely silence, the best strategy of all. But steadily the list grew.

On the 'third day of the third month, 1952', Jack Horner was reporting from Van Nuys, California, that he had been auditing a fifteen-year-old girl who had reached the state of Clear with dramatic ease. She had begun to exploit her new powers by 'clearing up all the minor scars on the body'. She also learnt typing from scratch, achieving twenty-five words a minute after merely studying the keyboard chart for fifteen minutes.

'Because some of her teeth were bad', Horner reports in a letter, which contains not the slightest sign of corroborative evidence to back up these claims, 'she had decided to make them fall out and grow new ones in their place. She decided that a mole on her cheek would look good so she grew one, then decided it didn't look so good after all and made it disappear. . . .'

Another magnificent specimen of *homo novus* was the former motor mechanic, H. R. 'Wing' Angell of Denver, Colorado, who made a name for himself in the fifties, thanks to a lecture tour in which he amazed audiences with accounts of the wonders he had performed—or could if he could only be bothered to. At one session, when asked directly what changes in himself he had actually experienced, the following dialogue took place:

Angell: Well, when old man Hubbard wrote a book, I got it the first week in June 1950. As I sat down to read that book with my thick glasses, my trembling hands, my paroxysmal tachycardia kicking against my ribs, my indigestion and my general attitude that the world owed me a living and was damn sure not doing anything about it . . . I was a mess. Now I know my body from one end to the other and it's a friend of mine, a part of me. I know the Universe around me better than I ever have before, and I enjoy everything in it. What more could you want?

Q: And the tachycardia and the various things like that?

Angell: They went away—I didn't need them any more!

It was as simple as that. Later, when asked about growing teeth, he replied:

> 'Yeah, I'd like to talk about teeth in a broad general basis. I discovered that a person can grow new teeth if he wants 'em, and *I've done so*. But that's parlour tricks. They aren't even teeth that would have been valuable to me one way or the other. It was just an experiment and it worked.'

For years Wing Angell was known primarily for his claim to have grown new teeth, and he certainly made the most of it. It is possible that he was even behind an anonymous company which launched advertisements in a number of the occult and psychic fringe periodicals in 1956 stating in bold letters:

GROW NEW TEETH!
IT CAN BE DONE! IT HAS BEEN DONE!
Write Box . . .

It is barely necessary to assure readers that none of the tooth regeneration claims were ever attested by independent medical, dental or scientific authorities, and one suspects that Angell's new dentition was about as functional as Howes's proposed anti-gravity machine. Of the little glut of early Clears, incidentally, few appear to be connected in any way with Scientology now, or with Hubbard. Howes is a successful salesman somewhere in America, Miss Bianca and Jack Horner's protégé cannot be readily traced, and Wing Angell died of a heart attack while still a youngish man some years ago. But, by the end of 1952, the fashion for producing Clears had died away, and some serious rifts in the movement were beginning to appear.

Thought Has Mass

JUST OVER TWO years after its sensational beginnings, a critic attempting to survey the status of Dianetics and Scientology might at first be inclined to the view that it was in a sturdy condition. The name of the founder was known all over America and in many other parts of the world. Literally hundreds of thousands of people—perhaps as many as a million—had had some first-hand experience of auditing and were familiar with the principles of Dianetic therapy. Many claimed to have received some positive benefit from it. Furthermore, the philosophy (as expounded through Scientology), with the concepts of the Thetan and its limitless past lives, its immortality and potential omipotence, and also the strange but imaginative idea that life was a game played by Gods—ourselves—who had temporarily lost their God-like powers, had struck a spark in many quarters.

On closer inspection everything in the garden was revealed as anything but lovely. True there were numerous claims of the successes of Dianetics therapy—but there is nothing remarkable about this. It is well known to any qualified medical practitioner or psychologist that neurotic symptoms—often quite spectacular ones—may dramatically yield as soon as the sick individual acquires a strong faith in something. This faith may be in magic, in spiritual healing, in Christian Science, in some quack doctor, in herbal remedies or whatever. Provided it is strong enough, neurotic symptoms will yield, temporarily. And such was turning out to be the case with the first Dianetic cures, and with the inevitable relapses came the inevitable disillusionment.

Furthermore, through his constant claims that the therapy worked, and that it could be made to work even better, Hubbard seems to have got himself into the difficult position of having constantly to supply marvels in order to simply stay in one place. Hence the repeated announcements of dramatic new techniques 'hundreds of times more effective' than the previous ones, etc., etc. But at each step, of course, the time between the making of the claim and the request for explanations as to why it didn't work, became shorter and shorter.

Even Hubbard's most solid converts, Campbell and the physician, Dr Joseph Winter, fled the field—the former by turning quietly back to science fiction of the space-ship variety, the latter by a public renunciation of Hubbard in his interesting book *A Doctor Looks at Dianetics*. Winter had been wildly enthusiastic in the early days, and for a medical man showed himself to be quite credulous. After the split with Hubbard which came partly, as we have said earlier, because Hubbard was 'prescribing' his weird mixture of vitamins—GUK—to accompany auditing, and partly, perhaps, because of Hubbard's rooted disinclination to have anyone in his entourage who might constitute a rival, Winter set up in practice with his own version of Dianetics. This he persisted with until his death a few years ago.

Another man to fall out with Ron was his fellow science fiction writer, A. E. Van Vogt, who also set up to practise a modified version of Dianetics in California. Van Vogt and Hubbard later made it up for a while, the former writing a fantastic science fiction novel, *The Universe Makers*, in which a man gradually acquires super powers through various Scientological insights and ends up creating and destroying the Universe at will. At the time of writing Van Vogt is still true to the principles of Dianetics and still practising them on a professional basis.

The story of the association between Purcell and Hubbard and its ultimate demise is worth telling for it helps one to understand the abrupt transition between Dianetics and Scientology which took place in the early fifties, and which is otherwise so puzzling. There are several versions of the tale each with minor variations, but most agree on salient points. In 1950, after the first raving runaway success of Dianetics when, briefly, orthodox medicine and psychology turned curious eyes on the cult and its techniques, there were signs of important rifts in the upper echelons of the movement. These, it appears, were occasioned by the conflict of goals and interest between Hubbard himself and the numerous intelligent, and often very well-educated, professional men who had become involved in Dianetics. Some of these, like Frederick Schuman, Professor of Government at Williams College, Massachusetts, who, in a letter to the *New York Times,* declared that 'History has become a race between Dianetics and catastrophe', went completely overboard on the topic. Others, like Winter, gradually cooled their enthusiasm. All were united however at one time with the aim of getting Hubbard 'organized', in other words moulding his personality and ideas into some sort of traditional or establishment form, and thereby making Dianetics and its practice academically and professionally 'OK'. In this enterprise they were doomed, for if there is one person on earth who dislikes being organized by others it is L. Ron Hubbard. Tensions grew steadily, with matters complicated by the fact that Hubbard's second marriage was hitting the rocks. He had been divorced from his first wife, Margaret Louise Grubb, in 1947, and married his second, Sarah Northrup, somewhere about this time—and she had become enthusiastically involved in Dianetics. For some reason or another, and quite possibly with some justification, Hubbard began to suspect that his wife and other Dianeticists, including Dr Winter, were planning to take control of the organization out of his hands. According to his son Nibs, he even entertained the notion, altogether less plausible, that the red hand of Communism was at work attempting to steal the secrets of Dianetics from the West and, after a peculiar incident in his New York apartment when he believed he had been drugged and 'brainwashed', Hubbard packed a few belongings and, with characteristic decision, left for Puerto Rico. A great flap arose in the Dianetic Research Foundation when it was discovered that the leader had departed, and press interest was also considerable. It was at this point that the millionaire Purcell intervened. After tracking down L. Ron in San Juan he persuaded him to return with the promise that Dianetics would be put on a business footing—which in Purcell's eyes meant establishing it along formal company lines. This Hubbard agreed to, though with what alacrity is not known. In return Purcell launched and partly financed the Hubbard Dianetic Foundation at 211 West Douglas Avenue, Wichita, which now replaced Elizabeth, NJ, as the focal point of Dianetic activity. There was a big snag, however. Convinced that Hubbard needed 'organizing' Purcell had persuaded him to assign the rights of his books, recorded tapes, techniques and all the titles and paraphernalia of Dianetics over to the Foundation. Hubbard's stake in the whole business was no longer that of the autocratic creator, but rather that of something equivalent to a company director. According to acquaintances of his this proved too much for his roving intellect, and in February 1952 he did another disappearing trick and, grabbing a typewriter and not much else, moved to Phoenix, Arizona, to start all over again. But alas he now found himself in the maddening position of being legally unable to practise or even write about his very own brainchild—Dianetics!

Lesser men might here have given up and turned to cactus growing or to Christian Science, but not Mr Lafayette Ronald Hubbard. With magnificent aplomb he launched, from its new headquarters in Phoenix, the latest brand new science to supersede Dianetics—Scientology. Before long this was issuing its own journal replete with such headlines as 'Source of Life Energy Found!', photographs of his 'Desert Research Laboratory', and warnings about something called 'Black Dianetics'.

What exactly went on in this scholarly haven is not absolutely certain, but there is little doubt that some remarkable thoughts passed through L. Ron's head. One discovery that he seems to have made at this time was that it was relatively easy for the Thetan to leave the physical body at will. This could be accomplished by the simple expedient of the auditor saying to the preclear: 'Be three feet back of your head'. One didn't need even to be a sensationally advanced Scientologist to do this and Hubbard claimed that sixty per cent of humanity could achieve 'exteriorization', as the trick was called, on the first attempt. This is still one of the basic features of any sustained period of auditing today, and most Scientologists will tell you that they can achieve it. Unfortunately they never seem to be able to do anything useful or interesting when exteriorized. It is no good, for example, asking them to read something written on a bit of paper in another room or even to describe an object hidden behind their backs, for you will be told loftily that such tricks can't be done to order or, more maddeningly, 'I could if I wanted to, but right now I don't want to'. Exteriorization may have been going on since the early 1950s but, to be frank, it seems to be one of Man's most useless metaphysical accomplishments.

It was also in this period of hiatus that Hubbard, or one of his organizations, is reputed to have offered for sale the typescript of a work called *Excalibur*. This allegedly contained data so staggering that it was 'not to be released during Mr Hubbard's stay on earth' and would-be purchasers would be sworn 'not to permit other readers to read it'. 'Gold-bound and locked', individually typed and retailing at fifteen hundred dollars, it is hard to say, without reading it, whether it was worth the money or not. Nor can it have been a joke, for the blurb for *Excalibur* warned that 'four of the first fifteen people to read it had gone insane'.[1]

Meanwhile back in Wichita, the Hubbardless Dianetic Foundation pottered slowly on, feebly attempting to quantify the ephemeral phenomena of the cult, desperately hoping to achieve academic and professional recognition. Within two years, despite its hold on Hubbard's earlier books and the world famous name of Dianetics, it was teetering on the edge of bankruptcy. Purcell and his colleagues learned the hard way that whatever the cult was called and however professionally it was organized, it was nothing without L. Ron.

With supporters melting away and no new Clears to speak of, things in Scientology were beginning to look almost dull. Fortunately there appeared on the scene a simple but impressive piece of gadgetry which has caused as much controversy as any of the stunts connected with Scientology and which is now perhaps one of the most important features of any standard Scientological auditing session. I am referring of course to the magnificently styled 'electropsychometer'—or more simply, the 'E-meter'. In modern cults quasi-scientific gadgets often play an important role, as we shall note in later sections of this book. Because of the importance of the E-meter to Scientology theory and practice and because of the muddled image—a mixture of witchcraft, brainwashing and electronic hocus-pocus—which the press publicity has unfairly created

[1] The author has made strenuous attempts to trace individuals who bought and read *Excalibur* without success. Is this because they were holding to their oath of secrecy, or perhaps because they went mad on finding what they had paid $1,500 for?

for it we shall take a close look at the device. Before doing so, however, it will also be necessary to take a brief refresher course on the techniques of auditing.

It will be recalled that engrams and hang-ups of various kinds evaporate when the individual 'confronts' them and shows that he can control or manipulate them at will. The auditor directs the patient or preclear along the track of his past lives and zeros in on any point where the memory seems either particularly acute or resistant. Once the incident is spotted, the preclear is ordered to control it by suitable fantasies —he may be invited to 'destroy it' or 'recreate it' a large number of times, and make it smaller or bigger by suitable use of his powers of imagination until he feels able to 'handle it' and reduce or erase its oppressive hold on him.

For example, let us suppose that the auditor has discovered that his preclear is 'stuck' with an incident involving a dead crow—it may have been the last thing he saw before he died in the Battle of Hastings, or something along those lines. Now one way of eliminating this incident would be for the preclear to acquire mastery over the mental images of dead crows, and the auditor can help achieve this by requiring him to manipulate, in his mind, various mental pictures—they are called 'mock-ups' in Scientology jargon. He may be asked to destroy dead crows, 'burn' them, imagine himself eating them, watch other people eating them, etc., etc. When he has done this many times and he begins to seem a bit *blasé* about it all, the incident is reckoned to be erased and eliminated as a debilitating engram. In the early days of Dianetics many dramatic cures were reported to have arisen as the result of processing of this kind.

It is important to realize that to Scientologists the mental images which most of us can observe and manipulate in our mind's eye, so to speak, are not just fantasy creatures of the brain, but have a real and objective existence in their own space time continuum where the Thetan with his omnipotent powers has created them. In principle it should be possible to create such an image to be so 'real' that other people could see it as well as oneself. At this point the object has 'reality' for them as well as for you. The universe we inhabit at the moment, according to the Scientologists, is simply the result of a whole bunch of Thetans—you, me and everyone else—at some time agreeing to share reality on a number of these mock-ups and these now constitute the world around us.

This explains the great weight attached in Scientological processing to the ability to handle these mental images with skill, and it is tough luck on those members of the human race who don't have the necessary vivid visual imagination, for they can be slow to advance in Scientology.

Returning now to the point from which we digressed, even those familiar with the marvels of auditing will appreciate that in the early days it was one thing to *talk* about identifying the points in the memory track where the significant or repressed incidents occurred, and another thing to actually *find* them. At best an auditor would have to rely on getting some signal—such as a twitch or gasp from his preclear—when he got near some critical point and it might be all too easy to be misled by such unreliable incidents. Then, in late 1950 or early 1951, an individual named Volney Mathison turned up in Elizabeth, NJ, bearing a strange but intriguing box, equipped with wires, handles, a dial, etc., which he claimed was capable of measuring thought.

To anyone engaged in the tricky business of tracking down thoughts and memories, Mathison's device would seem to be just what was wanted, but Hubbard, who never seems to care for developments in Scientology which are not his own, was at first rather suspicious of it. However, the staff at the Research Foundation felt sufficiently curious to look into the matter further and sought a demonstration of its worth.

The trick, Mathison explained, was to hold one handle in each hand, set the meter needle at zero, and then start to think of something. When any unpleasant or dramatic thought occurred, lo, the needle would swing dramatically across the dial. To many people the electropsychometer was a truly marvellous device, and its potential for auditing was not lost on the group present. On the other hand, anyone who had ever tinkered with electronics or taken a course in experimental psychology, would immediately have recognized it as a device for measuring what is known as the galvanic skin response—a change in the electrical conductivity of the skin which occurs during periods of even slight excitability or emotional stress.

The basic principle is that the individual, by taking one of the two terminals of the set-up in each hand, becomes part of an electrical circuit via a little amplifier and recording meter —in scientific jargon, the psychogalvanometer. Changes in the resistance of this circuit will cause deflections of the needle on the meter.

Now there are various ways in which this resistance can be varied, as the first psychologists working with the 'galvanic skin response' in the nineteenth century discovered. In the first place, if the terminals are held in the hands of the individual and the grips gently squeezed, this will produce a better contact between metal and skin surface, thus lowering the resistance and inducing a corresponding change in the reading on the meter. Another cause of reduction in the resistance of the circuit is the production of sweat, even in minute amounts, on the surface of the skin, for the saline acts as a conductor which again causes needle deflection. Since both these effects, particularly the first one, are under the voluntary control of the individual linked to the galvanometer, the device in its simplest form is more or less useless as an objective measure of his psychological state. Obviously anyone wishing to induce a needle change may do so simply by squeezing the terminals, and with a little practice one can soon cause the needle to do just what one wants it to.

There is in fact a third important phenomenon involved. This is a very minor change in the electrical conductivity of the skin itself which is part of the general sensitizing process occurring when a human or an animal is alerted or aroused— and this slight change, which is *not* under conscious voluntary control but pretty well a reflex act, can be measured by a sensitive galvanometer. In order to rule out artificial results caused by squeezing, sweating, etc., the proper use of the galvanometer requires that small electrodes, coated with a neutral jelly, are attached to the palms of the hand. When set up in this form (a standard laboratory demonstration in university psychology courses) the needle will then be seen to move about spectacularly when the subject is threatened with a pinprick, when some taboo word is spoken or a grisly photograph shown.

Now Scientologists dispense with the primary precautions outlined above and the preclear simply hold the terminals— they look like small tin cans—in his hand. Thus the significant incidents in his past life, or lives, which the E-meter is supposed to root out, can be produced pretty well at will either by conscious or unconscious effort on the part of the person being audited. Even when the meter is not being watched by the preclear himself, but is being monitored by the auditor, it is of course perfectly easy for the latter to give unconscious signals to the other as to when he wants the needle to move. (Such unconscious signals are exceedingly common and contributed enormously to the early 'evidence' for telepathy when subjects under tests were not hidden from each other by screens.) Significantly, the final steps to the state of Clear are approached by a long period of 'solo-auditing' in which the subject monitors his own E-meter at each stage.

When tackled on the question of using cans rather than electrodes in an effort to rule out voluntary control of the E-meter, Scientologists argue that the kind of deflection caused by a squeeze is very characteristic, and that trained auditors know how to disregard such artefacts. They even hold that the movements caused by an increase or decrease in sweat output, etc., produce responses which are detectable to the trained operator, and that there is a further class of needle activity, due to none of the above causes, which is the real meat of the matter. The important point, they claim, is that the mental images of past happenings, whether traumatic or not and whether in this or in any previous life, are *real* events which have an objective existence outside their representation in the memory store.

In other words, thought has mass and when an object is imagined it acquires a reality which may be sufficiently substantial to influence the circuitry of the E-meter. Changes in the circuit occur because at one moment there is just the person and the gadget, but when he creates his mental image or recalls his engram, this intrudes as an extra in the system. Sometimes the thought may have relatively *low* mass and needle deflections will be small or slow; on other occasions, such as in the so-called 'Rock-slam'—a very important incident in the auditing and one which denotes a major traumatic incident in the past—the mass detected may be so great that the needle gives a wild and erratic kick.

True, the 'Rock-slam' was a phenomenon unknown, at least by that name, to the psychologists who tinkered with the skin galvanometer a hundred years ago, but there is no reason to suppose that they were not aware of it as just another example of the gadget's capricious and unpredictable behaviour. What Scientologists seem to have done is to explore the whims and oddities of this particular box of tricks to a completely novel extent, lavishing far more attention on it than it has ever received before. This conclusion is supported by the austere British Psychological Society which, in 1970, had a long cool look at the E-meter and judged it to be no more than an unreliable version of the old GSR. To the simple-minded amateurs who hung around Hubbard's *ménage*, however, such critical thoughts did not occur and Mathison's device was a winner from the word go—particularly when he showed how it might be used to spot blocks or engrams before the preclear himself was aware of them. For those few sceptics who had a sneaking feeling that there was something familiar about the gadget, Mathison proudly produced the US patent number on the base of the device which he considered ample authentication of his claim to be its inventor. This should have squashed all traces of scepticism had not some unpleasantly suspicious auditor (even among Scientologists there are to be found occasional naughty fellows who won't swallow everything they're told) decided to note the number and check with the US Patents Office. He was rewarded, if puzzled, with the discovery that the patent number referred not to any device for measuring thought invented by Volney Mathison in 1950, but to a special kind of threshing machine developed in 1860 by some long-forgotten mid-west farmer. Despite this, it was agreed that the E-meter, whoever invented it, worked very nicely and ever since then we find it featuring heavily in all Scientology literature. It is also an essential prerequisite to anyone seriously thinking of a career in Scientology, and most students now proudly own one. These days they cost about £60 ($150) and are equipped with pretty dials and nice handgrips.

But even the innovation of the E-meter had little effect in arresting the steady decline in interest in Dianetics which was taking place in the early fifties and the relative lack of enthusiasm for its more philosophically oriented successor, Scientology. In the meantime Hubbard began to look overseas for fresh fields to conquer. The most promising areas would seem to have been the English-speaking countries including Australia, South Africa and New Zealand, where his fame had in some measure already spread, and, of course, England.

To English people, judging by the patronizing comments published at the time of the fad's peak moments, the craze for Dianetics and the success of its effusive founder were merely another example of the American characteristic of falling for such sensational nonsense as flagpole squatting and underwater weddings. It is interesting and ironic that nowadays Americans, who have forgotten the original fuss, view Scientology, with its flock of attendant hippies and its suggestions of sexual broad-mindedness, as characteristically British and are inclined to assume that the whole thing had its roots in the market town of East Grinstead. But in 1953, at about the time Martin Gardner was writing in his *Fads and Fallacies* that the cult had burnt out, Hubbard looked not to traditionally staid Britain for room to start afresh, but to those far-flung remnants of the British Empire, Australia, and South Africa. Accordingly, while keeping his headquarters in Phoenix, he took off on a round-the-world trip with special long stops in Sydney and Adelaide, Johannesburg and Durban. Here he found small knots of supporters waiting to greet him, and the nucleus of branch headquarters, generally in some small rented office, either set up or just about to be.

The technique employed in establishing formal Scientology organizations across the world was straightforward and followed a similar pattern in all English-speaking countries. In the first instance local groups existing in major cities (these would generally have come about as the result of a bunch of characters, often science fiction fans, getting together to audit each other) would be visited by a member of the Phoenix staff. He would act as Hubbard's personal envoy, giving a number of lectures to the natives and perhaps doing a little paid auditing. If things looked well, he would arrange for the setting up of a formal office with a small staff and a stock of books, tape recordings of Hubbard lectures, etc. Before long the local branch would begin giving official courses in Scientology, leading to the award of certificates of proficiency which would allow the individual to practise a special kind of psychotherapy using Scientology techniques.

For those sufficiently motivated or with enough money to spend, one could even take a course leading to the 'degree' of Bachelor of Scientology (B.Scn.). If you think that this abbreviation might make the unwary believe that the holder had a degree of Bachelor of Science (B.Sc.), then you are right. This qualification, which might set one back £100 or so, would allow one to set off on the greatest trail of all—the quest for the highest Scientological award, the Doctorate (D.Scn.), cheap at the price you may feel, for a further £200. The value of having a doctorate (never mind what it's in) to anyone engaged in the practice of psychotherapy is obvious, and the course was a popular one.[1]

In 1955, after duly surveying likely parts of the Commonwealth, Hubbard arrived in England where he found the nucleus of activity centred in the 'Scientology Clinic' in Notting Hill Gate. It is not certain who in the Scientology organization chose the loaded word 'clinic' to describe the movement's rather poky set of offices and rooms in Notting Hill. It is hard, however, to imagine policy decisions of this kind coming from anyone other than Hubbard himself. The practice of so describing Scientology centres was not confined to Britain and in issue 34-G of the American journal *Scientology*, in a longish article on 'Scientology Certificates', we are told that the 'degree of "Doctor of Scientology" is awarded only after a person has . . . completed his training as a Bachelor of Scientology in the Advanced Clinical Course Units'. The 'powers' of a Doctor of Scientology, the article continues, are 'considerable'. He may train, examine and revoke certificates and he may 'found clinics'. The maximum fee for the acquisition of the Doctorate at the time, via a mandatory sequence of lesser degrees, was fifteen hundred dollars.

In considering the motivation and orientation of Scientology and its practitioners, in its early if not its later stage of development, one is obliged to take into account the considered use of doctorates and such expressions as 'clinic', 'advanced clinical course', etc. (The OED defines clinic as 'a private hospital to which patients are recommended by individual doctors' or as an 'institution attached to a hospital'.) Both Scientology clinics and Scientology 'doctors' disappeared quietly from the scene at some uncertain date in the late fifties or early sixties as the movement continued its shift from a predominantly therapeutic to a largely 'spiritual' role.

[1] Scientology policy today is that D.Scn. stands for Dean of Scientology.

One of Hubbard's first moves on his arrival in England was to give a series of public lectures at the New Lindsay Theatre Club in Notting Hill. These were attended by enthusiastic audiences who had longed for a glimpse of the man in person. The lectures attracted almost no attention, either hostile or friendly, from the press, and the audiences were almost entirely composed of committed Scientologists or fellow-travellers.

This of course has been very much the case right back to square one. Ever since the unfortunate encounter at the Shrine Auditorium he has picked his ground with great care, preferring to address conferences of Scientologists only, where fairly steep admission charges are made and dissident elements will be non-existent. This partly explains the uneven quality of Hubbard's platform talks which contain material so badly organized that only the most committed of audiences would be prepared to tolerate them. Nevertheless, with his disciples they are undoubtedly successful and tape recordings of them are listened to with great attention and devotion at special meetings and congresses which Hubbard, for various reasons, seldom attends these days.

It is a pity that a record or tape of one of these speeches is not available to go along with this book. The very highly motivated may like to know that such tapes can be purchased for about £12.50 *per reel* from Scientology branch shops, but most non-Scientologists will find that their value, even as humorous or historical pieces, could never approach that figure. They generally last a bit less than an hour, and for anyone not absolutely convinced that he is hearing the words of the Messiah, listening to more than one of them can be a tedious experience. Hubbard's voice, it is true, is an interesting one, rich and well-modulated. His platform timing is excellent, and he sprinkles the talk with mildly humorous anecdotes of a personal nature delivered with enough skill to raise a laugh from his eager audience.

What is really at fault is the tenuous subject matter which seldom has a consistent theme or bears much relation to the announced title of the talk. In one tape on *The History of Dianetics* for example—which ought to make an interesting talk whoever were to give it—all one is treated to are a lot of anecdotes about Hubbard's life in the navy, some reminiscences of the famous Commander Thompson and a lot of joking or sardonic attacks on psychiatrists, revealing a particular obsession of Hubbard's which runs like a vein through all his works and utterances.

When the title of the talk is on something like 'Becomingness' or 'Confrontingness'—typical Scientology jargon—the message is even more obscure and yet the audience laugh and applaud as enthusiastically as ever. The truth of the matter is probably that indoctrinated Scientologists lower their critical level below the point dictated by common sense, and one gets the feeling that were Hubbard to stand on the platform and recite the telephone directory backwards he would still receive a standing ovation.

To give Hubbard his due, he has made imaginative use of modern methods of communication and must have been one of the first people to recognize the propaganda and financial worth of the tape recorder. Since the very early days of Dianetics, he has recorded special lectures, personal auditing sessions, etc., which have then been distributed all over the world and sold or rented at considerable profit. Nowadays the high point of the year among the faithful is the release of *Ron's Journal*, an annual verbal message to all Scientologists. This takes a form of a kind of cosy fireside chat—recorded in fact on Hubbard's ocean-going flagship—in which details of more sensational advances in Scientology are announced. Violent attacks are also made on the world of politics and big business, which he now declares are out to crush him.

Sometime in 1955 Hubbard evidently decided to quit America and settle in England. After a brief spell in a hotel he moved to a flat in London, holding open house for the small but ardent Scientology fraternity in the city. The movement was at this time at a very low ebb and remained so for at least five years before, after a slow rise, it suddenly leapt into spectacular prominence once more.

These were the years in the wilderness. The 'clinic' in Notting Hill Gate attracted only a sprinkling of visitors, a mixture of idlers, coffee-bar intellectuals, chronic neurotics, a few would-be bogus psychotherapists and the inevitable drab collection of cult-hunters who have worn and discarded in turn the garb of Christian Scientists, Theosophists, Spiritualists, Astrologists and Yogis. Hubbard himself seems to have been still fairly well off, though the London Scientology Organization itself was in a poor way. At meetings collections were made for the 'building fund', which was intended to produce some day 'Hubbard House', but when in 1956 about half of Notting Hill fell to the wreckers' ball, only a generous gesture by a friendly business man (neither the first nor the last of many) allowed a move to other, more spacious premises at Fitzroy Street.

More spacious accommodation was also needed for Hubbard's family by his wife Mary Sue, whom he had met and married in Wichita. By 1959 they had four children and the premises in Old Brompton Road were beginning to seem a bit squeezed. Emissaries were sent forth to scout for more suitable premises and one returned with a real catch in his net. It was Saint Hill Manor, the Maharajah of Jaipur's beautiful residence on the outskirts of East Grinstead in the green and leafy Sussex countryside. With eleven bedrooms, eight bathrooms, a ballroom, swimming pool and numerous living rooms it was spacious enough for almost anyone and its many acres of private grounds promised seclusion and isolation should they ever be needed. The selling price is stated to have been £16,000 and if so it was a bargain.

The Master of Saint Hill

WHEN LAFAYETTE RONALD HUBBARD first moved to Saint Hill Manor it looked to many outside observers as if Scientology was on a slow slide into oblivion. Public interest was low, new recruits were depressingly few, professional auditing no longer paid off, and of course there was still no sign of any Clears in view.[1] The attempt to recapture the gaudy days of Dianetics all over again in England seemed to have failed, and in some ways even the type of person interested in Scientology had changed. Gone were the intellectuals, the university graduates, the slightly off-beat professionals who had made up a substantial proportion of the pioneers. In their place was a mixture of men and women more likely to be small businessmen from Hounslow or aggressive secretaries from Melbourne with no pretensions to university life and no acquaintance with Kant or science fiction. Scientologists could argue that this was a shift in the right direction, a move from the pseudo to the honest which could only be beneficial, but it also suggests that Hubbard's original capacity to titillate the curiosity of the intellectual and the academic was waning.

It is reasonable to ponder here whether Hubbard himself was beginning to tire of the movement he had created and whether the shift to Saint Hill was the first move in a considered attempt at dissociation. This point of view, which would no doubt be hotly denied by Scientologists today, nevertheless appears to be supported to some measure by an examination of his public utterances and press interviews of the time. The most striking of these is probably the interview he granted to the magazine *Lilliput*, which was at that time

[1] Early claims of the Sonia Bianca, Ron Howes variety had one way or another apparently been brushed under the carpet.

in its death throes and attempting to contort itself in the kind of magazine *Playboy* is today. The article, not the most erudite or critical that has ever appeared in a British magazine, was entitled 'Sex Life of a Virile Cabbage', and it made practically no reference to Dianetics or Scientology. Instead the reporter, Charles Hamblett, found himself treated to a run-down on Hubbard's most recent researches which were to do with (as the title partly implies) the psychology of vegetables and Hubbard's successful attempts at communicating with them. According to Hubbard, whom the *Lilliput* reporter described as 'possibly the best-informed man alive today, besides whom Albert Schweitzer is a well-meaning medievalist and Aldous Huxley a naive mescaline pundit', it was vital to learn how to communicate with plants if we were to use them to the fullest advantage of mankind. By 'psychological observation' it was possible to deduce that there were amazing similarities between horticultural and human processes. 'There are mean plants, just as there are mean people', the reporter was informed. There were some plants that wanted to kill everybody and others that love everybody. The first were 'really vicious, the psychopaths'. Harping back to his exploring days, no doubt, Hubbard then told of the 'killer trees on the Amazon who seek to entwine their branches around the necks of explorers and choke them to death', of 'a certain common cactus in Arizona that will jump at the unwary passer-by' and even of the dreaded 'sparomomentum' of the South Pacific that would 'tear the shirt off a man's back'. As for the good plants, the 'easy-going ones', well they 'are gentle. They don't mind being eaten. And, boy', Hubbard is quoted as saying, 'are they sensitive!'[1] When he found that tomatoes 'scream for mercy when their skins are peeled and the lettuce howl when they are sliced' he was 'put off salads for days'. Hubbard was quick to point out that references to the squeals and howls of vegetables were figurative—a special instrument was needed to detect their cries of protest and outrage. The instrument itself was shown to the reporter and he calls it the 'Hubbard electrometer'—presumably another name for the E-meter, that

[1] Ten years later, interest in the topic of plant sensitivity and emotion has been aroused by the experiments of Mr Clyde Backster who is convinced that the vegetable kingdom can feel pain and register distress, and uses an E-meter-like device to detect their reactions.

most versatile of instruments in what many will agree is its most spectacular role to date.

The *Lilliput* article makes puzzling reading, and it is not clear how seriously the interview was taken by either party. However accurate or inaccurate the reporting, the whole episode goes some way at least in explaining the otherwise mysterious entry against Hubbard's name in the American *Who's Who in the South and West*, where he is described not only as a writer, explorer and nuclear physicist, but also as 'a pioneer in horticulture'.

As it happens it was this novel side to his scientific interests rather than Scientology that was stressed in his first interviews to the local press shortly after the removal vans had dumped their contents at Saint Hill Manor. A reporter from the Brighton *Evening Argus* secured an interview with Hubbard in April 1959, and wrote: 'The scientist grandson of a Montana cattle baron is the new owner of Saint Hill Manor, the millionaire mansion a mile from East Grinstead. He plans to escape from the "hammer and pound of the big city", writing and *experimenting with plant mutations*.'

'My hobbies are horticulture and raising flowers', Hubbard is stated to have told the reporter, adding 'I'll probably be setting up X-ray machines to make plants do strange things; to get them to mutate. That's one of my chief interests.' He also told the reporter that he had been working recently on 'technical stuff like nuclear physics' and aimed to finish a study of Scientology and retarded children.

Before long the horticulturalist-extraordinary was taking a dynamic interest in the affairs of East Grinstead and revealing yet another string to his well-strung bow. On 6th November 1959, the local paper reported that 'Dr Hubbard', after reading that the East Grinstead Road Safety Committee were seeking a Road Safety Organizer, 'placed himself and his organization' at their disposal after informing them of his world experience in this field of community service in the US. The result of all this was that the Committee duly invited Hubbard to attend their next meeting 'to tell them something of his vast experience in Philadelphia' and what he had been able to observe on road traffic conditions in this country. After addressing the Committee and proposing, among other things, an interesting string of linked traffic lights throughout the town, he was promptly elected East Grinstead's Road Safety Officer, a position he held for a brief period, receiving on his retirement from the post a 'vote of thanks' from the local council for services rendered.

For at least a year the honeymoon between the town and its eccentric millionaire scientist continued. The local paper reported his jaunts abroad to attend 'scientific conferences' in Australia, South Africa and America, and the word Scientology is rarely to be found. A competent photographer, Hubbard took pictures all around East Grinstead, advertising its shopping and other attractions in a little booklet which was later distributed free to Scientologists and townsfolk alike. He even seems to have acquired a butler who, suitably attired, would bring Coca Cola to his master on a silver tray.

All seemed set fair for Hubbard to slip gently into the role of eccentric country gent and local benefactor, and thus things might have stood today had it not been for the fact that in 1960, or thereabouts, against general expectations, Scientology began slowly to revive. It was also the beginning of the end of the honeymoon between Hubbard and the citizens of East Grinstead.

The cause of the steady return of Scientology to prominence at this time is hard to define. Had the long-promised state of Clear been suddenly achieved on a big scale there would have been no cause for surprise. But apart from the routine sensational news in the movement's unconvincing publications, there was no obvious sign of progress in that direction. The most probable reason would seem to be the move of Hubbard himself to this country, on a more or less permanent residential basis, thus making London, and later East Grinstead, the focal point of visits from overseas students. When the inadequate premises in London caused the overflow to Hubbard's own home, Saint Hill, the magnet gained even more strength; Scientologists were coming not just to a convenient point, but also to sit at the feet of the Master himself. A second possibility, much harder to argue (but far more interesting), is that at about this time Scientology began to exhibit the first real signs of metamorphosis from a questionable school of amateur psychotherapy into a definite, if rather eccentric, system of religious belief. This metamorphosis is very important and is worth looking at closely.

A study of the recorded beginnings of Dianetics reveals little hint of even the most unorthodox of religious belief being built into its philosophy. One might even hazard that in its early days Dianetics was almost anti-religious with its talk of creating supermen, and its implicit contempt for establishment beliefs in any form. Conversation with 'pioneers' of Dianetics seems to confirm that at this time orthodox religion was felt to have been totally outmoded by the discoveries of Hubbard, and that people of a religious mind tended to find it all rather offensive. There were some odd moments in the very early days of Scientology, it is true, when Hubbard seemed to be steering the whole concern into the realms of occultism. No better testimony to this can be found than the early issues of the journal *Scientology*. Issue 3-G, for example, with the incredible front-page headline SOURCE OF LIFE ENERGY FOUND, has as a sub-heading 'Scientology enters third echelon far ahead of schedule; revival of dead or near-dead may become possible'. The article reports that Hubbard had discovered the energy of life to be 'not a different thing from impulses such as electrons and protons but . . . the upper band of the same wave source which produces in the physical universe the energies earlier measured by James Clerk Maxwell, DeForest, Marconi and Edison'. Many answers to 'the riddle of human being-ness' had already been isolated by Hubbard, to whom the remaining answers came 'in a swift torrent'.

As one might expect, neither issue 3-G, nor issues 4, 5 or 6-G either, are specific about explaining the solved riddle of human beingness, and the article continues by saying that Dr Hubbard expected some scepticism in the face of his announcement—particularly that regarding the revival of the dead. Such scepticism was unjustified though, when one considered the 'considerable quantity of earlier knowledge known to the race'. For example, the Greek gods 'probably existed' and the 'energy glow and potential of Jesus Christ and early saints are common knowledge'. People had been trying to attain this level of potential for millennia without success. With Scientology 'the recovery of this energy potential and the ability to use it has become suddenly a matter of two to twenty-five hours of competent practice'. The state to be achieved was known as 'Theta Clear'.

This absurd stuff is quoted here merely to indicate the aura of fantasy which bathed the movement in its early days. It also serves to remind one of the kind of claims that that were being made by Hubbard and his colleagues in the name of Scientology at the time—made with no less confidence than are the claims of less miraculous and far more diffuse achievements today. For those who maintain that Dianetics and Scientology were never employed as an active form of psychological or even quasi-medical therapy, early issues of *Scientology,* or its stablemate *The Professional Auditors Bulletin,* will make revealing reading. Issue 15-G (1953) of the former features a column by Hubbard entitled 'The Old Man's Case Book' which quotes what it claims are extracts from 'the casebook of Dr Hubbard or advice he has given in letters or personally to auditors concerning the running of cases'. One such case concerned that of an eighteen-month-old baby, apparently suffering from leukaemia and 'expected to live one week according to medical opinion'. The English auditor had telephoned Hubbard for advice as 'medicine had as usual given up the case . . . and the family doctor had insisted that a consulting Scientologist be brought in'. Hubbard writes: 'He was informed of procedures as follows: Leukaemia is evidently psychosomatic in origin and at least eight cases of leukaemia had been treated successfully by dianetics. . . . The source of leukaemia has been reported to be an engram containing the phrase "It turns my blood to water".'

For those who saw the role of the Scientologist as a replacement for the doctor or psychotherapist rather than for the priest, there must have been some uncertainty when the news was released that on 21st July 1955, The Founding Church of Scientology had been incorporated in Washington DC. True, the reasons given for this link with formalized religion were pragmatic rather than idealistic. One point of view was that qualified Scientologists could now be ordained as 'Ministers of religion', and as such could not be denied entry to a hospital to administer Scientological processing to those in need. In an executive letter to senior officials in the movement at a much later date (12th March 1966) Hubbard explained the alteration of the *British* body into a church with these words: 'As all auditors will be ministers, ministers have in many places special privileges including tax and housing allowances.' He added significantly, 'Of course, anything is a religion that treats the human spirit. And also parliaments don't attack religions.'

At the time of this formal change there was a moment when the whole thing was taken so seriously that those who had been ordained ministers in the movement were requested to wear dog collars and other suitable garb. This at least one senior member of the London office refused to do, and dog collars today appear to be optional, though pretty well each 'Org'—or centre—has got a clerically garbed individual known as the 'Chaplain' somewhere around.

Nevertheless, the acquisition of the trappings of religion has advantages other than the purely fiscal, and there is no doubt that many people feel happier being zealous in the cause of a growing religion, than in the promotion of a rather complex and expensive system of psychotherapy. Proselytizing became, for the first time in the history of Scientology, a proper part of the duties of the rank and file, and the impact, as one might expect, was first felt in the neighbourhood of Saint Hill. Before 1960 was out the first murmuring of complaints was beginning to sound in East Grinstead.

Throughout 1961 the number of visitors to Saint Hill grew and grew, and the fame of the Manor expanded. By 1962, apparently cutting back on the unprofitable research into communication with tomatoes, Hubbard appeared to have regained any confidence he may have lost, demonstrating this with a personal letter to the White House on 13th August. In this he warned President Kennedy that the Russians were clearly interested in Scientology for their own nefarious reasons, and freely offered the President his assistance 'and help of Scientology in narrowing the gap in the space race'.

If you are wondering what Scientology could possibly have to commend itself to the rocket men at NASA, then the answer is simply that it could dramatically shorten the time required to train astronauts. Hubbard pointed out that in Scientology a 'whole body of skills exist which are peculiarly applicable to flight or space flight. All necessary conditioning for flight can be done thoroughly and permanently without any of the conditioning drills now used. The perception of a pilot or astronaut can be increased far beyond human range and stamina can be brought to an astonishing level, not hitherto attainable in a human being.' No beliefs or faith would be needed, and hypnotism and drugs were not used. The government would only have to 'turn over to us anyone it desires to condition to space flight or flight or anyone whose IQ it desires to have raised and we will take it from there'.

In an amazing paragraph Hubbard draws the President's attention to the famous letter from Albert Einstein to Roosevelt way back in the forties when the great mathematician advised that the atom bomb could be made, and points out how sensible Roosevelt was to take heed of its contents. 'This is another such letter', he remarks portentously, adding that he planned to visit the United States in the near future and could be contacted at his personal office in Washington.

President Kennedy never replied to the letter—somewhat to Hubbard's surprise according to a close associate of his at the time. However, Scientology did attract Government attention, but certainly not of the kind he had been seeking. On 4th January 1963 officers of the US Food and Drug Administration made a sensational swoop on the Washington headquarters of the movement, seizing books and pamphlets and carrying off E-meters by the armful. It was a blow to the movement's prestige, but like all such actions on the part of authority it merely served to tag Scientologists, for the very first time, with the label of martyrs. From that moment on the movement headed for a boom.

Brush with Authority

IN ITS RELATIVELY long history, neither Dianetics nor Scientology ever found itself brushing with the establishment—either in the form of government or the law—on any significant scale until the FDA raid of January 1963.

The Food and Drug Administration is one of the Federal agencies which flourish within the powerful Department of Health, Education and Welfare of the United States. Its function, which stems from its original association with the Department of Agriculture, is to look after the interests of Americans by keeping a careful watch on the standards of the food which they buy and the drugs which they are prescribed. The link with the Health Department gives the FDA a wide brief—rather too wide for some people's tastes—and has led to its campaigning on such matters as cigarette smoking as well as more obvious targets like the illegal dilution of milk. It is particularly unpopular with the big drug companies for its frequent tirades against the habit of taking vitamin pills, a hobby much cherished by Americans. It is also interested in quackery in all its forms—bogus doctors, phoney tonics and cure-alls—and all gadgetry used in unorthodox medical or psychological treatment.

As far as the controversial raid on the Washington Scientology headquarters is concerned, the E-meter was the principal target and the seizure of books and pamphlets was merely to provide reading matter to back up the FDA's investigation. The raid seems to have come as a complete surprise to the Scientologists, who by all accounts were simply going about their business auditing each other, or attending to the routine administration of the establishment. The press, however, who had been tipped off in advance by the FDA, were present in large numbers and we are thus favoured with photographs of solemn-looking US Marshals trudging out of the building with armloads of E-meters. (They can't have been very selective in what they took, for after filling two trucks with E-meters, books and pamphlets, they had to send for two more, ending up with a reported total of three tons of literature and equipment.) After this haul the agents, who with their Marshals numbered over two dozen, roared off back to their depot in Baltimore with an armed police motorcycle escort. Presumably someone was then landed with the unenviable task of reading through the three tons of Scientological literature which had come their way.

The raid was clearly a tactical error of the first order, and gave the Scientologists just the kind of ammunition they enjoy. FDA RAIDS CHURCH is the headline in a Scientology account of the event in which it is stated that the agents burst into the Church offices '. . . with their armed Marshals, and loudly if incoherently demanded and threatened all in sight. . . . Showing no legal warrant the agents and heavy deputies pounded their way up stairways bursting into confessional and pastoral counselling sessions, causing disruption and violently preventing the quiet pursuit of the normal practice of religious philosophy.'

The reference to 'confessionals' in the above paragraph is an interesting one, for it was an early instance of the phrase to describe the practice of auditing or processing. Today the word is freely used in Scientology publications and highlights even further the movement's partly controlled swing towards a formal religious structure and function. A recent pamphlet, *The Character of Scientology,* for example, explains that 'A Scientology Minister is called an Auditor, as this names his prime function', and that 'He gives Confessionals and in Scientology the Confessional is called Auditing'. Later it adds: 'The confessional in Scientology is not solely the recounting of sins or wrongs that the person has done. The purpose of Auditing is to make the person more spiritually able, more aware, more free.'

Anyway, in 1963 Scientologists made the most of their status as a registered church in pounding back at the FDA for religious intolerance. To many the argument might seem a bit stretched, but on one point there is no doubt—the FDA were unable to come up with anything to provide them with a useful case. In fact, after a rather embarrassing silence lasting four years, they finally produced a belated and unconvincing case against the E-meter, conscious perhaps that the 'Church' itself could not be charged under the famous First and Fourth Amendments.

Their real trouble, of course, was that the E-meter, as used by Scientologists, is a more or less innocuous gadget, and it should by now be clear that it is not, as many people—possibly including the FDA—seem to have assumed, a device for *treatment* of illnesses, whether physical or psychological. At its worst it is an unreliable aid to diagnosis, which might just bring it within the purlieus of medical malpractice. At the public trial in Washington, in which the FDA made their case against the E-meter, just about the hardest thing that could be said about it was that it was totally unscientific. The most mysterious thing was felt to be its price. When the question was aired as to whether Scientology was a business, religion or both, the Court Commissioner thought that the selling price of the E-meter might serve as a good guide. Its cost to manufacture was estimated at about £5, and its selling price was quoted as about £50. 'Such profitability', the Commissioner drily reported, 'while not at all conclusive, is indicative of a commercial operation.'

With these exceptions Scientologists emerged from the aftermath of the FDA raid with few battle scars. The same was not to be the case following the famous Anderson Commission in Australia.

The events precipitating the now famous inquiry seem to have started in November 1963 when the Hon. J. W. Galbally, an Australian MP, alleged before the Legislative Council of the Parliament of Victoria, that Scientology was being used for blackmail and extortion. It was a statement that kicked off a chain of action leading to the rapid appointment of a formal Board of Inquiry into Scientology, commissioned on 27th November 1963. This was the movement's second brush with government power, and quite definitely its unhappiest to date. It threw Scientology into the spotlight of world publicity at a time when its growth rate was steadily rising.

The Board of Inquiry, conducted by Mr Kevin Anderson, QC, at the request of the Governor of the State of Victoria, was appointed to study the aims and objects of Scientology, the people involved in it, its methods, practices, equipment, etc. Particular attention was paid, to quote the official wording of the brief, to: 'the illnesses or ailments, mental or physical, treated in the course of carrying on, practice or application (of Scientology) . . . and whether such treatment is in any and what way harmful', 'the nature and amount of fees charged' and 'whether persons or organizations (in its practice) . . . have indulged in any and what unlawful, improper or harmful or prejudicial practices or activities'.

It proceeded to subject Scientology to the closest scrutiny it had ever received, and after hearing over four million words from 151 witnesses in 159 days, it published a report in 1965 which constituted a 'damning indictment' of the principles and practices of Scientology, and led to the outlawing of its teaching, practice and advertising within the State Boundaries. It is also a document which has been widely quoted around the world, the most memorable phrase being that describing the cult as 'evil', and it is one which Hubbard and the Scientology organization have been working hard to live down ever since. They have had a hard job, for the Anderson report, which filled out 202 pages, refused to mince its language. For example, in one sensational paragraph, it says:

'Scientology is evil; its techniques evil; its practice a serious threat to the community, medically, morally and socially; and its adherents sadly deluded and often mentally ill. Its founder is Lafayette Ronald Hubbard, an American . . . who falsely claims academic and other distinctions and whose sanity is to be gravely doubted.'

In its devastating conclusion the report declares: 'If there should be detected in this report a note of unrelieved denunciation of Scientology it is because the evidence has shown its theories to be fantastic and impossible, its principles perverted and ill-founded and its techniques debased and harmful. . . .

'Its founder, with the merest smattering of knowledge in various sciences, has built upon the scintilla of his learning a crazy and dangerous edifice. . . .

'The HASI claims to be "the world's largest mental health organization". What it really is, however, is the world's largest organization of unqualified persons engaged in the practice of dangerous techniques which masquerade as mental therapy.'

These were strong words and Hubbard, who had refused to give evidence at this inquiry unless his personal expenses and return fare from England to Melbourne were met by the Commission (he was consequently not seen), was clearly enraged. In a venomous rejoinder against what was described as the 'Kangaroo Court', a special Scientology publication reminds readers that the residents of Victoria are almost entirely the descendants of convicts, 'the riff-raff of London's slums—the robbers, murderers, prostitutes, fences, thieves—the scourings of Newgate and Bedlam'. It adds, 'A society organized for criminals will eventually be run by criminals, who will seek in turn to turn decent people into criminals and enjoin criminality upon them.'

Despite the terrifying material in the Anderson Report there is no evidence that the movement suffered immediate practical damages—except obviously in the State of Victoria itself where 250 Scientologists packed up their bags for fairer fields. Interestingly enough, the Anderson Commission did not recommend the banning of Scientology itself, feeling that this would be ineffective as the cult would simply pop up again in a different guise. Rather it proposed a law forbidding unqualified people from practising Scientology, hypnosis and mental therapy and the setting up of a council to register practising psychologists and hypnotists. In fact the Government of Victoria went the stage beyond the Commission's recommendations and specifically banned Scientology with fines of from £100 to £250 for first offences connected with its practice, and jail sentences of two years for second offences.

In England the indignation of Scientologists knew no bounds, but with the label of martyrs now firmly strapped around their necks they continued to move on, seemingly from strength to strength. But what of Hubbard himself? One feels sure that he, of all men, could least relish the role of martyr. In fact, more than once, in following the history of Scientology one can detect signs of his incipient boredom with his creation. His jaunts abroad, while providing a change of scene, nevertheless simply served to dump him down among another bunch of Scientologists and there must have been times when he wished that he could have found himself in some un-processed, un-audited world where conversation revolved around topics other than preclears, E-meters, Thetans and Orgs. In the early days at Saint Hill he seems to have made one attempt to break loose without any lasting success. Over five years later the indications are that he tried again, and once again was frustrated.

At the end of 1965, with the clamour of the Anderson Commission still ringing in his ears, L. Ron Hubbard visited South Africa and, after a brief stay in that country at the Johannesburg Org, he moved on northwards to Rhodesia, at that time building up to its Unilateral Declaration of Independence. Here he showed signs of beginning to make himself at home and he is alleged to have bought a luxurious house in Salisbury for £16,500. He is even believed to have said that he was considering launching or financing several factories.

According to a former close associate of his, who spent some time with him in Rhodesia, Hubbard seemed unusually happy in Salisbury. For the first time for years he widened his circle of acquaintances enormously to include many non-Scientologists and in various other ways launched into the kind of social life that one might expect a talented and wealthy writer to lead. Parties were thrown at which the leading lights of Salisbury society were to be seen, including many politicians and people of influence in the community. On at least one occasion the founder of Scientology met Mr Ian Smith, the Prime Minister, though it is not known whether they talked about Scientology or politics.

Before long L. Ron was saying some rather curious things which, when relayed by various sources to Saint Hill, caused some surprise. For example, he is stated to have said that he was a Rhodesian. He also apparently appeared on television there and announced that he was planning to live in Salisbury permanently and, most interesting of all, that he was no longer active in Scientology. This latter comment in particular, assuming that it was correctly reported, must have sent a quiver through Scientology Orgs across the world. It was a tense moment.

But the best laid plans of mice, men and even L. Ron Hubbard sometimes go astray. In early July he was staggered to find that the Rhodesian authorities had tersely rejected his request for an extension of his visitor's visa and that he must leave the country by 16th July, just six months after he had arrived. Thus, enigmatically and with a few strokes of an official pen, was ended the brief career of L. Ron Hubbard, Rhodesian business magnate.

The news of his impending return to England was greeted with great excitement amongst the faithful, and two hours before his 'plane was due hundreds of Scientologists, many of them with children and babes-in-arms, had gathered at London Airport. The East Grinstead headquarters itself provided several coachloads. There was also a large number of banners, which could not be unfurled following a directive by the airport police. While awaiting their leader's arrival, the Scientologists busied themselves handing out leaflets and taking photographs, and showed themselves to be on the whole an extroverted, smiling bunch with a large smattering of attractive-looking girls among them. A few were dressed in unconventional style, forerunners of the flower people that were just beginning to appear on the scene.

For many of the press on hand it was their first glimpse of Scientologists *en masse* and an indication that the movement was beginning to acquire a newsy feel. It was also many people's first introduction to the idea of Scientology as a religion, for leading the crowd of supporters was an American sporting a dog-collar and silver crucifix who indicated that he was the 'Chaplain' of the headquarters organization.

As Hubbard emerged from customs a great cheer and shouts of 'Welcome back, Ron!' went up and police had to restrain the crowd, which had surged forward in excitement. Smiling broadly Hubbard granted brief interviews to the press, denying that he had been thrown out of Rhodesia. Nevertheless, he told the reporter of the *Sunday Telegraph*, 'I'm normally a cool man, but the last few days have been unnerving'. Then, a portly figure in a huge sun hat, he gave a final wave and, stepping into a large yellow American convertible, was swept off to his mansion at East Grinstead.

His return was the signal for the biggest burst of expansion that the movement had known since its early days. To meet the growing flood of students more space was needed at the Manor. As far back as 1962, when Hubbard had barely left the East Grinstead Road Safety Committee, the Council refused permission for classrooms to be built at Saint Hill. The plans had called for three linked buildings, comprising single-storey classrooms, two-storey offices and administration area and also a 'postgraduate' training school. Plans were agreed, however, for a chapel, a reception office and changing rooms in the 'pleasure garden' and subsequently the Minister's Inspector allowed the Scientologists' appeal against the Council's original refusal.

Shortly after this an incredible structure began to arise in the grounds near the Manor. As the months went by this gradually revealed itself as a kind of Norman castle in miniature, complete with turrets and battlements. There are many stories which attempt to explain this curiosity—the most popular is that Scientologists had discovered some ancient regulation stating that no one could be refused permission to build a castle, so a castle was built. The building needs to be seen to be believed, and whatever motivated its Robin Hood style of architecture, it is built of solid stone and will probably last a very long time.

Slowly but surely the influx of Scientologists began to cause unease among the townspeople. There were complaints to the police about wild parties and excessive noise, and a house which was being used as a hostel by Saint Hill students became the subject of a public inquiry.

The organization at Saint Hill became increasingly authoritarian, with a kind of internal police force, the 'Ethics Officers', wielding considerable power. Hubbard himself was often abroad, gradually acquiring the little fleet of ships which were to provide the next step in the saga of Scientology, but a ceaseless flow of telex messages passed back and forth between him and the headquarters where his wife, Mary Sue, reigned in his place as 'Guardian'.

Then came a series of scandals, all of which attracted national press coverage, and which varied from simple allegations that Scientologists were infiltrating local schools, to suggestions that they were deliberately brainwashing people to the point of madness. One local school for autistic and maladjusted children fought vigorously against the Scientologists' plan for expansion by informing a planning inquiry that 'the presence of about a thousand Scientologists in the area has already threatened the work of the school and training centre in trying to restore normality to maladjusted young people'.

They added that the school could no longer allow its young people to go outside on their own for walks because they would be accosted by Scientologists who, they feared, would try to process or audit them.

By now local MPs, notably Mr Peter Hordern, member for Horsham, and Mr Geoffrey Johnson Smith, member for East Grinstead, were being pestered to take action, and on a number of occasions questions were raised in Parliament.

In the meantime other sensations continued, some alarming and some just ludicrous. On the silly side, one local caterer, Mr William Harewood of Tunbridge Wells, who ran a mobile canteen which used to provide snacks for Scientologists, was declared a 'suppressive person' for running out of apple pie. On the seamy side, a twenty-year-old youth, who was reported as 'suffering from latent schizophrenia' and who was stated to have been interested in Scientology, was found semi-conscious in the street at East Grinstead and died later in hospital from an overdose of barbiturates. On another occasion a girl who had been under psychiatric treatment and was subsequently taking a course in Scientology, suddenly turned up at her mother's house in the middle of the night. After an emotional scene she took off again, this time to the police station where a doctor, recognizing that she was in a hysterical condition, gave her sedatives before admitting her to hospital.

By this time there was enough smell in the air for some official government statement and on 6th March 1967 the then Minister of Health, Mr Kenneth Robinson, blasted out against Scientology in the House of Commons, describing it as 'a hollow cult which thrives on a climate of ignorance and indifference', and stated that Scientologists tended to 'direct themselves deliberately towards the weak, the unbalanced, the immature, the rootless and mentally and emotionally unstable'. He refused, however, an official inquiry into the cult, but added that he would be keeping his eye on it.

In early 1966 the first 'Clear' (new style) had been announced, a South African named John McMaster. Within weeks others had followed and within months the number of Clears had risen into the hundreds. As might be expected the announcement of the breakthrough spread across the world and caused an unprecedented flood of students to batter on the doors of the Manor.

On 31st March 1968, or 'A.D. 18' (the 18th year after Dianetics to use Hubbard's new calendar), *The Auditor* proudly announced the clearing of Mr Lyle Sudrow, a New York 'Film and TV actor'. It was an historic moment as the journal explained: 'A mere two years and two weeks since the announcement of John McMaster as the world's first Clear, 1000 Scientologists have achieved this state of Clear.'

This wonderful achievement cut little ice with the British Government, however, and on 25th July, the Health Minister, following questions in the House of Commons from Mr Horden and Mr Johnson Smith, announced sweeping restrictions on the entry of Scientologists into the country, which were clearly designed to clip the movement's wings. Commenting on Scientology in the House he said: 'It alienates members of families from each other and attributes squalid and disgraceful motives to all who oppose it; its authoritarian principles and practice are a potential menace to the personality and well-being of those so deluded as to become its followers; above all, its methods can be a serious danger to the health of those who submit to them.'

In this same statement Mr Robinson announced that Scientology centres would no longer be recognized as educational establishments, foreigners arriving for courses would not be given extensions of stay, and no work permits to foreigners working at its centres would be granted or extended.

This was intended to be a painful blow, and so it turned out to be. Almost immediately 'students' found themselves being turned back at Southampton and at London Airport, and various odd aliens who had attempted to evade the new restrictions were later unceremoniously turfed out.

At East Grinstead a great flap began. Hubbard seems to have chosen this moment to be difficult to find, although cables flashed out to his last recorded location—a boat somewhere in the Mediterranean. Mrs Kember, the 'Deputy Guardian' at East Grinstead, told a *Telegraph* reporter, 'Mr Hubbard is abroad. I don't know where he is and if I did I wouldn't tell you.' One suspects that they were looking for instructions on what to do next.

After a few days of ghastly hush, there came a dramatic telex message from 'Somewhere at sea', to be followed by a second a few hours later. The first message apparently announced Hubbard's retirement or abdication and read:

> I have finished my work; now it is up to others. I retired from Scientology directorships over two years ago and have been exploring ever since.
>
> I gave Scientology to the world with hopes of good usage. If it is a decent world, it will use it well. If it is a bad world, it won't. I finished my work; now it is up to others.

The second message, slightly reiterative, said:

> I retired from directorship in Scientology organizations two or more years ago to explore and study the decline of ancient civilizations and so learnt how this current one is going.
>
> My conclusion is that they declined because of intolerance and inhumanity to man. Efforts to stamp out philosophy and bar our students is a shadow of the injustice soon to be visited on all.

Readers detecting a touch of pique in the above cable will not be surprised at its conclusion: 'England, once the light and hope of the world, has become a police state, and can no longer be trusted.' The cable was signed, 'Love, Ron'.

If Hubbard was annoyed at the Health Minister's removal from Scientologists of their status as students he must have been even more offended when, a day after his rejoinder, the Home Secretary, Mr Callaghan, used his powers under the Aliens Act to refuse him re-entry into England. Within twenty-four hours every immigration officer in the country had been told of the ban.

A third telex now arrived at Saint Hill, in which Ron indicated, if obliquely, who it was he really felt was getting at him. It was not, after all, the British Government.

> There is no Government attack on Scientology. What appears to be an attack is only an attempt by private groups of older practices to protect their governmental appropriations, as the public, having long since lost faith and confidence in them, no longer supports them.

Presumably, the 'private groups of older practices' are Hubbard's old enemies, the psychiatrists. The cable went on:

Perhaps it is out of fear that the Government will cease to contribute such vast sums of money that these older practices use the Government to protect their vested interests. Their motive is not evil, it is only self-protective and greedy.

It was a grave moment for Scientology. Within a week, from being a thriving, though controversial, movement it had lost in two sharp strokes its recognized status as an educational organization and had seen its beloved founder branded as nothing more or less than an undesirable alien. The headquarters organization pulled itself together and called a private meeting at the Café Royal in London for four hundred leading followers of the cult. Few reliable details about the meeting are available, but the movement's chief spokesman, Mr David Gaiman, later told the press that he had reassured those present that the ban did not mean the start of a witch hunt. Afterwards, at an informal press conference, Gaiman defended charges that Hubbard had made a fortune from the movement by saying that if he had 'made fifty million pounds from it he would have been entitled to it'.

After tottering momentarily against these knocks from the establishment, Scientologists seemed to rally rapidly, all things considered. In a timely PR move, Saint Hill Manor was thrown open to the public for an 'Open Weekend' in August. Considerable crowds took advantage of this to satisfy their curiosity by a visit to the mysterious Manor itself. What they were expecting is hard to imagine, but most were probably disappointed. The zaniest thing in sight was probably the new castle, and the most alarming the difficulty of finding somewhere to park. All visitors were asked to register and could take, if they wished, a 'free ability test'. Outside the chapel, a smiling young man in clerical garb invited all and sundry to attend services.

Earlier, in that same chapel, in which a bust of L. Ron featured prominently, tape recordings of some of his speeches were relayed through hi-fi speakers. In these one could detect some of the strain that Hubbard must have been going through in the previous turbulent years.

Apart from the usual statements about the progress of his research and a few brief anecdotes about the trials and tribulations of these researches (such as when he first broke through 'the wall of fire', a fearsome barrier on the route to Operating Thetan), much of the tapes were devoted to petulant assaults on politicians and newspaper barons, including the then Prime Minister, Harold Wilson, and Cecil King. According to Hubbard, Scientology is the victim of a concerted attempt to squash it by a small group of intensely powerful and evil men. Mr Wilson and Mr King were not in this group—they were just its uncomprehending puppets.

The service which followed began with the chaplain reading the 'Creed' of Scientology. This turned out to be a completely innocuous, if slightly windy, set of principles with the ring of the Declaration of Independence about them. After this came an address by Mr Gaiman pointing out how unreasonable people were to attack L. Ron and Scientology. Finally came the reading of some poems by John McMaster, the movement's first Clear, which sounded on first hearing like very early Auden or possibly late Hardy. All seemed totally harmless, and many of the curiosity seekers must have wondered what all the fuss can have been about.

Meanwhile, somewhere out at sea, the Founder himself surveyed his shrinking world.

All at Sea

For some time the Master of Saint Hill had owned a small yacht, the pretty ketch *Diana* (formerly *Enchanter* and renamed after Hubbard's good-looking daughter). This was a spruce little craft equipped with diesel auxiliaries, echo-sounders and expensive ship-to-shore radio, and on this in weather fair and foul Hubbard and his family would explore the coastal waters of Britain and the Eastern Atlantic seaboard. Its 30-ton displacement had also allowed L. Ron to take along with him the occasional Scientologist, sufficiently high up in the hierarchy to attract his attention and keen enough on the salt sea breezes to make the trip tolerable.

Sometime in 1966 or 1967 the Hubbard Exploration Company, one of the very many registered companies small and large which make up Ron's straggling empire, made a more ambitious purchase—the 414-ton trawler *Avon River*, which had originally plied its trade in the North Sea out of Hull. Then in 1967, when many Scientologists must have been speculating slightly nervously on what possible use a 400-ton trawler could be to their movement, came an announcement which was received with some surprise.

For a reported sum of £60,000, the Hubbard Exploration Company had landed an even bigger fish—the 3,400-ton former Channel ferry, *Royal Scotsman*, which was at the time lying in berth at Southampton. Naturally it wasn't too long before the press got to hear of this unusual investment and a great mystery grew.

On 19th November reporters from the *Sunday Mirror*—a newspaper with an ear acutely tuned to the dafter doings of this world—visited Southampton hot on the trail of the usual rumours which follow the Scientologists wherever they go. The rumours mainly concerned the planned role for the new boat—some stated that it was going to be a floating casino, others that it was to be staffed entirely by women, others again that it was going to be involved in some dramatic undersea exploration.

In fact it was to be none of these things, though the *Mirror* representatives were surprised (not unpleasantly) to find themselves welcomed aboard by a good-looking girl, aged about twenty-five, who introduced herself as Mrs Jill Van Staden, the ship's third officer. Dressed in a smartly-cut uniform of a naval type and with a dashing peaked cap on her head, Mrs Van Staden allowed herself to be photographed alongside the ship's wheel. Questioned about the ship's ultimate destination—assuming that it was ever going to leave dock—the third officer indicated that in 1963 Hubbard had done some 'survey work' in the English Channel with promising results, and that the ship's mission would be to study 'the geology of the sea floor where recently much oil and gas have been found'. Most of their work, however, would be done in the Mediterranean. The sharp-eyed reporter commented that notices pinned up in the saloon, signed by 'L. Ron Hubbard, Commodore', declared that the ship was going to be run on 'Scientology lines'.

The first sign of things not being quite what they ought to be came from the Board of Trade, who ungenerously refused to re-certify the thirty-one-year-old vessel as fit for a sea voyage unless certain alterations were made. For two weeks the Scientologists pressed their claims without avail, and then, evidently giving up in despair, the *Royal Scotsman* hauled down the red duster and replaced it with the national flag of Sierra Leone. The boat had been re-registered in Freetown, and was thus outside the Board of Trade control.

On Tuesday 29th November, the flagship of the Hubbard fleet pulled out of port and set sail towards the Bay of Biscay. On board was the Commodore himself, and as the boat left speculation was rife that the Scientologists were pulling out of Britain—a possibility which seem heightened when it was learned that earlier in the month the former trawler, *Avon River*, had left Hull. This also headed southwards, arriving after some misadventures in Gibraltar.

The story of the trawler's first voyage under the auspices of the Scientologists as related in the *Daily Mirror* is a weird one. Wisely it had been decided not to attempt the trip through some of the stormiest waters of the world with an untrained Scientological crew, and the skipper appointed was a Captain John Jones, who was supported by the only other professional seaman aboard, the chief engineer. Before they had got under way Captain Jones had been warned that he had to run the ship according to the rules of *The Org Book*—a handy manual written by Hubbard to tell people, among other things, how to manage boats. To the Scientologists aboard this was a book of rules, the words of the Prophet, and consequently to be obeyed to the letter. Describing the hair-raising consequences of this on his return, thirty-nine-year-old Captain Jones told a *Daily Mirror* reporter:

'It was the strangest trip of my life. My crew were sixteen men and four women Scientologists who wouldn't know a trawler from a tramcar. But they intended to sail this tub 3,000 miles in strict accordance with *The Org Book*.

'I was instructed not to use any electrical equipment, apart from lights, radio and direction finder. We had radar and other advanced equipment which I was not allowed to use. I was told it was all in *The Org Book* which was to be obeyed without question.'

There were, however, at critical times, strange tests with E-meters (another interesting role for this marvellous device). 'We tried these methods', the skipper recalled. The result was that 'getting out of Hull we bumped the dock. Then, using *The Org Book* navigation system based on radio beams from the BBC and other stations, we got down to Lowestoft before the navigator admitted we were lost. I stuck to my watch and sextant, so at least *I* knew where we were.'

At this point there was a huge row about who was in command, and as a result when the boat pulled in to Falmouth for fuel the chief engineer and skipper began to pack their bags intending to walk off. After a great flap, and lots of telephoning to East Grinstead, the Senior Scientologist was ordered ashore by Hubbard and Captain Jones resumed command. 'He begged and pleaded', said the skipper, 'but he had to go. Hubbard had spoken.'

On the voyage south, during which many of the crew were seasick, Captain Jones had leisure to observe some of the Scientologists' odd habits, including their frequent recourse to the

E-meter and *The Org Book*. The sleeping arrangements were another strange feature, all the Scientologists sharing the same saloon with a blanket dividing the men's section from the women's. There was no fear of impropriety, however, for *The Org Book* said that 'anyone guilty of sexual misconduct would be instantly sent back to the Scientology headquarters at East Grinstead'—easier said than done!

With his mind reeling slightly, Captain Jones left the *Avon River* at Gibraltar, to take a post as navigation officer on another boat. He decided to leave *The Org Book* behind.

Things were just about as daft aboard the *Royal Scotsman*, if we are to believe *The People* of Sunday 18th February, which reported the ex-channel ferry's voyage from Southampton to Valencia.

'AHOY THERE!', shouted the headline gleefully, 'it's the craziest cruise on earth!', adding that the Chief Officer was a carpenter and the 'skipper' (L. Ron of course) 'says he's been to Venus'. Accompanying the text is a photograph of the *Scotsman* in berth with, in the foreground, the ubiquitous Mrs Van Staden again. This time she is not only wearing a peaked cap and uniform, but boots as well. She has a stern expression on her face and is clearly taking everything very seriously.

The Chief Officer in question was Mr Stanley Churcher, a twenty-four-year-old carpenter, who was hired by Hubbard to serve on the ship in a purely professional capacity. At first he had no reason to suppose this was anything other than a perfectly normal voyage until he found that the big boat was manned by Scientologists who had never been to sea before, and that there were only two or three other professional seamen aboard—including the chief engineer and the boatswain. On arrival on board he was accosted by an officer who accused him of being a journalist, but relented after he had seen his seaman's log. It wasn't long before someone discovered that Churcher knew a bit of navigation, and in one dramatic day he found himself rocketed from carpenter to Chief Officer. This promotion, which probably made naval history, was duly recorded in his log. After this he set the ship's course most of the time and generally ran things pretty well as he pleased.

There were seven other officers, four of them women, all resplendent in uniform, peaked caps, etc., but 'knowing next to nothing about seamanship'. Hubbard, who was on board as

'Commodore', had 'four different types of peaked cap', and his wife, Mary Sue, also 'had an officer's uniform made for her'. Everyone, according to Mr Churcher, seemed to enjoy playing sailors, and when he offered to give them all seamanship lectures they reciprocated by giving him a free beginner's course in Scientolology! This completely baffled the Chief Officer, who told *The People*: 'I was given a test on their E-meter, a sort of lie detector, and a woman officer asked me a lot of personal questions, including details of my sex life. I could never make head or tail of their instruction but I played along because it made life easier!'

The former carpenter found the whole thing so blooming mysterious that he questioned some of the Scientologists about what they were doing on board. He got some odd replies. One elderly lady of seventy-five told him that she was there because she was convinced that Mr Hubbard would fix her up with a new body when she died.

Eventually when the ship arrived in Valencia, Churcher himself was declared to be in a 'Condition of Doubt', as was the boatswain. This didn't prevent them both from packing their bags in a totally decisive manner and leaving the ship.

It is now time to consider the evolution of Scientological ideas at about this time and attempt to explain the curious hierarchy of the movement and various 'Conditions' in which an individual or group may have been said to find himself or itself.

In all his writings Hubbard has continually stated that first Dianetics, and then Scientology, were exact sciences with a rigorous logic and an extremely high success rate when applied correctly. A close study of the logic reveals that it is anything but rigorous, and the illusion of coherence is achieved only by Hubbard's adoption of a specialized jargon which makes it impossible frequently to decide whether a particular statement is meaningful or meaningless. Within the system there is probably a limited coherence, but this soon collapses when an attempt is made to integrate it with the other philosophical and technical systems which exist outside.

Now the admitted deficiencies in Scientology are attributable, according to Hubbard, not to flaws in the system or the ideas, but rather to their implementation. In other words if some individual, or some organization in Scientology, is failing for some reason it is not because Scientology is wrong, but because it is being inappropriately applied at some point, or not being applied at all.

There are three possible sources of success or failure which in the Scientology jargon are known as 'Ethics', 'Admin' and 'Tech'. To give an example of the strands of interaction here one can imagine an individual who is well trained in the techniques of Scientology (in which case he would have a high 'Tech' rating) and who is good at carrying out or administering these techniques (he would then have a high 'Admin' rating). This same individual might, for one reason or another, have a less than positive attitude to Scientology, in which case his 'Ethics' rating would be low. Now Scientologists believe that an individual can be located fairly accurately on the rungs of a ladder on each of these ratings. When an individual or an organization (Org) have high ratings in all three, then by the principles and theory of Scientology, that individual or Org will be successul in all spheres of activity.

Conversely, one can reason that if an individual or Org shows signs of inefficiency or of failing to succeed, then this must be because somewhere, someone or something is lacking in either 'Ethics', 'Tech' or 'Admin'. The location of this weakness and its eradication or enforced improvement will then cause the system to continue on the success road once more.

Hence the aims of Scientology are to 'get Ethics, Admin and Tech in to 100% level'—at which point, inevitably, nothing will be able to stop the expansion of Scientology.

Since 'Tech' and 'Admin' are largely a matter of training and teaching, weaknesses are far more likely to lie in the sphere of 'Ethics' according to Hubbard, and thus the decision to form a Scientology Ethics Department with the hierarchy of Ethics Officers who may have very considerable power. For this vital arm of the movement a headquarters safe and secure from physical and psychological assaults on the part of the non-Scientology world (the 'Wogs' to use the cult's homely descriptive term for outsiders) is required. For this reason, it seems, the 'Sea Orgs' were brought into being.

Thus one of the first tasks of these boats was not, as the press had assumed, to evacuate all Scientologists from Britain, but to form an *élite* central body, a special 'police force', who would sally out from their mobile headquarters to any land-based Org suffering from what are known as 'Down Statistics'. The boats are euphemistically known as 'Mission Schools' which can dispatch 'missions' as required to recalcitrant Orgs. Their task is to seek out the suppressive person who is the cause or to find the 'Out-admin' or 'Out-tech' who is applying the brakes.

It would be a mistake to underestimate the intensities of belief in operation here. To the detached individual reading about these odd capers, the comic and ludicrous side is always apparent. Scientologists take all this in deadly earnest and the members of an Ethics Mission, arriving at a Land Org dressed in naval-type uniform with high boots and peaked caps, strike something very close to fear in the hearts of the suspected suppressives. To get some idea what they look like, a small photograph in *The Auditor*, Number 42, shows three tough-looking characters with peaked caps like American police, open-necked shirts, lanyards and grim-looking expressions on their faces. The caption reads: 'Sea Orgs officers specially trained by Ron as Supervisor Class VIIIs are teaching the Advanced Org Class VIII course.' Hubbard has written that missionaries must be tough, and to that end judo is taught and also, according to some ex-Scientologists, karate.

In the chaotic days when the Ethics Department was at the height of its power, and an atmosphere of paranoia was beginning to permeate the world of Scientology, even the famous headquarters at East Grinstead suffered visitations from missions, about which we shall hear more in a moment. At the successful conclusion of a mission, incidentally, the retiring Ethics Officers, with a charming gesture, were wont to fix a notice to that effect to the Land Org's notice board with a Sea-Org throwing knife.

The decision to send out an Ethics mission, or to take any form of disciplinary action, is based on an assessment of the relative severity of the suppressive individual, or Org's condition. If things are merely slightly stagnant, then no direct action other than the dispatching of some pep-up letters (Scientology Orgs are great letter writers) will be taken, but if the Org is sliding in some way, a mission will be launched.

On 11th July 1968 the staff and students of the London Org in Tottenham Court Road learned, no doubt to their dismay, that a 'Worldwide Mission to London' had been instigated with 'TOTAL ETHICS POWER' (to quote their special Bulletin, Mission Order 22) 'to get Ethics in and production rearing'.

In an unpleasant letter signed by 'Jon Rappoport, Mission-in-Command', the London Org was warned that a 'Suppressive Person attempts obsessively to stop this goal [of Total Freedom] from being achieved' and that the 'effect of a suppressive person on an individual can be quite harmful to his state of being', and therefore that all contact with this individual must cease. There followed a list of over a hundred names of various people, some longstanding disciples of Hubbard, from whom all Scientologists were to disconnect themselves immediately and totally. The letter closed with the ominous reminder that 'refusal to disconnect from a declared Suppressive Person is a Suppressive Act'. Thus might friends be cut off from friends and a man severed from his family—if he wanted to remain in Scientology.

The sliding scale of success or failure is an interesting one and each level on the scale has its own punishments or rewards, as the case may be. At the top of the scale is the Condition known as 'Power' (one rarely achieved) carrying very special privileges such as a pay rise with bonuses and 'free gifts'. These may be quite valuable, such as a typewriter or tape recorder.

One step lower down is the still exalted condition of 'Affluence', when special pay bonuses are again granted, and there are also some free gifts, though less magnificent than those awarded to the power people. In fact the free gifts are rather marginal, such as hair-do's for the women and free razors and bath soap for the men. (The emphasis on soap, etc., will become slightly clearer as we proceed down the ladder.)

Most people working away in an Org are likely to be in the Condition of 'Normal Operation'. Here they are given normal pay and (I quote from a Scientology bulletin): 'can shave, wear make-up, bathe, wear decent clothes and have hair-do's'. They have to pay for their soap, however.

Below 'Normal' is a Condition known, dramatically, as 'Emergency', and there the bonuses metamorphose into penalties. Members of an Org in this Condition find themselves not only deprived of their lunch hour but also expected to put in overtime without pay. Their pay scale is also reduced. Small wonder that anyone labelled as 'Emergency' struggles hard to move back up the ladder and, perhaps even more, fights to avoid slipping down further to the unhappy rung of 'Danger'. At this level things get decisively worse, the penalties reflecting the cranky outlook that lies skin-deep in most Scientology philosophy. Those in 'Danger': 'may not bathe, wear make-up, have hair-do's or shave'. They have no lunch hour, of course, and are expected to work at night. They are on the lowest pay scale of all.

Grimmer yet is a still lower Condition with the tragi-comic title of 'Non-Existence'. Here not only are bathing, shaving, make-up, etc., barred, but individuals must wear old clothes which they may not change. Nor may such individuals leave the premises of the Org. The farcical Condition of 'Non-Existence' (which is taken completely seriously by Scientologists) is not, incredible though it may seem, the lowest. Further on yet come the states of 'Liability', 'Doubt,' 'Enemy' and 'Treason', and according to former Scientologists these are socially and psychologically demoralizing. In a condition of 'Liability' for example, no uniform may be worn and a dirty grey rag must be tied around the left arm. One is also supposed to eat only stale food and drink only water. Worse yet, in the condition of 'Doubt' Scientologists are supposed to wear handcuffs on their left wrist (the ex-Scientologist Cyril Vosper claims that these could be 'symbolic', being made of paper clips). One can also be locked up or ejected from the Org premises. There are many reported cases of erring Scientologists being literally cast overboard, presumably when in a condition of Doubt or worse. *Auditor* No. 41, for example, publishes a picture captioned 'Students are thrown overboard for gross out-tech and bequeathed to the deep'. It is a relief to learn that they are fished on board again afterwards. In the dreaded condition of 'Treason' Scientologists or 'suppressive persons' are stated to have become 'Fair Game' and in the weird words of Hubbard's original dictum 'may be deprived of property or injured by any means by any Scientologist without any discipline of the Scientologists. May be tricked, sued or lied to or destroyed'. This penalty, plus 'all penalties for all lower conditions' and all other relics of what Mr David Gaiman was to describe in court as Scientology's 'puritanical' period, were abolished in 1970, no doubt in the face of pressure from within and outside the movement. One feels that there are few people, whether Scientologists or outsiders, who will regret their demise.

Details of life on the Scientology boats are hard to come by. The application to join a Sea Org involves filling up a long form composed of questions which seek to ferret out one's background and anyone suspected of being a journalist or in any way hostile to Scientology is unlikely to get aboard for any length of time. Once on board one's first obligation is (or was until quite recently) to sign a document binding oneself to the Sea Org for a billion years. This preposterous piece of paper, which is decorated at the head with the picture of two sea horses, reads:

> I, . . . do hereby agree to enter into employment with the Sea Organization and, being of sound mind, do fully realize and agree to abide by its purpose which is to get ETHICS IN on this PLANET AND THE UNIVERSE and, fully and without reservation, subscribe to the discipline, mores and conditions of this group and pledge to abide by them.
>
> THEREFORE, I CONTRACT MYSELF TO THE SEA ORGANIZATION FOR THE NEXT BILLION YEARS.
>
> (As per Flag Order 232).

As ever with Scientologists, whether on land or sea, a rich thread of unconscious comedy is laced through their activities. But there can be a black side as well. Boats are boats and, when at sea and outside territorial waters, are little empires in themselves. Scientologists who have left the Sea Orgs (and Scientology as well at the same time) have spoken of their terrifying feeling of isolation from society and of their awareness that they were effectively totally committed to an encapsulated Scientology world-in-miniature. And indeed the outsider and the non-Scientologist can think of few less welcoming environments than that on a boat of Mr Hubbard's strange fleet as it ploughs the waters of the world on its enigmatic mission.

Ethics and Uniforms

In 1968, following increasing assaults from press and parliament, many sparked off by the Anderson Report, organized Scientology began to harden its position and to counter-attack wherever possible. The famous 'Disconnect' orders requiring Scientologists to dissociate themselves totally from any individuals labelled as 'Suppressive Persons', which could, and occasionally did, cut husband off from wife, or parent from child, are in fact just one further sign of the movement's drift into group paranoia. The actions of the Ethics Department, intended to preserve total discipline (Ethics) within the movement and to discourage outside interference, was another step along these lines. Over the years, following the continued rejection of himself and his movement by establishment bodies such as Church, orthodox medicine, government, etc., Hubbard's own attitude had moved from jovial tolerance of the world's stupidity, to angry counterblasts both in word and deed.

His main target has always been psychiatrists and the established methods of medico-psychological treatment, and there are constant references throughout his writings to 'medical imperialism', 'psychiatric sadism', 'electric-shock psychology', etc. In an issue of the magazine *Certainty*, under the somewhat curious title 'Join the Crusade for a Happy Healthy England', Hubbard, in giving a rapid 'history' of psychiatric treatment in the years before Dianetics, says that Pavlov's principal belief was that men were 'animals' and could be conditioned 'like dancing bears or dogs'. Freud is dismissed as an 'Austrian Jew' whose 'concentration on sex gave the subject considerable popularity'. He adds that 'the results of psychiatry are physically damaging, consisting of various brutalities, and often injure the patient for life and kill him outright'. Psychology is 'more concerned with and financed for warfare'.

Such ramblings, provided that they are confined to the Scientologist's own bizarre periodicals and Hubbard's own books, are relatively harmless. For a period, however, when the Scientologists were at their most aggressive, a far more sinister and dangerous situation began to arise. This seems to have been started by Hubbard's direct call for overt action on the part of Scientologists to back up their personal beliefs.

The story broke when *The People* of 20th March 1966 reported that they had tracked down a number of private detectives who had been hired by Hubbard to investigate the private affairs of various critics of Scientology. High on the list, of course, came the psychiatrists.

Answering an ad in the personal column of the *Daily Telegraph* a private detective, Mr Vic Filson, was hired by the Scientologists at £35 per week (plus car expenses) with the fantastic task of 'investigating the activities of psychiatrists in Britain and preparing a dossier on each'. The first person on the list was to be Lord Balniel, who at the time was Chairman of the National Association for Mental Health.

There was to be no messing about. Hubbard has been reported as stating the following: 'A psychiatrist today has the power to take a fancy to a woman, drug or shock her into temporary insanity, use her sexually, sterilize her to prevent conception, kill her by a brain operation to prevent disclosure.'

Psychiatrists violated not only persons but groups such as Scientology, and they had 'very dirty hands'. The shrill blast continues: 'We want at least one bad mark on every psychiatrist in England, a murder, an assault, or a rape or more than one. This is Project Psychiatry. We will remove them.'

But it was not only psychiatrists who were seeking out Scientology's destruction. In the magazine *Certainty,* Vol. 16, No. 3, we find Hubbard declaring that every time he had investigated the background of a critic of Scientology he had found '*crimes* for which that person or group could be imprisoned . . . we did *not* find critics . . . who do not have criminal pasts'. Over and over again, Hubbard states, they had proved this. In one of his most unbalanced passages he declares: 'Politician A stands up on his hind legs in a Parliament and brays for a condemnation of Scientology. When we look him over we find crimes—embezzled funds, moral lapses, a thirst for young boys—sordid stuff. Wife B howls at her husband for attending a Scientology group. We look her up and find she had a baby *he* didn't know about.'

And so on. The message is crude but simple. When you find a critic of Scientology tell him that unless he desists 'we will look up—and will find and expose—your crimes. If you leave us alone we will leave you alone. It's very simple,' Hubbard continues. 'Even a fool can grasp that.' Such people, like the worst kind of Suppressive Persons, were of course declared 'Fair Game'.

Recently, in an attempt to erase the unsavoury image the founder has acquired for Scientology by such formal statements, spokesmen for the movement have interpreted this order as denoting that individuals who are 'Fair Game' are merely deprived of the protection of the Scientology Organization and Ethics Office. A re-reading of the order, however, makes this hypothesis seem a bit thin and it is impossible not to feel chilled at the terrible phrases so callously written down, and their effect on people attempting to break away from the cult.

Like many other heads of bureaucratic organizations Hubbard seems to believe that anything that is not written down is not true; the spoken word is ephemeral and has no mass to it, while something written on paper becomes fact. This perhaps accounts for the obsession with paper-work, the countless bulletins, directives, sub-orders, memos, policy letters, etc., which Scientology Orgs circulate and file. It also accounts for the telex network which links all major Orgs across the world, a communications system of great efficiency that allows Hubbard, wherever he may be, to be in constant touch with any outposts of his empire.

A vivid account of the muddled administration network within Scientology has been given by Cyril Vosper, a former senior official within the movement whose recent book *The Mindbenders* is interesting in as much as it gives one the valuable opinion of an insider turned outsider. Far from producing efficiency it appears the obsessive paper-pushing wastes a colossal amount of time and is a constant source of gripe to the ill-paid minions who staff the various Orgs. From the Hubbard headquarters, wherever they may be, come policy letters and directives at all times of the day or night, listing new rules and regulations, occasional great thoughts from the Master himself, and details of the latest dramatic promotions or relegations, which are a feature of the frenetic Scientology scene. Each individual in an Org must have a 'Comm basket' to stack piles of paper which move to and fro throughout the day, and the colour of the star on his basket indicates his status, whether 'Power', 'Non-Existence', etc. No one is spared, and one of the most heinous of Scientology crimes is to leave work with a full 'Comm basket'.

On the boat even Hubbard's children find themselves with jobs as messengers, propagating the network of noise and paper. It is communication for communication's sake, and in the fantasy logic of Scientology this in itself is good enough. The quality or substance of the message being passed does not matter. All is done in the name of efficiency, and Scientologists pride themselves—in theory—on the streamlined operation of their Orgs.

'Scientology is the most vital force on this planet and Saint Hill staff its select team of leaders', we read in *The Auditor* No. 12. 'Now is your chance to join this fabulous team', it continues, adding that 'Ron says that by 1966 we will have expanded to 266 staff members and occupy twice the space.'

In this same issue we also see the first signs of uniforms which appeared in Saint Hill in 1965. Making it clear why it is necessary to have uniforms *The Auditor* continues: 'Scientologists are in the forefront of society today. Their alertness, their enthusiasm are visible to all and in this unaware, aberrated world a group of Scientologists stand out from their fellows like beacons. Scientology is the most vital philosophy in the world today, in fact that the world has ever seen.'

Waxing ever more enthusiastic, the article goes on, 'The leaders of this rapidly growing movement of truth are the Org staff members. So it's only fitting that they have a uniform . . . that they can wear in the full pridefulness of what it stands for; Truth and the establishment of good order and freedom for Man to attain higher states of existence'.

After this stirring message it is disappointing to find out that the uniform consists of grey flannel trousers and blue blazers for the men and grey skirts with blue blazers for the women.

Within a few years, however, uniforms were to seem a good deal less attractive to the staff of Saint Hill. In 1967, with Hubbard out of the country and the emphasis shifting steadily to the Sea Orgs, a decline in the fortunes of the East Grinstead headquarters—imperceptible at first but steadily becoming more noticeable—took place. In September of that year a cable from Hubbard's boat told the flabbergasted crowd at Saint Hill that they had been declared in a 'state of Non-Existence'.

To most of the staff and students this was a real blow, and the penalties associated with this Condition were sorrowfully but meticulously obeyed. These it will be recalled, included the working of overtime without pay and an embargo on bathing, washing, shaving, etc. To others, in particular those who had been with the movement from the early days and many of whom were personally acquainted with Hubbard, the restrictions were ridiculous and intolerable. Several felt that it must be all some kind of mistake and carried on in their usual fashion, trying to ignore the stink that began to arise from their unwashed colleagues who had meekly toed the party line.

Presumably news of the partial refusal to obey orders must have been passed to the Ethics Department, for late one evening a car pulled up in the driveway of the Manor and four uniformed Ethics Officers, one a young girl, swept through the offices where overtime staff were still working away.

One of the most senior Scientologists present, a man who had worked for many years in the organization, relates that he was working at his desk when the members of the 'Mission' appeared in his room. They presented him with a policy letter stating that Saint Hill was being taken over by the Sea Org. The three men and girl had 'total ethics power'.

Then occurred a grim little incident, trivial perhaps in itself but hinting strongly at the unpleasant undercurrents which were coursing through the movement at the time. After handing over their orders, which gave them virtually dictatorial powers, one of the party ordered the Scientologist (he recalls) to take a cigarette out of his mouth. Understandably he refused, whereupon one of the men present seized him and removed his cigarette forcibly. It was done with strength, speed and a coarse brutality.

When he recovered from the shock, he got up and walked out of the Manor. For ten seconds he had seen an ugly face of the movement he had served and a decade of involvement with Scientology, much of it in an official capacity, was ended.

By now the growth of the symptoms of a dictatorial bureaucracy, including even the trappings of a uniformed police force, were attracting increasing attention from the press. In the late summer of 1968 Hubbard, or some of his associates, must have decided that a period of liberation was overdue. Perhaps news of the rough handling of Scientologists by the Ethics Officers were beginning to cause dissatisfaction and fear within the movement.

The phrase 'Hubbard, or some of his associates' above is not an error. 1968 was the year which saw what seems to have been L. Ron's controlled handing over of the reins of power to the directors of Scientology as a business organization and as an incorporated religion. In theory this all began on 1st September 1966 (shortly after his return from Rhodesia) when he claimed to have quit all directorial posts in Scientology. On this date he sold the 'goodwill' of the name 'L. Ron Hubbard' to the Scientology movement for the tidy sum of £100,000 and, as the result of a special agreement, Orgs had to purchase the use of his signature.

One might fairly assume that this was an easy method for Hubbard to increase his own considerable fortune, but he is quick to dispel this illusion. In another of his famous letters he says that the real reason for requiring Orgs to buy his signature rights was because 'the public demonstrably stays away from Orgs that do not bear the name "L. Ron Hubbard" and I do not wish to damage their traffic volume'.

Hubbard's personal fortune, which it is claimed he has amassed from Scientology, has always been in dispute, though it is hard to see how he can fail to have made immense sums from it. Hubbard can be—and has a right to be—unforthcoming about exactly how much he is worth, but according to a report in the *Daily Mail* of 3rd August 1968, he was telling close associates, just prior to leaving England in 1966, that he had nearly £3,000,000 in a secret Swiss bank account. There was a 'personal account' in his name at the Pictet Bank in Geneva and the *Mail* claimed that money from Scientology Orgs all over the world has been channelled into this account, or into another 'trustee' account in the same name. The Scientologists deny this strenuously.

Hubbard claims that he has loaned Scientology literally millions of pounds which he is prepared to forget. Reliable sources state that he used to draw a percentage, usually ten per cent, of the gross income of all Scientology Orgs, and even allowing for the waxing and waning in popularity of particular centres this would amount to a really meaty sum—the income of Saint Hill has been as high as £30,000 in one week for example. How much all this is affected by his supposed resignation as the head of Scientology is very unclear. Certainly he is now listed as 'Founder' on letter-heads, and there are increasing signs of the reins being taken up by hands other than his—if very diffidently at first.

The cost of training at most levels in Scientology is high, and it should be remembered that levels follow each other up along a ladder which appears to have no topmost rung. Let's take a look at one typical ladder, bearing in mind that the frothy nature of the surface of Scientology and the frequent 'break throughs' that occur at regular intervals, lead to unpredictable changes which may well make this ladder when the book is published. (Details are taken from *The Auditor*.)

At the bottom of the scale, you may take 'Free Membership' in the Scientology Organization for six months, simply by applying in writing to your nearest Org. No obligation to take any courses or to spend any money accompanies this trial period, though if you do join you will be sent a string of letters and pamphlets urging you to buy this book or that, attend this or that Congress or purchase a tape of Hubbard talking. If you respond to any of these and actually part with any money, then the Org will shift gear and you will be invited to take an introductory course.

At the time of writing the bottom rung of the ladder is represented by the 'Hubbard Apprentice Scientologist Course', which lasts a total of ten to twenty hours. This is followed by the 'Hubbard Special Dianetic Course', which lasts about a month. Both these courses cost less than £50 between them and provide one with certificates. These in turn let one ascend the ladder from the lowly 'Hubbard Apprentice Scientologist' to the more senior 'Hubbard Qualified Scientologist'. At this point, when with the cost of books, etc., the student will have parted with about £100, he may be sufficiently ambitious to take the course for 'Hubbard Recognized Scientologist'. Here he may be disappointed to realize that he is still, after all these exertions and certificates, only on Grade O of the seven rungs of the ladder leading to the state of Clear.

If still persistent and solvent he may now press on, parting with fees from between £10–£50 at each rung, from 'Hubbard Trained Scientologist' through 'Hubbard Certified Auditor' and on to 'Hubbard Professional Auditor'. Above this lie the goals of 'Hubbard Advanced Auditor', 'Hubbard Validated Auditor' and the impressive 'Hubbard Senior Scientologist'.

By now, if his senses are not reeling with the glory of his achievement, he will have noted that the fees have suddenly become really substantial, the 'Saint Hill Special Briefing Course', which moves one up from rung Five to rung Six of the ladder, costing £323. He can now become a 'Class VII' Auditor and the goal of Clear is near, there only remaining the little matter of 'Power Processing' at £417 a shot, before one settles down to the clearing course itself.

And what does one get for all this? Not all that much if one is to believe the stories of those who have taken this lengthy course and later come to regret the money spent.

One individual, whose name is numbered among the first hundred Clears, doubts whether Clears really have anything to show for all their trouble—at any rate anything likely to impress the non-Scientology world. The trouble is that the kind of person who gets involved in Scientology in many cases tends to be either young, naive and idealistic—and these often drop out to move on to other 'religions' or 'philosophies' or political movements—or the lonely, neurotic or inadequate for whom the extrovert social involvement of a Scientology course, and the constant statements about 'great improvements' and 'evolving states of being', etc., have a definite tonic effect. That tonic effect may well be temporary, as some disgruntled ex-Scientologists will testify, but by the time this is realized the individual may be too highly committed financially or ideologically to be able to back out easily and yet retain his own psychological self-esteem.

In addition there are many rewards of a minor, though at

the time seemingly important, kind along the trail—the numerous certificates, the constant optimistic statements of other Scientologists and the hyper-confidence of Hubbard's writings and lectures. There is also the mystery-magic of the E-meter—which to many in the cult is a totally marvellous device—and the sense of achievement associated with the acquisition of a complex jargon, plus the increasing involvement with what appears to be an in-group as one ascends the scale.

There are also the occasional curious experiences known as 'releases'. A release is described, by those who have experienced it, as a kind of emotional or psychic discharge which suddenly engulfs most Scientologists at some stage or another in their training. It appears to be akin to a minor mystical or religious experience, such as is often associated with conversion and it is accompanied by a sense of euphoria and apparently heightened perceptual awareness. If so, it is a phenomenon not at all rare among those with mystical, hysterical or even psychotic traits and its aura is of short duration and may be accompanied by a depressive hangover. Scientologists treat it as an objective and permanent personality change achieved as the result of the elimination of some major engram or hang-up.

The biggest let-down of all seems to be the state of Clear itself. It will be remembered that in the palmy days of Dianetics, it was believed that Clears, when they finally came along, would be immensely superior human beings—simply because they would be free of the huge accumulation of psychological garbage that they had acquired in numerous traumas since their birth and even before.

Beyond this was the state of Operating Thetan. This is a condition in which the Thetan (which it will be remembered corresponds to the human spirit or soul) can emancipate itself from the body and use its amazing powers at will. The Greek Gods, with their control of thunder and lightning and their other magical powers, Hubbard explained, were simply Operating Thetans who happened to be roaming around the world at the time amazing the yokels with their supernatural powers.

Even this fantastic stage of being, Hubbard and followers believe, should be reachable by humans using the techniques of Dianetics and Scientology.

All this was twenty years ago, and while the states of Clear and Operating Thetan still exist in the Scientological terminology, their supposed qualities have changed drastically with time. Gone, in the case of Clear, are the presumed telepathic ability, the 'total recall of all perceptics', the acquisition of a photographic memory, the freedom from body aches, pains, colds, etc., which made the goal exceedingly tempting to the pioneer Scientologists. In their place we now find a Clear defined as a person who has 'attained the state of being in which he is *at cause* over mental factors, is wholly himself, can follow his own basic purposes and is not reactive'.

This statement is meaningless outside the framework of Scientology. In fact so vague are the attributes of Clear that no one can dispute them. For example, if Scientologists claim that a Clear is genuinely 'at cause' over mental factors, or is 'wholly himself', then it is impossible for one to deny or even comment on this because there is no way of making an objective test of statements of this kind. On the other hand if it is claimed that Clears are more intelligent, better looking, have a greater resistance to pain or illness, then it is in principle possible to examine these claims and test them.

Scientologists reply to this kind of argument by saying that to a Scientologist the phrase 'at cause' has a very precise definition, but can only be so defined within the logic of the philosophy of Scientology. This is fair enough, of course, provided that it is realized that this is now not a transferable system—in other words the supposed attributes of a Clear mean nothing to the outside world and have no practical objective application in it. At any rate it is a far cry from the times when Clears talked of growing new teeth, making anti-gravity machines or living to be four hundred.

The new goal in Scientology, not achieved at the time of writing, is that of Operating Thetan. Like the road to Clear, that to Operating Thetan consists of a series of carefully delineated steps or stages, each costing money—it now runs into thousands of pounds. One asks what are the attributes that will go with the state of Operating Thetan for those who achieve it? Will thunder and lightning crackle at their finger-tips, as at those of their predecessors, the Gods of Olympus? It seems very unlikely. And furthermore, when the state is achieved, who, apart from the Operating Thetans themselves, will be impressed?

On 26th August 1968, not more than a month after he had been told that he would not be granted re-entry into England, and in the wake of the biggest press blast—almost entirely unfavourable—that Scientology had received, Hubbard announced that 'Security Checks' were being abolished. These 'checks'—and also the kind of prying by private detective, amateur spying, accumulation of gossip, etc.,—which led to the declaration of individuals as 'Suppressives' and their subsequent labelling as 'Fair Game' were abandoned for a number of reasons. The first and foremost, which comes in amazing contrast to earlier statements, reads: 'We have no interest in the secrets and crimes of people and no use for them.'

Another was frank and revealing: 'There is public criticism of security checking as a practice.' This statement, with its strong suggestion that the founder of Scientology was becoming bothered about public criticism, is in its way a landmark in Scientology, a welcome sign of pragmatic realism.

But this was just the beginning. On 14th October Hubbard announced a new Auditor's Code to guide the conduct of professional Scientologists when auditing or processing other people. This manifesto, with its twenty-eight points, was described as superseding all other codes and was to be learnt by heart by all 'auditors and students under training'. The points range from the obscure (i.e., jargon-ridden) such as 'I promise to grant beingness to the preclear in session' or 'I promise never to run any one action beyond its floating needle' to the dramatic such as 'I promise not to permit sexual liberties or violation of the mentally unsound'. There are, in addition, certain very direct commands, which, one feels, are intended to clarify the shifting role of Scientology in answer to its critics. For example, Code No. 15 reads: 'I promise not to mix the processes of Scientology with other practices except when the preclear is physically ill and only medical means will serve.' While No. 24, in similar implicit vein states: 'I promise not to advocate Scientology only to cure illness or only to treat the insane, knowing well it is intended for spiritual gain.'

Both these codes clearly attempt to define the role of an auditor *vis-à-vis*, say, psychotherapists or even physicians, a definition which in many people's eyes was long overdue. Even in this solemn-sounding catalogue, Hubbard couldn't resist the temptation to get in his traditional dig against psychiatry. Code No. 26 states: 'I promise to refuse to permit any being to be physically injured, violently damaged, operated on or killed in the name of "mental treatment".'

Keeping the ball rolling swiftly and continuing the policy of 'liberalization', on 1st November 1968, Issue 42 of *The Auditor* carried a giant headline 'INTERNATIONAL AMNESTY'. In a terse statement, signed by himself, Hubbard declares: 'To celebrate the advent of Standard Tech, an international amnesty is declared for all Scientologists and Scientology Organizations and franchises over the world effective 1st November, A.D. 18. All acts before that date are freely forgiven.'

This magnanimous gesture, which amounted to an effective ending of the Condition known as 'Fair Game', and to the general harassing and persecution of ex-Scientologists and the movement's antagonists—psychiatrists included—is another obvious response to protest from within and without the movement. The official reason given, however, is the achievement of 'Standard Tech', another of the major advances which occur so frequently throughout the cult's history, but which are rarely explicable to anyone not thoroughly steeped in the jargon. A short piece in the same issue of *The Auditor*, 'What is Different About Standard Tech?', attempts to explain, but succeeds only in adding another puzzling article to the many thousands that have already been published in this journal.

'Isn't it the same Tech? Isn't it the same Scientology? Same drills same Processes?', the article begins breathlessly, and continues in the same vein:

'Yes. It is. It's the same Scientology, the same axioms, the same grades and OT sections.

'But the APPLICATION is STREAMLINED.

'Instead of fifteen possible actions to correct something on a Case, Ron worked it down to one action that fitted the lot.'

It's as simple as that. 'Like tuning up a motor', it adds incomprehensibly. If you don't know anything about motors then you have a hard time getting one to run, and when it doesn't run you don't get full performance out of it. Then along comes a new handbook written by an expert, and the results are dramatic.

'It's the same motor, same tools. But wow look at it go NOW!'

The above extracts will serve to give something of the flavour of the material propagated by *The Auditor*, and by all accounts eagerly devoured by its readers.

In line with the new policies, and presumably the new image of Scientology, the New Year issue of *The Auditor* reaches new heights of effusive bonhomie. Wishing 'a happy 69 to you', Hubbard gives a brief message to his clans:

'As Scientology enters A.D. (After Dianetics) 19, we have big plans and purposes to make this a better world for everyone in Scientology.

'Less Ethics, more tech, bigger orgs, new civic groups and all the truly good things in life.'

'But be that as it may, what I want to say is, I'm hoping for a really good year for YOU personally. I'm doing all I can to make it so.'

The piece is signed, 'Love, Ron'.

On the same page, in an article on 'The Value of Scientology', Hubbard refers to the 'screaming apes' of the press and the 'cold sadists who run the learned societies'. He also comments that 'mental "health" has been perverted into an excuse for a Belsen or an Auschwitz by the older practices in the field'. There may have been an International Amnesty, but this article suggests that L. Ron still keeps his enemies in his sights.

From Psychotherapy to Religion

WE HAVE EXAMINED in detail the historical development of Scientology from its earliest and somewhat mysterious beginnings in 1949 or thereabouts when, as Dianetics, it was hailed as a breakthrough in psychotherapy, to its present turbulent existence as an organized cult striving to be accepted, in popular terms, as a formal and valid religion. We have also paid some attention to the interesting and controversial personality of the man who created the movement and shepherded it from its initial boom, through a period of depression, and up again to its more recent renaissance.

Scientology would have been nothing without Hubbard. It is his personal, unequivocal brainchild, and he has nursed and enlivened it for over half his adult life. Its concepts, jargon, logics, its rules and regulations are the product of his own thoughts and have been implemented only through the power of his will and the magnetism of his personality. Of the millions of people who have at one time or another involved themselves, whether flirtatiously or committedly, with Scientology precious few have made a major or durable contribution, political or ideological, to the structure and function of the movement. If one is to trust the statements of those Scientologists who once held positions relatively high in the movement's hierarchy but subsequently dissociated themselves from it, creativity and signs of originality are not welcome in Hubbard's entourage. Those who show any soon run into trouble.

This is attested by more than one ex-Scientology notable who found that their own rise to prominence in the movement attracted Hubbard's baleful attention. The only people with a vestige of real power have been his present wife, Mary Sue, and to a lesser extent his firstborn child, Nibs. The latter, of course, is now in disgrace having testified on behalf of the FDA in their case against the E-meter, but his married sister, living in Los Angeles, is still a keen Scientologist, and all Hubbard's children by Mary Sue are deeply involved. The oldest daughter was recently married, incidentally, aboard the *Apollo* to another young Scientologist, both proud parents being very much in evidence at the ceremony.

There are a number of reasons for the dramatically pyramidal structure of the Scientology Orgs—an effective dependence upon Hubbard which could well cost them dear in the event of his demise. The simplest reason is that Hubbard is himself, undeniably, a man of considerable intelligence, boundless enthusiasm, one hundred per cent conviction of his own rectitude and, very possibly, with the unshakeable zeal of a man who believes that he is a figure of destiny. Friends and acquaintances from the early pre-Dianetics days recall that he stood out at the time as a remarkable figure, bursting with personality and seemingly equipped for great deeds of one kind or another. A fellow SF writer, Damon Knight, believes that Hubbard was gifted beyond the ordinary as a writer and might have become a major literary figure had he been capable of imposing more self-discipline in his work. Other areas where Ron might have excelled would seem to be politics, the theatre or cinema, perhaps even some footloose scientific topic such as anthropology. But it was not to be. Dianetics and Scientology were to be the major fruits of his talents. Little wonder, therefore, that in an organization not particularly attractive to those of academic or scientific bent, Hubbard stands out like a beacon.

The second reason is probably a more pragmatic one. Hubbard must be aware, when he can bring himself to think about it, of the flaws in the principles and practice of Scientology, of its numerous contradictions in word and deed, some of which have been brought to the fore in this book. No amount of decorative jargon can disguise the fact that the original claims of Dianetics, made twenty years ago, have not been met. The simple concepts of that time—engrams cause most of Man's ills, and their erasure will bring him to an emancipated state of power—have now become hopelessly clouded. The proximity of too many sharp-minded and critically inclined individuals would, one suspects, cause Hubbard to dwell unduly on the gaping flaws in the fabric of Scientology and their presence would thus be unwelcome.

Finally, Hubbard is, like any other creative man, justly jealous of the material wrought from his brain. There is evidence that he has always feared that certain individuals or groups, for one reason or another, are persistently out either to steal the ideas built into Scientology or to destroy it. In fact, in this strange world of ours, there is almost always a basis of truth in even the wildest paranoid fantasy. Scientology and its founder have, from the word go, been under sustained pressure and assault from the outside world. Sometimes the pressure is benign, as when the millionaire Purcell attempted, in the early days of Dianetics, to put the subject on a serious business and scientific footing. Sometimes dissidents have attempted to form 'rival' Scientology organizations of their own. Such breakaways are known to loyalists as 'Squirrels', and most fade away into ignominy or oblivion through simple lack of talent, *panache* or both. Occasionally the squirrels are individuals of real ability—such as the science fiction writer A. E. Van Vogt who runs his own version of Dianetics in California. Van Vogt seems relatively happy without L. Ron and publishes a little magazine chatting on about Dianetics, rather as if it were still 1953 and Scientology and its later flowerings had never come into being. Others, less self-confident, somehow manage to remain only parodies of the Master. Jack Horner, a former high priest of the movement, fell out with Ron some years ago and now runs his own tiny circus under the drearily unimaginative banner of 'Dianology'. Its impact on the world psychological scene at this time must be counted as minimal. Sometimes squirrels (and these are the interesting ones) deviate so far from the old line that the origins of their movements appear to have been forgotten by public and adherents alike. One such movement is 'The Process', about which a few words must be said.

The Process was the brain child of a Mr Robert de Grimstone and his wife, Mary Anne. Both were at one time Scientologists (hence the carry-over of the word 'process') who left the movement for ideological reasons which today have vanished into the mists of forgetfulness. At first they appeared to be practising fairly straight Scientology, using 'processes' out of the auditor's manual, and even maintaining the practice of staring people in the eyes with a long and unblinking gaze, an aggravating habit much in vogue among Scientologists and amateur psychologists the world over. At first they operated from a small flat in Wigmore Street, charging modest fees of three or four guineas an hour. As their following grew they moved to larger premises—a complete house in Balfour Place, one of London's most exclusive residential addresses. The reported rental of over £3,000 per annum gives some measure of their financial standing at the time, as does the rumour that the lease of the house cost £40,000.

Meanwhile a strange change was being wrought in Mr de Grimstone. His hair grew and grew and grew, and the expression on his face, to judge by photographs, became exceedingly pious. By 1968, some years after parting from L. Ron & Co., he looked, one cannot deny, like a Hollywood version of Jesus Christ. Perhaps this explains why *The People* reporters, who infiltrated The Process at their headquarters in 1970, found that he was actually known to other members of the cult as 'The Oracle' or, more simply, 'God'. His wife was known as 'The Goddess'. This aura of sanctity spread over lesser members of the group as well, and individuals who had previously laboured through life with names like Smith, Brown or Robinson, suddenly sprouted beards and were metamorphosed into Brother Micah, Alban, Lars, etc. There were even to be found 'Sisters' flitting around the place, all wearing The Process's unisex outfit of black jeans and sweaters. The next development—predictably—was the shift of the organization into a formalized religious body under the slightly ominous name of 'The Church of the Final Judgement'.

Interested visitors to The Process's headquarters at Balfour Place in the late sixties must have asked themselves where the Church of the Final Judgement got all its money. The building, which occupied four or five floors, was expensively furnished and decorated in a style which can best be described as tasteful opulence. An engraved metal plate on the front door bore the organization's emblem, a square with radiating arms, vaguely like a modernized version of the swastika. The money can hardly have come from profits on the organization's little coffee bar, selling nut-and-watercress sandwiches, in the basement. Nor can any really large sums have been raised, one would have thought, from the street canvassing undertaken by the more ardent members of The Process, who, wearing flowing cloaks, would invite members of the public passing by to 'subscribe to animal welfare'. Anyone who felt inclined to ask what kind of animal welfare was implied before parting with his coin, would be told that the supplicants belonged to a Church which actively opposed vivisection. Thus, money going to the Church would ultimately support animal welfare. Nor yet could much revenue come from sales of The Process's slick and professional magazine which, richly endowed with photographs, colour illustrations and expensive artwork, must have cost six or seven times its selling price to produce.

The most likely clue probably comes from the pages of the magazine itself, wherein people were invited, in the most open-hearted way imaginable, simply to dispose of their fortune to the Church. Issue number 4, for example, thanks readers for their 'magnificent response to the appeal which appeared in our last issue for fortunes to dissipate'. 'However', the magazine continues, 'we have successfully dissipated all of them in absolute record time and are eagerly awaiting more.' Those readers who had not quite left themselves destitute were adjured not to 'hold out on us'. Anyone unfortunate enough to have 'millstones of money hanging round their necks' should relax and let The Process remove the same. It would be only too delighted to do so. A photograph on the same page shows a group of black-garbed people, eight male, two female and two indeterminate, seated around a table with a globe on it. 'Invest in the end of the world' reads the discouraging caption.

Blatant appeals to people to dissipate their fortunes may seem like undergraduate whimsy, but there is some evidence that the joke was on anyone but The Process. More than one exceedingly well-to-do young person, and some with connections in upper-crust British society, saw this strange outfit as providing spiritual or psychological haven, and more than one hearty cheque has been written out to the Church. There is of course nothing illegal in a religious organization appealing for funds, all one can say is that one hopes that the donors got good value for their money.

A study of the pages of The Process's magazine gives a fairly clear picture of the movement's philosophy and makes it evident that it is more than simply an intellectually upgraded Scientology, which is how a number of critics have attempted to dismiss it. Traces of Scientology remain—an obsession with the idea that Life is a game played by fallen Gods, a preoccupation with communication for its own sake, and a distinct tendency to be paranoid about psychiatry, electro-shock therapy, cortical surgery, etc. On the other hand the frenzied tub-thumping of Scientology is gone, as is the uncritical adulation of leadership, so typical of many modern cults. The focus is sharper, the mood cooler, the view of the outside world sardonic rather than jaundiced, and there are traces of self-criticism and an ability to laugh at oneself, which are very sparse in Scientological literature.

What exactly is the philosophy? Well, members of the Church of the Final Judgement are, as you can imagine, enormously interested in the forces of Good, the omnipotence and totality of God and his various messengers on Earth—Christ, Buddha, Krishna, etc. But to complicate matters (for outsiders) the Church is also interested, and no less so, in what one normally takes to be the forces of Evil, the virulence and power of Lucifer and his various henchmen. There are, in The Process's theology, three Great Gods of the Universe, Jehovah, Satan and Lucifer, who, when welded together into one, become a super-cosmological entity called, for want of a better word, GOD. Life is the interplay of the forces of the three master players, and human beings are the pieces—pieces which can, however, choose the side they will play on, and who may by one means or another (mainly joining the Church of the Final Judgement) even rise ultimately into the role of players. The really important thing, The Process believes, is that one must be firm in one's alignment and one's commitment. It doesn't matter in absolute terms whether one allies oneself on the side of Christ or Satan for no one is 'better' than the other. One side is Black and the other White. The only real sin, the one essential corruption, is to fail to take up a positive position with either Black or White forces, and thus become Grey, an advocate of compromise and indecision.

The world, as it turns out, is at present run by the Greys. Photographs in the magazine indicate who these are—The

Pope, Mr Harold Wilson, the TV personality, David Frost, etc. The Whites include Jesus Christ and the Blacks are represented by such charming chaps as Adolf Hitler. If you, like most people, would find H. Wilson and D. Frost very much preferable to A. Hitler, then you are either one of the Greys yourself or have rather missed the point of The Process's message. Jehovah and Lucifer, you must understand, work not against one another, as all other religions hold, but hand in hand. Both have returned to earth with a very singular purpose—to root out the Grey forces utterly from every sphere of society and destroy them. Or, as the magazine puts it: 'To bring every grey government to its knees and to replace it either with utter chaos and anarchy or with a militant dictatorship.'

This is the message of The Process. The extremes of viewpoint inherent in the Black/White division of forces is reflected not only in the editorial matter of The Process's magazine, but also in its readers' letter page. 'The picture of Robert de Grimstone sent me reeling', writes J. Smith of Leeds, 'I've never seen a face with such impact. It's Christ come again was my first thought.' On the other hand, 'Anon' of London writes, 'I want you to know I think you're evil, straight from the devil. Whenever I see your magazine anywhere I make the sign of the cross.' There are other examples in both veins. Perhaps one should leave the last word to 'Valerie' of London. who seems to have it all summed up pretty well when she writes: 'Ooh, you lovely lot, beards, long hair and all. I don't know what you're talking about but I'm with you. Can I have the one that looks like Rasputin?'

In the past year or so the Church has somehow or other pulled up its roots from Balfour Place and has shifted its base to America. A major Chapter has opened in Chicago with a number of English *émigrés*, including the wealthy daughter of at least one peer of the realm, in residence. The Chicago group have philanthropic pretensions, raising money for sick children, etc., and appear to be moving rapidly towards a commune kind of existence. They wear black tights, silver pendants and bracelets and have the emblem of The Process emblazoned in red on their clothing. Wherever members of the Church go, large Alsatian dogs (known as German Shepherds in America) are to be found in attendance. Not just one or two Alsatians, but *lots* of them. The dogs lead fairly uninhibited social and domestic lives and are taken to be symbolical of something or other—perhaps it is the Church's devotion to the cause of animal welfare. At one point in its history the movement acquired a centre in Mexico, at a seaside spot called Xtul. Photographs in the magazine show it to be a place of sun, palms, sand, surf and Alsatian dogs and it has to be admitted that everyone looks as though they're having a pretty good time.

Other notables have at times tried seizing Scientological limelight, and their heads have rolled as a result. Hubbard's second wife, Sarah Northrup, was apparently accused of seeking to take over Dianetics and use it for selfish and evil reasons. An equally bitter family quarrel later arose when Hubbard, for one reason or another, parted company with his son Nibs who had achieved some prominence within the movement.

Hubbard also believes that major forces within the world are gathering in an attempt to crush Scientology, and much of his more recent writing reflects this persecution complex. Many Scientologists consequently believe that a sinister international group is out to sit on them, this group being made up of a motley association of crooked politicians, psychiatrists (of course), greedy businessmen and various insane and malevolent journalists. As we have said, in a weird way this paranoia is justified. The world, or some vocal and powerful sections of it, *is* out to suppress Scientology, as the action of the FDA, the British Parliament and the State of Victoria, to name but three, demonstrates conclusively. The open question is, how justified this persecution really is?

Persecution is a loaded word. To some extent it implies wrongful suppression by a big and powerful body of some relatively blameless minority. When the Germans set out to eliminate the Jews from the continent of Europe they were clearly guilty of persecution. On the other hand, if a country acts through its legal forces to eliminate an undesirable minority—let us say professional pushers of heroin—then we are all disinclined to use the word 'persecution'. Though we are talking here of two extremes on a continuum it is important, if we are to get Scientology in perspective, to decide which of the two extreme cases cited above most clearly fits the case of Mr Hubbard and his followers. Does society, which to some extent penalizes them, do so justly or unjustly?

This is a crucial matter. Western societies set much store by —or at least pay lip service to—the concepts of religious freedom and tolerance. If Scientology is, as it claims to be, a religion then why should its free practice not be permitted in society? The simple answer put forward by its opponents is that it in fact only *pretends* to be a religion, and in any case it is a harmful organization. How reasonable is this point of view? Is Scientology (*a*) a religion, and (*b*) harmful?

These very issues were raised in an interesting way during a recent remarkable High Court action in which the Church of Scientology of California sued the MP for East Grinstead, Mr Geoffrey Johnson Smith, alleging that he had libelled them in an interview on the BBC TV programme, *24 Hours*. They claimed that statements he had made on the programme had meant that they were a 'harmful organization, acting in an improper way towards members'. After an incredibly lengthy action (the longest in recent legal history), when no fewer than thirty days were given over merely to hearing evidence, the jury found that the words spoken by Johnson Smith were not defamatory of the sect and the case was dismissed. The Church of Scientology was ordered to pay the immense costs involved —which were estimated as being as much as £70,000.

The action is important, for, as was pointed out at the outset by the Scientologists' counsel, Mr Ronald Shulman, issues of great significance, some relevant to the whole basis of religious freedom within the country, were implicitly raised. In fact, Mr Shulman remarked, it was 'surprising that in the twentieth century such a right as the freedom of religion should be challenged in court'. The trial was 'probably the freedom trial of the century'. Scientologists were not different from anyone else. They believed in an Almighty and in the immortality of the human spirit. Scientology was not a joke, nor was it a 'trumped-up religious enterprise'.

In fact the Scientologists made a somewhat braver showing in court than many had anticipated, and witnesses were brought from all parts of the world to support their case. The most dramatic of these was probably the evidence of an American, William Benitez, who stated that through Scientology he had broken free of a history of nineteen years of drug addiction, which had included thirteen years in prison for drug offences. He was now the founder of an organization for the cure and rehabilitation of drug addicts which, using some of the principles of Scientology, claimed '85% success in dealing with addicts'.[1] There was also some medical testimony from doctors who had used Scientology in their practice, and even one Californian psychologist who stated that he included some of its principles in his introductory lectures on psychology. But to most observers the debit side must have loomed largest. Much discussion centred around the oft-quoted 'disconnect orders' and the infamous policy order indicating that selected opponents of Scientology were labelled 'fair game'. Mr Shulman did all he could to argue that the horrendous phrase 'may be lied to, cheated or destroyed' merely implied that the defaulters were no longer granted the protection that Scientologists normally gave to each other, and that the words 'lied to, etc.' were not to be taken literally. Neither judge nor jury looked convinced.

After the result had been announced Mr Gaiman stated that in his view the evidence produced at the trial had served to clear the air on certain important misunderstandings and had merely reinforced their belief that the previous government (Wilson's 1964–70 administration) 'did act against us without proper investigation'. This, Gaiman told a newspaper, is 'the most vital point to have emerged from this hearing'. Although this chirpy pronouncement probably reflected no more than the usual Scientological optimism and superconfidence, the action, while financially unpalatable, may have yielded certain fringe benefits for the movement. In the first place, as we have said earlier, they put up a better showing than their unkindest critics might have predicted. Some of the witnesses impressed the court with their honesty and general demeanour, and at the very least anyone who had seen the trial through from end to end must have been left with the impression that Scientology could, in certain circumstances, actually do some good. If one is to retort that there are very few things in the world that do not do *some* good, then that is probably fair comment. It is, nevertheless, true to say that Scientology's PR front has been consistently so bad that

[1] Narconon seems to be making headway; *The Auditor* No. 81, published late 1972, lists official affiliations all over the world. It is claimed that the Mexican and Swedish governments and the state of Delaware provide funds for the Scientology-based movement.

evidence that it can do some good must inevitably improve its image. Furthermore, one was left with the undeniable impression that Scientology was evolving out of a murky past into a somewhat more balanced and creditable future. The question now arises as to what are the benefits which people report as the result of taking Scientology courses or after becoming involved in the movement.

Scientologists themselves wax eloquent over the great improvement that they feel as the result of 'processing', and at this level one has to admit that the treatment probably has some specific benefit. If so it may well be a benefit very much akin to the spiritual lift and heightened sense of well-being that comes from achievement in any field, in particular when this is hitched to a religious experience of some kind. Like all such subjective experiences, which resist any kind of quantification, that lift is often temporary—particularly when for one reason or another the individual is unable to proceed any further up the endless ladder of grades and qualifications that Scientology puts in front of its adherents.

A study of some of the personal success stories by Scientologists themselves, as given in *The Auditor*, No. 12, reveals only too clearly the subjective nature of the improvements as the results of processing. For example, Bob Musack, who had been on the Clear Course, writes: 'Here's a rundown of my gains since Power Processing. With most of my old habit patterns broken up (thank God) it took a while to get reoriented in the environment. Not that the environment in any way seemed dangerous to me, in fact I found it contained scarcely any significance unless I put something there, but a certain reluctance in creating any effects unless I was certain I would take responsibility for them. This is a definite gain as I formerly did things on pretty much of an impulse basis. My postulates on making money are working better than ever. Another gain is recognizing and confronting entheta characters around . . .' Etc., etc.

Even more obscurely, John Lawrence writes: 'The gains and wins I have made since power processing are many and the nature of my gains is such that there is only one gain worthwhile to me and that is becoming me as I know I can be. The gain is just being more me and having it be alright with me and have it this way and knowing I will continue to progress.'

Gertrude Brown has this to say: 'Since my Power Processing I am becoming more and more certain. I am more able to Intent. I have more and more ability to validate myself. Stage V was where I had my big win. With the exception of R6 Solo auditing, Power Plus Processing was the best auditing I've ever had. For me they truly were orientation processes. I am doing fine.'

It all sounds fine, even if a bit like an advertisement for a new kind of petrol, but not, as far as one can see, in substance, distinguishable from the kind of testimonials one reads to the successes of nerve tonics, relaxation belts, win-friends-and-influence-people courses, lucky charm necklaces or yogic meditation. And it is, of course, far more expensive than any of the above. But subjectivity itself is no crime. If people feel better and say so, or declare and believe that their life state has been changed for the better by Scientological methods, then Hubbard and his followers are entitled to face their critics with these successes. A reply that most successes are only transient is not really enough—why should they occur at all? In other words, what is there about the techniques that works, if only at a restricted level?

There are probably two major reasons for the successes when they occur, one of which must, in fairness, be credited to the philosophy of Scientology. This is linked to their notion of improving the effectiveness of interpersonal communication. Hubbard has always stressed the importance of communication as one of the most fundamental principles in the operation of the universe. Thetans are effective in what they do to the extent of their ability to communicate with each other and also with other objects in the world around them. Without such communication nothing useful can take place and individuals become moribund, inward-looking creatures, stagnating intellectually and physically. Really bad communicators, according to Hubbard, may even 'believe themselves to be' things like rocks, etc., and may remain thus for millions of years in gloomy self-induced seclusion. Vast improvements in personality, intellectual ability and general human effectiveness can be brought about by sharpening up the individual's talent for communication, and thus introductory Scientology courses concentrate heavily in this area. Students are given a series of drills consisting largely of question-and-answer sequences, some of which may be apparently trivial or nonsensical, such as 'Do birds fly?'. The answers given to the questions are generally counted as more or less irrelevant, the important fact being that an answer is given at all. 'Two-way communication' has been set up and from this step all the subsequent techniques of Scientology can begin to take effect.

From a psychological point of view it must be admitted that exercises aimed at inducing introverted individuals to become more 'outgoing' could be of real value. For many a lonely, shy and mildly neurotic individual the introductory Communication course might work wonders, and no doubt has done.

The second major reason for Scientology's successes, when they occur, is probably its reliance on a stratagem which is as old as the hills and known to soothsayers and quacks as well as to reputable ministers of religion and qualified psychoanalysts. This is the blazingly simple technique of giving people some undivided personal attention. In our society the neurotic individual dives for such systems as yoga, health food fads, Scientology, etc., simply because the orthodox doctor has neither the skill, the time nor the patience to spare for the chronically insecure individuals who frequent his surgery with their burden of neurotic complaints. The average psychiatrist, similarly, can do little for these victims of the malaise of our own society and can only offer the affluent few the lengthy course of psychoanalytic treatment, which occasionally can produce permanent improvements in personality. The only 'free' treatment remains the comforts of orthodox religion, with prayer and spiritual guidance from the priest or minister, but with galloping speed the decline in the credibility of orthodox religious philosophy is cutting the power from these quarters.

Scientology, even in its present confused state, seems to offer a real and, to a certain type of person, entirely plausible alternative to either psychoanalysis or orthodox religion. It produces a superficially watertight belief structure with clear-cut boldly spoken answers to questions of the 'Why are we here?' and 'Where are we going?' variety which human beings, understandably, seem to need to ask. Furthermore, it phrases these answers, which are of a generally mystical kind—eternal life being, as always, firmly stressed—in a language more suited to the second half of the twentieth century than any of the major religions of the world. It is a language with a technological and psychological ring, with phrases drawn from science fiction, from psychoanalysis, from computer technology, yet subtly blended with the spicy flavours of Eastern mysticism. This language appeals most directly to that section of society which finds itself most affected by the collapse of religious belief and the failure of modern psychology to make more comprehensible the workings of the human mind.

This is not for the older, poorly educated working class, whose problems are still largely economic and social and who have little time for 'the mind' and even less for neurotics. Nor is it for that growing band of highly trained and intelligent professionals whose intellectual sophistication is sufficient to allow it to ignore (or repress) the awesome mysteries posed by the gaps in our scientific knowledge, and whose interest in the mind will most generally be channelled into the crossword puzzle of psychoanalysis.

Rather it is for the moderately intelligent, reasonably well-read and self-aware individuals who by reason of lack of opportunity of one kind or another are denied higher education or who are temperamentally unsuited for it, that Scientology makes its strongest pitch. For them the self-assurance of Scientologists, the rapid induction into a private jargon and the acquisition of Certificates, Diplomas, etc., the immediate feedback from others of their kind, and the promise of achieving miraculous goals, provide a glowing beacon of hope. Once within this movement, with the feeling of identity with a cause building up, it would be odd indeed if major personality changes failed to take place. All along the line in Scientology, from the lowest rung to the misty heights of Operating Thetan, the willing individual may get attention at any level—provided that he pays his way—and there is nothing that the unsettled souls of our society require more desperately than the personal, unqualified, unjudging attention of another human being.

The auditing session in Scientology is called the 'Confessional' and it is no misnomer. For, if the truth is faced, the auditor with his magical E-meter is a workable substitute for the rapidly outdating confessional of the orthodox church. The ritual progression of the 'process' is more likely to be effective in the second half of the twentieth century than the act of praying to a God who shows so little sign of hearing and in whom so few people today really believe.

The point I am making is that despite all its faults, Scientology is making a serious bid to become one of the significant religious movements of this decade, perhaps even of this century. Its evolution seems to be demanding this, and there is some evidence, while Hubbard still firmly holds the reins and will continue as the Messiah figure for years to come (and certainly after his death), that the movement now has enough momentum to keep rolling on its own, modifying itself to fit the mood of the time as it does so.

Today, twenty years after its inception, it has swung full circle from claiming to be psychotherapy to claiming to be a religion. Like all young religions, it considers itself, with some justification, to have its martyrs. Indeed, until quite recently it had been getting progressively less house-room in English-speaking countries and were it not for Hubbard's brilliant idea of forming the Sea Orgs, it might be in dire accommodation difficulties. It has its seamy past and no doubt its seamy present too. It charges heavily for its services and a measurable portion of its income, there seems little doubt, has gone to swell Hubbard's personal fortune. But these are both criticisms not only of Scientology but also of many supposedly respectable business operations today. The cult is—or used to be—ruthless in disciplining its malcontented supporters and urges indoctrination of the children of its adherents. But so do numerous other cults—the Jehovah's Witnesses, for example, who push their singleminded beliefs to the point of danger, as with the controversial blood-transfusion ruling. Furthermore, outlandish though many of Scientology's theories are, it is doubtful if they are any stranger than the belief held by the Witnesses in the absolute truth of the Bible and in the coming intervention of Jehovah on earth.

To those who argue, with some justification, that (*a*) Scientology behaves more like a business than a religion, (*b*) it began as a pseudo-psychoanalytical system, and (*c*) it appears to have had, for at least one period recently, a history of harsh internal autocracy, it can be replied that these things, if true, nevertheless do not detract from its present role. One knows very little about the birth pangs of religious movements—even the more ancient and respectable ones—and the motives and personalities of their founders are unlikely to be those of 'normal' or 'average' men anyway. The main point seems to be whether their philosophies or practice have a vital spark of some kind within them (it need not be a truthful spark incidentally, just a vital one). If this spark is present, and the founder has enough personal dynamism and a sufficiently simple-minded view of the world to believe that he can change it overnight, then the system will grow and persist, modifying steadily to meet external and internal criticisms as it does so. Scientology's future, at the time of writing, is very uncertain, but it seems that it has probably passed the low-water mark of public unpopularity. The report of the recent Parliamentary Commission into the movement, conducted by Sir John Foster, considered the restrictive measures taken against them by the Labour Minister of Health, Mr Robinson, to be unjustified to some degree, and recommended a relaxation of those regulations which seemed to discriminate against Scientologists entering the country simply because they were Scientologists. On the other hand it had little specifically favourable to say about Hubbard and his followers and, in fact, made a strong recommendation that the practice of psychotherapy for reward should be confined to recognized organizations. It also made noises about the unique fiscal privileges accorded to religious organizations in this country. The publication of the report has been hailed by the Scientologists as a victory for their cause, and as an omen of better times to come. Close reading, however, suggests that they can draw less comfort from it than has been assumed, and the report, which quotes large slices of Hubbard's more eccentric prose with a few dry comments, is really a classic example of subtle British plonkmanship.

The extravagant claims made for Scientology's worldwide membership are very likely exaggerated, and are probably based more on all who have at some time taken an interest in it, rather than those who remain actively involved. At the time of writing, there are something between three and four thousand Clears (the figures are announced regularly in *The Auditor*) and this figure seems to average out at between five and six hundred newly cleared individuals per annum—indicative of steady, rather than growing interest in the cult. At this rate of expansion it is going to be a long time before Hubbard's declared goal of 'clearing this planet' is achieved and it should be remembered that the drop-out rate in Scientology is not confined to the rank and file. Clears themselves often leave or defect—to the organization's understandable dismay. The most staggering departure in recent years has probably been that of the much vaunted first Clear, John McMaster. McMaster, an intelligent and cultured individual, with much poise and an excellent platform manner, became the movement's unofficial PR expert and in the late sixties toured the world lecturing to enthusiastic audiences. Although he has severed all ties with Hubbard, he still holds (as do a number of ex-Scientologists) that the techniques of auditing or processing have something to offer mankind.

Whatever form it takes, students of sociology, psychology and religious history will watch any development of Scientology in the next decade with increasing interest, not the least reason being the fact that it offers a splendid opportunity to watch the metamorphosis of a flash-in-the-pan psychotherapy cult into an embryo religion. Official Scientology publications tend these days to play down the psychotherapy angles and stress the religious ones. The 1968 booklet *The Character of Scientology*, for example, has a colour cover featuring a stylized Disneyland choir boy with a golden aura, and includes pictures of religious medallions and crucifixes of special design. Religious services are held with choirs (singing the 'Factors'—see page 50), with sermons of a sort, and with the principal characters actually garbed in robes. When I have attended these services I have been impressed, it is fair to say, by the fact that they are only too clearly anything but PR exercises designed to pay lip-service to the movement's religious leanings. The audience, congregation or whatever, recite the 'Creed' with apparent reverence, and the sermon (normally an informal talk on communication or something similar) is listened to attentively. Discussion with young Scientologists about the religious implications of their movement often reveals a certain amount of philosophical confusion, but most are united in declaring that Scientology offers them a 'way of life' which is at least potentially all-embracing in the way that a religion is traditionally supposed to be.

This raises, I feel, a point of significance which has been almost exclusively missed by previous commentators on Mr

Hubbard's newsworthy organization; that the time has probably arrived when one should concentrate on what Scientology is all about now, and not be too diverted by its tumultuous past. In the book mentioned above Scientology is described as 'the first religious technology', and I am obliged to say that there is an element of truth in this. Perhaps a better description (from the point of view of an outsider) would be that it is the first science fiction religion; it has enjoyed relative success not because its techniques necessarily work any better than those of any other cults or systems of belief, but because it plays with the themes and terminology of this century in a way that few other systems do. One might even push this argument further and point out that Scientology seems to respond with immense readiness to the winds of fashion, and that this no doubt is another reason for its success.

In some cases it even seems to be anticipating public trends in a curious way. The involvement of the movement in the increasingly significant drug rehabilitation scheme in the USA —a number of former drug addicts appear to be facing life afresh through their association with Scientology—is one good example. There is also the matter of the current anti-psychiatric backlash which is pulling in a certain amount of media support at the time of writing. Scientologists for one reason or another have tended to make a platform of Hubbard's views on lobotomy and ECT (electro-convulsive therapy), two aesthetically and emotionally disturbing facets of current psychiatric treatment, and while they have been plugging away on these lines for a decade or more, it is only recently that they seem to have caught a prevailing popular mood. Their relatively new newspaper *Freedom*, for example, one of their most literate, yet still staggeringly immoderate, publications has taken on an almost political slant on these matters and is currently involved in a wrangle with the former Minister of Health, Mr Kenneth Robinson. If one were to try to sum up the flavour of *Freedom* in a word, one would describe it, I think, as anarchistic; indeed one can detect a hint of overlap between the pop anarchism represented by the readers of *International Times* and the more youthful citizens of Hubbard's empire.

Readers of the book up to this point may be surprised to find that after highlighting the absurdities, inconsistencies and smoky background of Scientology, I conclude without giving it a wholehearted thumbs-down. The reasons for this are quite straightforward. The closer I have looked at Scientology the more I feel that it is changing for the better, and the more eager I believe its leader and its adherents are to forget its past. Critics may reply that Scientology's past is so unpleasant that any change would be for the better, and they are entitled to this opinion. However, one asks oneself how much is really known about the founders and originators of the great classical religions of the past? How did they really begin? What were the true motives of their founders? What did their earliest supporters really feel they were getting for their sacrifices? Perhaps all successful and enduring religions in their early days go through sensational and controversial birth pangs, laced with wild talk, rash promises and extravagant behaviour designed to secure for the movement a precarious foothold in an aggressive world. It is only once a cult is established and its reality no longer questioned that the long haul to forget the failures of the past and glorify the successes of the present can begin. With this in mind one asks—in the most idle and speculative kind of way—a leading question. Supposing that the world rolls on for a thousand years and that people are still walking about on this peculiar planet, and supposing also that Scientology is still around (you may say 'God forbid' if you please) what then will the mythology of Scientology look like? And what stories will people be telling of Mr Lafayette Ronald Hubbard, his teachings and his first disciples?

PART II: THE SAVIOURS FROM THE SKIES

The Coming of the Saucers

SCIENTOLOGY IS A do-it-yourself psychology course which grew into a cult and now lays claim to being a religion. Its success has largely rested on the personality and restless energy of its founder and leader, but it could never have sprung into being without the avid support of its many thousands of adherents.

The cult, or cults, that have sprung up around the phenomenon of flying saucers—or 'Unidentified Flying Objects'—are based on firmer, or at any rate more defensible ground. Whereas evidence for the validity or objectivity of Scientology exists mainly in the minds of its devotees, a far more plausible case can be made out for the existence of UFOs and, more important, the active interest of their occupants in the inhabitants of earth. While the roll-call of reputable scientists, philosophers or men of academic achievement counting themselves as Scientologists would make brief reading, the list of those who have come to believe that spaceships from alien planets are whizzing around the skies of earth includes rocket experts, astronomers, politicians, military and air force leaders and some of the major personalities of our time. Those who have gone one step further and become involved in the specifically religious aspects of the matter are fewer, but a detailed inspection of the flying-saucer story and a study of the tenacity of belief in 'celestial crockery' lead one quickly to the conclusion that powerful emotional factors are at work pushing human beliefs in a definite direction.

This can be summed up as follows: The God of orthodox religion has been found wanting—on a simple credibility basis—and can no longer be relied upon when Man is in dire circumstances. In his place new Gods have arisen—super-intelligent beings who are technologically and, perhaps, morally superior to mankind. They come not from some outdated Dantean Heaven, but from one or many of the myriad planets which undoubtedly exist in the vast arena of the universe. They no longer ride on clouds or chariots of fire, but in fast and manœuvrable spaceships of a bewildering variety of designs, most commonly shaped like giant inverted saucers.

Public belief in their existence is, according to many official opinion polls, unusually high—in fact more than fifty per cent of the population have expressed belief on occasions. This suggests that people find nothing intrinsically unlikely in the idea of visitations from outer space, a point of view, no doubt, much fostered by science fiction movies and paperbacks and, more recently, by the observable achievements of many countries in space exploration.

For those who know a little astronomy, the possibility of the flying saucers being alien spaceships may seem quite high. Most astronomers now agree that the universe is sufficiently large to accommodate thousands of suns with planetary systems, and that many of these are capable of supporting intelligent life. Our own solar system appears to be in a relatively 'young' part of the universe, and by now in some other galactic region there could well exist civilizations immeasurably more advanced, scientifically and technically, than our own. The argument continues on obvious lines. If, after only three or four thousand years of recorded history, homo sapiens is navigating his local astronomical space, then why should not a civilization with, say, a million years of recorded history be traversing the entire universe at will, even visiting our own little planet from time to time?

The argument is superficially attractive and is based on the reasonably sound premise that advanced civilizations probably do exist in other parts of the universe. Unfortunately when one considers the probable distribution of the planetary systems within the universe and the staggering scale of the cosmos, then the simple-minded picture of alien races commuting everywhere in flying-saucers becomes less plausible. The rather freakishly close Alpha Centauri—our nearest stellar neighbour—is about four light-years away and, as any ten-year-old schoolboy will tell you, this means that a point-to-point voyage travelling *at the speed of light* would take four years. For most of the stars in our part of the galaxy, one to two hundred years at such gargantuan speeds would be required. Assuming that anyone considered such trips worthwhile, and on the further doubtful assumption that speeds approaching that of light could be possible for a spaceship, one would still feel that earth might be visited once in a very long while—perhaps every ten or fifty thousand years. Advance this argument to a flying-saucer fan and you will soon be asked why you assume that the upper speed limit for space travel should be that of light; may not some super-scientific civilization have developed a method of travel which transcends our puny knowledge of the laws of space and time so that their craft can leap across the stellar wastes in the twinkling of an eye? This, of course, is conceivable in the sense that all things are theoretically possible, but here the UFO protagonist has moved from his strong ground (that other parts of the universe are probably inhabited) into the swamp of pure guesswork (that they will inevitably be able to move around at a speed greater than that of light). The second assumption is unwarranted, but is frequently passed off as something more than total speculation.

Nevertheless we have witnessed, in the last two decades in particular, an astonishing social phenomenon with literally tens of thousands of human beings reporting the sighting of mysterious flying objects in the skies, and some even reporting mental and physical contact with their occupants. This has given rise to a major system of beliefs shared by a measurable percentage of humanity—that earth is being visited by superior alien beings—and to a number of sub-beliefs which have unquestionable religious connotations.

The historical background to the flying-saucer controversy which, as the great psychologist C. G. Jung declared, was to become one of the great myths of the twentieth century, has been fully, if erratically documented in literally hundreds of books over the past two decades, and we will touch on it only briefly here. Fighter pilots on all sides during the war years had been reporting mysterious flying objects in the skies, often apparently moving at speeds quite beyond the range of normal aircraft. These, when they turned up in post-flight reports, acquired the nickname of 'foo-fighters' and a minor, faintly serious legend matured about them, somewhat akin to the mythology that surrounded the 'gremlins' or flying fairies which plagued battle-weary pilots with practical jokes. With the end of the war foo-fighters and gremlins seemed to vanish into spray, until on a sunny afternoon in June 1947 an Idaho businessman, Kenneth Arnold, who was piloting his own plane on a trip over the Rockies, saw a group of metallic-looking, wingless objects flying in formation at incredible speed. Questioned by newsmen Arnold described their peculiar motion as flying 'like a saucer would if you skipped it across the water'—a phrase which was misquoted by the news agencies so that on the following day the world was told that 'flying saucers' travelling at fantastic speeds had been seen over American territory. Despite the fact that Arnold had said nothing about their shape, other than that they appeared to be wingless, from that time on it was saucers all the way.

Something about the event—perhaps it was Arnold's matter-of-fact, honest-to-goodness manner—excited public interest to a remarkable extent, and students of sociology will not be surprised to learn that within weeks saucer reports were flooding in from all parts of the world. So widespread, and often so convincing, were these reports, that the American Air Force itself launched a full scale investigation into them. A moment's pause for reflection will allow one to see why this should have been.

At the time of the Arnold sighting the United States and Soviet Russia were plunging into the darkest depths of the Cold War. Both sides felt that at any time they might suffer a surprise nuclear strike, and immense technological effort was being poured into the development of high-flying, high-speed aircraft and the first rudimentary ICBMs. Radar networks across the whole of the USA were in a state of constant alert and ceaseless aerial patrolling by spotter aircraft was taking place. Neither side could afford anything but maximum interest in reports, no matter how far-fetched, of unidentified aircraft violating its air space.

The state of Russian aerospace technology, while thought to be creaky, was still unknown and it was not certain what contributions the tediously inventive German rocket engineers, captured by the score, might be making to the Russian air effort. American experts had found some peculiar aerial weapons under advanced stages of development as the Allied armies moved into Europe, and a saucer-shaped craft would be no odder than some of the contrivances with which the *Luftwaffe* had been toying. The Americans had themselves been experimenting with a craft which, with a little imagination, could be described as saucer-shaped—it was actually known as the 'flying flapjack'—and while this was proving disappointing the Soviets might conceivably have gone one better. Thus the Air Force had good reason to follow the saucer 'flaps' (as the waves of sightings came to be called), and took a critical interest at every stage in the game.

Much of the criticism of the USAF attitude to UFOs (the same applies to the routine but small-time interest shown by the Royal Air Force) arises from a misunderstanding of the circumstances. The late Captain Ed Ruppelt, a former director of Projects Sign and Grudge—the first official UFO inquiries under the auspices of the Air Force—states that in 1947 top-ranking officers in the Pentagon were demanding precise information on UFO sightings and at one stage believed that the Russians were testing some spectacular new weapon. Public and military reports of sightings were scanned with the greatest interest, though with little co-ordination, and by the autumn of that year the lack of any coherent hypothesis to account for flying discs, cigars, sausages, etc., had led to press inquiries being met with ill-planned evasions, or even blank denials, that anything significant was going on. This mistaken strategy, which seems to have been adopted as the result of the genuine confusion and concern in the higher echelons of the Air Force, was later revised when formal investigations were set up—Projects Sign, Grudge, Blue Book, etc.—and realistic, considered press releases with details of numbers of explained and unexplained sightings were made at regular intervals. But by then the damage had been done and the myth that the Air Force was holding back some apocalyptic fact on flying saucers was already established.

In point of fact, the more the Air Force investigated the less it inclined to the view that the saucers were real craft of incredible performance, and the more readily they subscribed to prosaic explanations such as that the UFOs were weather balloons, meteorological phenomena, conventional aircraft whose distance and speed had been incorrectly judged, etc. A series of official Projects pronounced either neutrally or against

UFOs as extra-terrestrial objects and this official view began slowly to permeate through to the public, despite a number of sensational books such as Donald Keyhoe's *The Flying Saucer Conspiracy*, which argued the contrary. No matter how attractive the notion that UFOs were visitors from another planet might be to newspaper headline writers, by the early fifties the public at large were bored with saucers and their elusive and recalcitrant occupants. Only science fiction fans and the chronic seekers after the miraculous remained steadfastly loyal throughout. The publication of a sensational book, *Flying Saucers have Landed* in 1953, however, caused a dramatic resurgence of interest. This unscholarly work, purporting to be an account of the first person-to-person meeting between a human being and an alien life-form, hit the best-seller lists overnight and became a conversation piece across the world. It is also highly significant in another way, for it marked the beginning of a shift of emphasis in Ufology from quasi-serious science fiction to a mythology in embryo.

The book, in two sections, is an unlikely collaboration between the talented writer and electronics expert Desmond Leslie, son of the Irish novelist peer Shane Leslie, and a Polish-American of unusual ignorance, bogus astronomer and dabbler in psychics, George Adamski. Leslie was responsible for the first and longest part—a survey of the many thousands of peculiar objects which have been seen buzzing about the skies of earth since time immemorial. These range from Ezekiel's 'Wheel of Fire' (a hot-shot favourite with UFO antiquarians) which comes from that well-known book of wonders, the Old Testament, to more recent peculiarities such as those eyewitness accounts of a giant airship which passed across America in 1879, its crew for some reason or another all singing *Abide with Me*. Ezekiel's UFO sighting contains such passages as:

I. 4: And I looked, and, behold, a whirlwind came out of the north, a great cloud, and a fire unfolding itself, and a brightness was about it, and out of the midst thereof as the colour of amber, out of the midst of the fire.
5: Also out of the midst thereof came the likeness of four living creatures . . . they had the likeness of a man.
15: Now as I beheld the living creatures, behold one wheel

upon the earth by the living creatures, with his four faces.
19: And when the living creatures went, the wheels went by them; and when the living creatures were lifted up from the earth, the wheels were lifted up.
20: . . . for the spirit of the living creature was in the wheels.

Most readers no doubt will see the above passage as a typical piece of biblical enigma, rich in poetic imagery but low in informational content, but most UFO fans interpret it without difficulty.

Desmond Leslie, in fact, thinks that UFO sightings considerably pre-date the Bible, and seems to be sincerely convinced that flying saucers have been a highly significant part of Man's history since the year 18,617,841 B.C. when the first interplanetary vessel arrived from Venus. He makes no apology for the amazing precision of this dating which was 'calculated from the ancient Brahmin tables in 1951'. The plain fact is, he tells us, that the Brahmins were exceedingly accurate people.

He has also uncovered the fact that saucers and their occupants were active during the heyday of Egypt and the Nilotic civilizations, and in England in pre-Celtic times. This neatly solves some venerable problems which have foxed archaeologists for decades. We are referring, of course, to such matters as how the huge blocks which make up Stonehenge were moved from their apparent point of origin in the west of Wales to Salisbury Plain, and how the fifteen-ton casing stones of the Gizeh pyramids were lifted into place. The answer is simply that the great scientists of the time, who were as familiar with flying saucers as we are with jet aircraft, also had at their disposal a now-forgotten use of sonics to more heavy objects. Quoting from W. Kingsland's farcical book, *The Great Pyramid in Fact and Theory*, he reveals that to move the huge stones it was merely necessary to strike them with a rod, whereupon they would move 'through the air the distance of one bowshot. In this way they came eventually to the place where the pyramids were being built'. These magic rods, Leslie believes, were 'cut to precise lengths corresponding to the wavelength of the vibration required'. Whatever that might mean, it must certainly have provided an unmatched source of motive power and caused widespread redundancy among the captive slaves at the time. Hard though this idea of magic rods might be to believe, Leslie feels that 'When one looks at the seventy-ton blocks of red granite roofing the so-called "King's Chamber" brought from quarries six hundred miles away, it is difficult to imagine any other way of moving, and setting them, with such incredible precision'.

These few passages should serve to convey something of the book's spicy, near-historical tone. Unfortunately Leslie's researches were not always as critical as they might have been, as witness his account of the 'Ampleforth Abbey Sighting' which 'took place in the year 1290'. The story of this particular historical event appeared with an acknowledgment to someone with the unusual name of Mr A. X. Chumley for supplying the original information. It is of such a superficially convincing nature that several other UFO authors have repeatedly requoted, and occasionally embellished it—without taking the precaution of checking back to the original source. This was left to the well-known photo-journalist Samuel Rosenberg, who had the entertaining job of researching the historical aspect of UFO phenomena for the American Air Force for the *Condon Report* in 1968. It is to him that the credit goes for this amusing but important exposé.

The complete transcript, which appears on pages 22 to 23 of the original edition of the book (but is wisely omitted from the second edition published in 1970), reads as follows:

> oves a Wilfredo susceptos die festo sanctissimorum Simonis atque Judae assaverunt. Cum autem Henricus abbas gratias redditurus erat, frater quidam Joannes introivit, magnam portentem foris esse referebat. Tum vero omnes ecuccurrerunt, et ecce *res grandis, circumcircularis argentea, disco quodam haud dissimilis,* lente et super eos volans atque maximam terrorem exitans. Quo tempore Henricus abbas exclamavit Wilfredum adulteravisse (quo) de causa impius esse de . . .

Latin scholars may care to amuse themselves attempting a translation, but for those less learned or with less time to spare we will quote the original translation as offered by the mysterious Mr Chumley:

> took the sheep from Wilfred and roasted them on the

feast of S.S. Simon and Jude. But when Henry the Abbott was about to say grace. John, one of the brethren, came in and said there was a great portent outside. Then they all ran out, and Lo! *a large round silver thing like a disk flew slowly* over them and excited the greatest terror. Whereat Henry the Abbot immediately cried that Wilfred was an adulterer, wherefore it was impious to . . .

The important passage is, of course, that italicized reference to a flying disc, and Desmond Leslie interprets the story by suggesting that since it would be unlikely that the spacecraft arrived specifically to accuse the Monk Wilfred of adultery, it was merely a coincidence which the 'astute Abbot' seized on as an opportunity of admonishing him for his behaviour and 'the community for their lack of piety'.

Unfortunately for this charming tale, Rosenberg decided to do a bit of original checking himself, only to find that the entire Latin excerpt from *oves a Wilfredo* onward was a joyous fabrication by two schoolboys at the Ampleforth Abbey Public School who had perpetrated the myth in a letter to *The Times* on 9th February 1953. From there it was picked up by Desmond Leslie for his book, from which numerous other versions were duly pirated. By the time it reached Gabriel Green's totally uncritical work, *Let's Face the Facts about Flying Saucers*, published as recently as 1967, it had metamorphosed into something closer to a television script for the adventures of Robin Hood—'Yo Ho', quoth the good Friar, 'behold the silver saucer in the sky'.

For those with the unusual hobby of collecting hoax material of this kind—there is an enormous amount of it in the literature of the occult and the psychic anecdote as well as in Ufology—Rosenberg's chapter in the *Condon Report* (the American Air Force's final *exposé* of the UFO myth) is particularly recommended. He also includes an examination of spurious saucer material from the writings of the complicated mystic Madame Blavatsky and certain questionable Egyptian papyri.

Despite the unconvincing nature of much of the material amassed by Leslie, it is nevertheless important to realize that a very substantial number of people count this kind of inexact and highly selective historical research as on a par with the more scholarly, if perhaps less readable, works that come from strictly academic quarters. The fashion that Leslie set of hunting through a wide range of literature and producing evidence to push this or that theory to account for flying saucers is still with us today. Noted exponents are B. le Poer Trench (*The Flying Saucer Story, The Sky People*, etc.), G. Hunt Williamson (*Secret Places of the Lion, Road in the Sky*), and Paul Thomas (*Flying Saucers through the Ages*). A particularly good example of this genre is the book *Chariots of the Gods?* by the German author Erich von Daniken which has recently enjoyed a world-wide craze. This is an apparently serious attempt to demonstrate that the history of civilized man stretches much further back into the past than modern archaeology would have us believe. Earth has been visited on numerous occasions by alien spacemen who have been largely responsible for injecting homo sapiens with the main elements of his science and culture. The titles of one or two chapters —'Was God an Astronaut?', 'Fiery Chariots from the Heavens' and 'Easter Island, Land of the Bird Men'—sum up the emphasis of the work rather well.

Full of historical howlers or not, Desmond Leslie's section of the book has at any rate the merit of literary style, imagination and a suggestion that some basic research at least had been sunk into it. Adamski's account of his encounter in the Mojave desert with a long-haired Venusian wearing ski-pants with whom he engaged in telepathic contact, on the other hand, reads like a desperate travesty of the most simple-minded science fiction. We will not linger here on the details of their boring conversation, nor dwell on such matters as the unctuous expression on the Venusian's face as he warned earthlings of the displeasure that their naughty behaviour was causing to the 'higher beings', etc., who were watching us from the comfort of their spaceships. We will, however, pause briefly to wonder at the world-wide success of the book when it was published, unsupported by evidence of any kind other than a 'plaster cast of the Venusian's footprint' (Adamski just happened to be carrying plaster-of-Paris with him when he visited the desert that day), and a collection of photographs which have aroused considerable controversy in the past two decades, and which most experienced photographers hold to be crude fakes, being close-ups of a simple fabricated model. The most important of the pictures shows the underparts of a vaguely bell-shaped device with portholes along its sides and with three spherical objects—landing gear or table-tennis balls, as you will—below. Despite the fact that Adamski claims he had ample time to take pictures the detail is blurred and the background non-existent so that it is impossible to gauge the scale of the device. The late Frank Edwards, a pro-saucer journalist who was, however, immeasurably scornful of most contactee stories, believes that the spaceship was the 'top of a canister-type vacuum cleaner, made in 1937'—a device which he considers to be most unsuitable for extended space travel. Commenting at the same time on some suspicious lighting effects on the side of the object he concludes that these can be explained in one of two ways: (1) they are reflections from three floodlights used to light the model for photography, (2) that on the day Adamski took the picture, three suns were shining in the sky. A cautious man, Edwards selects the first alternative as preferable.

Adamski's adventure struck a chord of acceptance in too large a segment of the population for it to be lightly dismissed. The surge of publicity which flying saucers had had since 1947, backed by the endless speculation in magazines and newspapers as to their origin, can only have served to prepare an uncritical populace for the notion that some day contact between earthly and alien civilizations would take place. Furthermore, the vigorous attention which newspapers, etc., had paid to the saga also induced a crop of similar 'contact' stories, some more fantastically embellished. A number of contactees claimed that they had actually met with aliens some time before Adamski's adventure but had been 'too frightened' or 'too embarrassed' to tell anyone.

Another early contactee was a Mr George Van Tassel, who has since become an important international figure—at least among the dotty fraternity of flying-saucer fans—because of his claimed ability to be in more or less regular daily contact (telepathic, of course) with alien spacemen.

It all started on 24th August 1953, when he and his wife were sleeping out in the desert 'because of the heat'. At about two o'clock in the morning, Van Tassel related, he awoke to find a man standing at the foot of the bed, who immediately introduced himself as 'Sol-danda' and invited him to inspect his craft. He had a good, not to say splendid, command of the

English language, talking 'like Ronald Colman'. Leaving his wife, who 'seemed to be under some spell', Van Tassel went to inspect the spaceship, a bell-shaped craft whose dimensions he was able to measure quite precisely. After experiencing a feeling of nausea as he approached, he was levitated into its interior on an 'anti-gravity beam'. The inside of the ship, with its dials, seats and various pieces of equipment either revolving or glowing, lived up to, if it did not exceed the levels of imagination reached by science fiction 'B' features of the time. Van Tassel was not treated to a ride, but he was shown a number of rooms and something of the craft's motive unit which he thinks can best be described by the phrase 'wheels within wheels'.

Now known as 'The Sage of Giant Rock', George holds an annual convention of contactees at his home in California. By all accounts these are strange gatherings indeed. At the 1966 convention, for example, delegates heard Miss Gloria Lee, a former air hostess, tell of the messages she had been receiving regularly from a Jupiterian. Chiefly these concern the sexual mores of our planet and it is evident that in Jovian terms we have misconceived our sexual desires. On Jupiter, Miss Lee informed the group, there is no marriage and the inhabitants lead quite uninhibited sexual lives. Also present on this glittering occasion were such remarkable characters as 'Andy Sinatra, the Mystic Barber', who wears a daft-looking hat given to him by saucer men, and Mr Gabriel Green, founder of the Amalgamated Flying Saucer Clubs of America, Inc., who runs regularly for President of the USA on a straight flying-saucer ticket. So far the combined weight of the Republican and Democratic party machines have been too great for him to make much headway but each election time finds him soldiering on indefatigably.

To while away the time between conventions, George Van Tassel keeps his head open, metaphorically speaking, for messages from other planets. These he publishes monthly in the *Proceedings of the College of Universal Wisdom*—a journal of unparalleled interest to those who ponder the strange workings of the human mind.

We will not linger to consider the adventurers of Buck Nelson ('My Trip to Mars, the Moon and Venus'), or Orfeo Angelucci ('The Secret of the Saucers') or even of the late

Truman Bethurum ('The Voice of the Planet Clarion'). All have, as do most contactee stories, a common and significant theme. Earth is in danger of destroying itself and must learn the peaceful ways of the Cosmos or perish at its own hand. The space people, who have advanced scientific skills, also have moral and ethical principles to back them, and they wish nothing but kindness and well-being to humanity. For various reasons initial contact can be made only through a 'Chosen Few' whose job it is to propagate the cosmic wisdom as quickly as possible to all who will receive it. The day of a mass landing of saucers in Times Square or outside the Houses of Parliament may be a long way off, as the shock would be too great for the pig-headed autocrats of earth (probably a reasonable assumption incidentally), and initially the truth must be infiltrated rather than trumpeted.

Such is the message of most contactees whether they are favoured with rides in spacecraft, or are merely the recipients of strange telepathic signals. It forms the principal theme running through the majority of the explicitly religious groups that have sprung up in this area and we shall take a closer look at one in particular.

Jesus is Alive and Well and Living on Venus

ON A COLD Saturday morning in March 1954 Mr George King was washing up the dishes in his bed-sitter in Maida Vale when a voice boomed out from nowhere: 'Prepare yourself. You are to become the voice of Interplanetary Parliament.' Struck by the unexpectedness of the message George King dropped a plate.

Although he has subsequently claimed that he had never heard the voice before and had no real reason to suppose that he would ever hear it again, the experience, he tells us, had a devastating effect on him. Not the least of his puzzles was that he had never heard of the 'Interplanetary Parliament'. Nor could he imagine where the voice—which came from outside himself and not as some mere telepathic signal—had originated. Before long all these mysteries were to be cleared up and Mr King, with the resolute band of followers who joined him, were to become embroiled in interplanetary intrigue and skulduggery of the most fantastic kind—adventures which would put to shame the pathetic delvings of more pedestrian mystics and occultists and, on a different level, the feeble excursions into space attempted by Soviet and American cosmonauts. For from this original contact and the numerous and voluble communications which followed, arose a minor religious movement which is today the most potent and best-organized of these many groups across the world which relate themselves, in the religious sense, to superior beings from outer space. This is the Aetherius Society, which numbers its supporters in thousands, has branches in most English-speaking countries and offers a complete religious package-deal including prayers, chants, complex rituals, arduous pilgrimages and a fantastic and far-flung philosophy geared to the terminology and iconography of the space age.

Like Scientology it has evolved from its roots as a mixture of dramatized science fiction and personal revelation, into a clear-cut religion with numerous devout adherents. Stylistically and intellectually it is, however, more gauche and, with an emphasis on the divine power of healing rather than on an *outré* version of psycho-analysis, seems to pitch for, and attract, the middle-aged and elderly rather than the young. It also relies heavily on the personality and dynamism of its founder and leader, and similarly propagates its beliefs and achievements in a series of fantastically enthusiastic publications which scale—to the outsider—the strangest heights of fantasy. In this chapter we will examine this history and attempt an account of its philosophy, principles and practice.

At the time of his first contact with the Masters from Outer Space, George King was thirty-five years old. He hails from the West Country where his mother for a period ran a healing sanctuary complete with 'Holy Well' and other attractions for the spiritually minded tourist. After a spell in the now-defunct National Fire Service he moved into routine civilian life being employed in mundane jobs of the kind that earn one's bread and butter and devoting evenings and weekends to an enthusiastic study of mysticism and yoga.

According to his own account, the coming of the mysterious voice left him in a state of turmoil and bewilderment, and only the self-discipline of the practice of 'pranayama' (a yogic system of breath control) enabled him to hold on to his mental capacities. Eight days after the initial contact he was 'shaken to the core' by another amazing experience. A man dressed in spotless white robes walked through the door of his room (George immediately recognized him as a well-known eastern saint) and delivered a homily on the dire state of mankind and the need for its rapid spiritual regeneration. He also indicated that George had been selected to perform a great task, and that no matter how unworthy he felt himself to be, he had been chosen as one of the few capable of acting as servants of the Cosmic Masters. Advising him to continue to make himself ready for this task by the further intensive practice of yoga, the saintly visitor turned and left, passing through the door again with a magnificent gesture of contempt for material barriers.

The visit was soon followed by a truly momentous occurrence. George King found himself under the control of—he prefers to use the phrase 'overshadowed by'—a being calling himself the 'Master Aetherius' and hailing from Venus where apparently a full-blown, highly advanced civilization exists. Aetherius declared himself to be the spokesman of the Interplanetary Parliament which met on the planet Saturn and brought the news that this august body had agreed on George King as their 'primary terrestrial channel'. At intervals he would be required to surrender his brain and body to act as the link between the mighty civilizations of the solar system and beyond, and the ignorant masses on earth. His mission (on the guidance of Aetherius and others) would be to alert the world, or those on it spiritually elevated enough to grasp the truth, to the fact that man was not alone in the universe and that the time had come for him to awaken to his cosmic as well as his physical responsibilities.

Pondering this development in his bed-sitter, George King realized that it was incumbent upon him to spread the Gospel by all means available—firstly some form of public meeting and second via a newsletter or magazine. The first possibility was quickly explored and a meeting was held in the Caxton Hall, Westminster.

London's Caxton Hall is perhaps best known for its society and celebrity registrar weddings, but its secondary role is intriguing and important in a different way. Here, night after night, the casual visitor in search of spiritual or mystical enlightenment will find himself offered at least one, and frequently a selection, of public meetings expressing these fascinating cross-currents of the psychic, the occult, the bizarre and the simply cranky, which are so essential to the smooth operation of any complex society in our troubled world. Why the Caxton Hall has become the traditional centre for these borderline interests is hard to say. Perhaps the dark wood-panelled walls, the carpeted stairways and the giant throne-like seats for the speakers, add an air of conviction which might otherwise be lacking. At any rate it was in the tiny Tudor room on the first floor, in the latter part of 1954, that the Master Aetherius, entrancing the body of Mr George King, gave his first public audience.

Despite the fact that meetings of the Aetherius Society may now be held in packed modern halls seating hundreds, in places as far apart as Los Angeles and Sydney, and to audiences that accept the authority of the Interplanetary Parliament almost as much as that of the national governing bodies, the essential pattern of the event has changed little since those early days in the Caxton Hall.

Preliminaries and introductions at these meetings are generally kept to a minimum—the audience have come to hear the star performer and have no more desire to listen to the ramblings of some tedious minion than have Scientologists when Hubbard himself is due on the platform. George King sits quietly in a chair and after one or two deep breaths dons a pair of close-fitting dark glasses. The house lights may be dimmed at this point and after the briefest of pauses the first communicator comes through. Traditionally, this is not the Master Aetherius but an entity who announces himself, in a staccato voice, as 'Mars, Sector 6'. This individual's role seems to be that of a kind of psychic switchboard operator connecting two exchanges under difficult circumstances. He also conveys information about various celestial events from the arrival or departure of fleets of flying saucers to forthcoming terrestrial disasters such as earthquakes, tornadoes, etc. This is couched in clipped phrases with a quasi-scientific ring to them, and may include such sentences as: 'With an absorption measurement of 3, the greater percentage of magnetic power has yet to be established from a flux caused by recurrent reverberations within your atmosphere.' Or perhaps: 'Take those M-ions inside of yourself, then your brain cells will release an opposite female magnetic energy. This will counteract the hurricane-force.' Or even: 'Certain crops next summer will be very good as a direct result of even the low-scale absorption. It should be an excellent season for wool.'

After the edgy yapping of the Martian, the voice of the Master Aetherius, sounding like that of a working-class curate striving hard at the Bishop's tea party, comes as a striking contrast. It is unfortunately no more informative, though devotees of the Society seem able to listen to it for literally hours on end. Apart from his maddening habit of addressing everyone as 'My dear friends', he is also prone to phrases such as 'My heart bleeds that it is so', 'Go ye forth brothers!' and even, occasionally, 'Take heed, ye schemers!'

Despite the unpromising nature of this material, King's first meetings in a tiny room soon began to acquire a regular following, and it became necessary to move to one of the larger halls. In June 1955 interest was sufficiently high to allow the launching of a mimeographed magazine, at first entitled *Aetherius Speaks to Earth* and later, as its pretensions grew, *Cosmic Voice*.

Copies of early issues of *Cosmic Voice* are now collectors' items, and so great is the demand for them that the Society's headquarters in Fulham Road have issued special edited 'reprints'. These included the text of many of the first recorded transmissions from Mars, Sector 6 (and his occasional replacement, Mars, Sector 8), Aetherius and even those highly controversial communications reputed to come from Jesus Christ himself.

This latter development, which gave the Aetherius Society it first brush with the national press and brought charges of blasphemy to its door, came as a great surprise not only to the audience, but also to George King, the medium. For one or two meetings prior to the occasion, the Master Aetherius had made a number of passing references to 'the Master Jesus' who, he implied, was alive and well and living on Venus. The same evidently applied to such other great religious leaders as Buddha, and Rama-Krishna. In a section, 'Your questions answered', in the July 1955 issue of *Cosmic Voice*, it is indicated that there is nothing unique about the Immaculate Conception—this is the way all planetary masters are reborn on Venus. Furthermore, one of the first flying saucer sightings ever reported has come to be called the Star of Bethlehem and it was, of course, the space vehicle which brought Jesus to his earthly abode.

Today such stuff would pass pretty well unnoticed in the press, but in 1955 the climate of opinion still favoured the notion that England was an actively Christian country with an actively Christian press who were expected to take up the cudgels in the defence of the national ethic. In a swingeing attack on George King, the Aetherius Society and anyone vaguely connected with it, the Sunday *Empire News*—a newspaper which bit the dust in the TV boom of the late fifties—even took the line that the group were the dupes of Communism. This unusual accusation depended on the frequent warnings from Mars, Venus and elsewhere emanating through King which urged the suspension of nuclear tests and warned the world that it was rushing headlong into another major war—a theme which we have seen runs strongly through most of the contactees' stories.

The personal appearance of Jesus at the Caxton Hall also induced a great surge of interest on the part of the public and, following an attack on King by the specialist weekly paper *Psychic News*, tickets for future meetings sold out weeks in advance.

The voice of Jesus (it is possible to hear it by purchasing tapes from the Aetherius Society) is disappointing, not to say irritating. Nor is what he has to say particularly convincing, being mainly a collection of platitudes dressed up in a faintly New Testament style—'Lead them as you would a little child', 'within each heart there burns a flame of love', etc. Nevertheless, according to contemporary accounts of the early meetings, it had a startling effect on the audience, some of whom were visibly moved to tears. Whatever the stir it caused in the fifties, the Master Jesus, speaking from Venus, still 'overshadows' the leader of the Aetherius Society to this day and is a completely credible figure to most members, who accept his communications as untainted in any way with blasphemy.

Jesus survives as a major figure in the Aetherius cult though its adherents are careful to point out that he is 'but one of the Great Masters' and not the divine Son of God. Today the publications of the Society include occasional dissertations from him, all more or less in the same harmless and good-natured vein, and he has communicated through George King in numerous parts of the world, during the latter's extensive travels to spread the word. This has led to such amazing headlines as JESUS SPEAKS IN NEW ZEALAND (*Cosmic Voice,* May 1961) and to the solemn delivery, before a Los Angeles audience in Christmas of that year, of a completely new text of the Lord's Prayer. Somewhat longer than the orthodox version, its basic appeal is for divine power to be channelled personally to the supplicant and there are references to 'Inner Vision', 'Energy' and 'Higher Selves'. There is also a mysterious phrase with an Eastern ring—'Om Shanti, Shanti, Shanti'. The prayer is chanted enthusiastically by cult members, normally at the conclusion of a gathering or public meeting.

In the complex hierarchy of the quasi-deistic beings who communicate through George King (quite apart from the link-men Mars, Sector 6 and Jupiter, Sector 92) there appear such notables as the Lord Buddha and Saint Peter. There is also an entity, no doubt of Eastern origin, who labours with the unfortunate name of 'Saint Goo-ling'. All these individuals and many unnamed and unsung heroes besides are, the Aetherius Society would have us believe, labouring tirelessly to save the inhabitants of earth from damnation and cosmic disaster. The philosophy is tangled and its history incomplete, but by a careful perusal of the Society's written material it is possible to piece some kind of coherent picture together.

The main theme—one common to most religious belief systems whatever their vintage—is that the Universe is a battleground between the rival incompatible forces of Good and Evil. Unlike most other systems, however, which assign the duel mainly to 'spiritual' planes of existence, supporters of the Aetherius Society hold that the war is being fought in the physical universe of which we are a part. The opposing forces move from planet to planet and from galaxy to galaxy by spaceships of various kinds and, even when sufficiently hard pressed, by teleportation. Contrary to all the findings of astronautics, the planets of the solar system are well populated, only Mercury being barren. Certain planets—notably Saturn—are more 'spiritually advanced' than others, with our own earth (referred to ostentatiously as 'Terra' by Aetherius and others) rather low on the list. So spiritually decrepit is earth, in fact, that it would normally fall easy prey to any kind of all-out assault from the Forces of Evil, many of whom have highly sophisticated weaponry at their disposal. In fact were it not for the unceasing efforts of Mars, Sector 6, Aetherius and others, to say nothing of the holy Goo-ling, we would have succumbed long ago.

According to numerous accounts delivered through George King, the apocalypse has nearly been visited on earth several times recently, and while the vast majority of terran inhabitants go about their daily lives in doltish ignorance of the massive battles raging across the Universe, there are a few—a very few—enlightened ones on earth who not only appreciate the situation but can also do something concrete to alleviate it. Aetherius Society members make up a high percentage of this privileged group, but not for them the luxury of basking indolently in the glory of self-awareness or cosmic enlightenment. With this great knowledge go even greater responsibilities and the opportunity to play a dynamic role in the fight against the forces of evil. The principal, and by no means the least exacting, of these duties is to participate in the frequent bouts of activity known as 'Spiritual Pushes'.

The concept of the Spiritual Push is an important one and must be studied in some detail. All life forms are motivated by, and themselves may utilize, a vital power known to enthusiasts of yoga as 'prana'. This force, which is essentially non-physical, is itself neutral and may be put to use for Good or Evil, depending only upon the skills, knowledge and motivation of those employing it. Terrans, Aetherians believe, have largely lost the capacity to use this vital force except in an entirely automatic way, and our own planet is particularly weak as far as its own spiritual batteries are concerned. This naturally makes it particularly susceptible to assault from Black Powers of one kind or another. For centuries now, the White Powers of this solar system, represented mainly by Aetherius and his chums, have been shoving prana into the earth and its ungrateful inhabitants for all they are worth (Aetherius himself has been at the game for some time—when he first contacted George King in 1954 he revealed that he was 3,456 years old).

The main method of doing this is to bring a giant spaceship—the one generally used is known as 'Satellite Three' which is literally miles in length—into a tight orbit around the earth where it acts as a base for a 'push' of vital energy. Details of how this is effected are not at all clear, but if we remark that it involves 'metaphysical manipulations' and the beaming of 'magnetic energies' this should serve to give some idea as to what is going on. During the periods when Satellite Three is in orbit (it is covered by a radiation absorbing screen which renders it invisible and non-responsive to radar signals) members of the Aetherius Society assist by various spiritual exercises, prayers, meditations and the like, thus doing their bit towards re-charging the earth's dwindling batteries. There is no doubt that such assistance is appreciated. On numerous occasions the Masters Aetherius and Jesus, together with Saints Peter and Goo-ling, have been unstinting in their praise, and have hinted that the power of their allies' 'push' has been enough to tip the scales during very ticklish moments.

Anyone who feels that the threat of a take-over bid for earth by the Black Powers is exaggerated would do well to ponder the terrifying story of the 'Fiends of Garouche', related in *Cosmic Voice* No. 5 published in 1956. Writing about it at the time George King, while admitting that it read like science fiction, claimed that it was 'true in every detail'. He was able to vouch for its authenticity having been himself 'intimately concerned in the action'.

The saga runs thus. Some time ago our earth was inspected from afar by highly intelligent fish living on the water-bound planet known as Garouche, situated on 'The other side of the Milky Way'. These creatures, aptly described as fiends, made it their purpose to 'annihilate all humanoid life on Terra, by drawing the atmospheric belt' away from earth. This, Mars, Sector 6 tells us (erroneously), would not have affected the sea-dwellers on this planet for 'they take their oxygen from the water itself'. (For the pilot of a twenty-mile-long spaceship, Mars, Sector 6 is a bit dim about planetary physics.)

Happily the plans of these creatures were intercepted by the friendly Martians who intervened at a cost of great effort, and some loss of life. Mars, Sector 6 reminds us that 'many from Mars sacrificed themselves in the Cause to save Terra' and he asks those upon earth who 'have the decency that goes with humanoid life to realize this'. The skirmish—we are not told what weapons were used, but presumably they were of the spiritual push variety—did not destroy the fish-people from Garouche who then sent a radioactive asteroid to within a few hundred thousand miles of Mars. This was fortunately detected by the robot-miners of that planet, and the asteroid was 'deactivated'. 'Do not thank us', says Mars, Sector 6 magnanimously, adding that 'the Earth-receiver I am now using was nearly killed himself three times during that action'—suggesting that George King's role as intermediary between the beings from outer space and earth is not all beer and skittles.

The attack from the fiends of Garouche however was as nothing compared to the fearful duel which took place more recently and whose progress was reported, in serial fashion, like the Perils of Pauline, in successive issues of the Society's news-sheet. This epic, which went under the code name Operation Karmalight, involved George King and 'Five Adepts'—men living on earth in material bodies but who are of such a high state of spiritual development that they can emancipate themselves from these physical encumbrances whenever they please. Dr King (he acquired a doctorate at some stage during his travels in the USA) never claims to be an 'Adept' himself, though one rather gets the impression that he is, and many members of the Aetherius Society have no doubts on this score. Be that as it may, in the terrifying events during Karmalight, he was to need all the spiritual support he could lay his hands on.

The principal problem seems to have been an evil scientist by the name of Lubek who had 'for hundreds of years . . . thrown the whole of his energies into amassing occult data'. Being one of the chief scientific advisers to none other than Satan himself, Lubek made it his business to keep abreast of all the latest developments in science and technology and had devised a massive computer complex known as Egog which covered ten square miles of land—in the lower astral realms of course. Into this impressive instrument the evil scientist had steadily been feeding all the occult data of the universe and was also developing the software to match.

The possession of this huge data bank, which would in due course fall into the hands of Satan, posed a real threat to the Forces of Good, as the Five Adepts plus the 'Master Babaji' (a kind of spiritual President of Earth) were not slow to realize. Fortunately, Lubek, like so many terrestrial scientists of his ilk, became so wrapped up in the intricacies of his computer's mechanics and in the spectacular programming problems it provided, that he began to waver from his goal. As the Aetherius Society newsletter of July 1969 puts it, he 'became more and more the pure scientist and less and less concerned about the dog-eats-dog politics of the lower astral kingdoms. His whole mind was turned to the improvement of his computer system.'

Before long, Lubek found himself challenged by the feudal barons of the astral realms who, taking advantage of his preoccupation with the Egog, strove to unseat him in Satan's favour. It was at this point, with their enemies divided by internal bickerings, that the Adepts decided to strike. Backed by the concerted 'pushing' and other metaphysical efforts of Aetherius Society members on earth, and numerous emergency gatherings at their headquarters in London, Los Angeles and elsewhere, the Adepts began a James Bond mission to seek out Lubek's computer and destroy it.

It was a grim but stirring time. On 24th May 1969 at two o'clock in the morning, Dr King ordered the spiritual energy radiation switched on 'in the reciprocating fashion' in an attempt to stave off an assault from Lubek on his headquarters. This wonderful device—there are, unhappily, only too few on the planet—consists of a series of simple rotating parts, activated by an electric motor and allegedly emanating prana or some similar vital force in the common good. No one at the Aetherius Society's base in London, where they have one or two of these machines, seems totally able to explain the principles of their operation, so it is hard to assess their overall efficacy. Anyway, Lubek apparently received the spiritual equivalent of a thick ear from the device but, having the ever-curious mind of the scientist, could not refrain from sticking around to examine it in detail. It was a fatal error, for while thus engrossed he was attacked by Adepts Number One and Three, rendered unconscious and removed by them, very sensibly, to a special satellite which they had placed in orbit as a prison station. Explosive charges were than planted in appropriate places and the computer, 'so painstakingly built and educated throughout the years, disintegrated into a mass of twisted wires and shattered crystal in a matter of seconds'.

Lubek himself, the newsletter informs us, is now awaiting the Karmic repercussions for his past actions. And is this then the end of the fiendish scientist? It may look like it, but addicts of American comic books will be forgiven for wondering if, like the Joker and the mad scientist Luthor, those implacable enemies of Batman and Superman, Lubek will not somehow contrive to escape his prison to terrorize the world once again.

It is important to realize that this material, no matter how outlandish it may seem to the outside observer, is accepted almost without question by adherents of George King and his Society. Periods of Spiritual Push are taken with complete seriousness and crises such as that engendered by Lubek and his Egog are treated with the awe engendered in most people by major international upheavals. This highly uncritical acceptance of the bizarre and the fantastic is further illustrated by a series of witty, if rather cutting hoaxes which were played on the Society and its founder in the fifties.

The hoaxes began when, as the result of a complaint by King that scientists were too narrow-minded on matters concerning flying saucers, a letter appeared in the *Cosmic Voice* from a Dr Walter Wumpe, Ph.D., D.Sc., F.R.A.P.C., which seemed to suggest that far from finding the messages from Aetherius incredible, scientists across the world were examining their texts with interest. In fact, Dr Wumpe reported, astronomers had lately been receiving radio signals coming from a planetary system 'forty-three light years distant' in which the names 'Thereus' and 'Zaturn' could be detected. Commenting on this staggering development, the editor of *Cosmic Voice* wrote: '*Cosmic Voice* wishes to extend grateful thanks to that famous lecturer on astronomy, Dr Walter Wumpe, Ph.D., D.Sc., F.R.A.P.C., for the report from a meeting directly connected with the Geophysical Year Programme. I consider his paper to be of great importance to the work of *Cosmic Voice*.'

Dr Wumpe's colleague, another distinguished astronomer, evidently of Swedish origin, and with the slightly unusual name of Dr Egon Spunraas, also came in for favourable comment from the *Voice*, which added: 'The reference to the discoveries of Professor Spunraas is very interesting in the light of our Space Contacts. I would like to point out to readers that words "Thereus" and "Zaturn" as translated by Professor Spunraas, allowing for interference, picked up by his vibratory recorder, could quite well have originally been radiated as "Aetherius" and "Saturn". If this is the case', *Cosmic Voice* continued triumphantly, 'it stands as yet another unshakable proof of the authenticity of the contact with Aetherius, whose seat of Government is the planet—Saturn!'

Later issues of *Cosmic Voice* offered even more conclusive evidence of the growing interest of professional scientists. There was an article on 'Mescaline and Flying Saucers' by a Dr Dominic Fidler, which was later to be challenged for scientific inaccuracies by a Professor Huttle-Glank. If members of the Aetherius Society showed any puzzlement at the queer names of these great men of science, they raised no querulous sounds, for subsequent issues of the magazine included references to sages with even weirder names including a Dr N. Ormuss (and his assistant Waathervan), two Dutchmen Drs Houla and Huizenass and even the ridiculously obvious Dr L. Puller. Presumably the hoax would have escalated even further had not the literate Spiritualist newspaper, *Psychic News*, which casts a baleful eye on mediums who spout nonsense and had already had one or two verbal tussles with King and his Society, exposed the whole joke under the sardonic headline, THESE NAMES MADE NEWS. The offending articles have been blue-pencilled from later reprints of *Cosmic Voice* for obvious reasons. The incident remains, however, as a salty comment on human credibility and lack of critical acumen.

Despite the press controversy over the weekly manifestations of Jesus at the Caxton Hall, the fiasco over the Egon Spunraas hoax and the successful excursion into space by Russian and American rocketry (Mars, Sector 8 claimed that Man would never be permitted to set foot on the moon, and that the first Russian lunar rocket had been destroyed before impact by 'Magnetic Beam Neron six five') the Aetherius Society continued to flourish and before long small branches were being established in many cities of the USA. By 1959 it was becoming evident to its founder that other parts of the world would benefit from his personal visitation, and thus when the command was finally issued to him by an unidentified Martian to go to America he did not waste time hanging around in London. In addition a new and major enterprise on the part of the Society—code name 'Operation Starlight'—was under way and would need to be implemented in all parts of the world.

Operation Starlight, which was launched in July 1959 and continued until August 1961, represents one of the most spectacular religious rituals ever undertaken and is a tribute to the zeal and sincerity, if nothing else, of George King and his followers in their saga to follow the instructions of the Cosmic Masters. The operation consisted of the personal ascent, by George King and colleagues, of certain 'holy' mountains to 'charge' them with spiritual power. These mountains, which were selected for their own inscrutable reasons by the Cosmic

Masters, were named one by one, and led George and his band a merry dance across the globe. The earlier ones, including such neighbourhood pimples as Holstone Down in Devon or Ben Hope in Scotland, presented few problems, and literally crowds of Aetherians made the ascents, bearing sandwiches and Thermos flasks. Here they saw their leader raise his arms to the skies and proclaim the mountain charged, after which the Society's symbol (pyramid and mystic scribble) was marked in white paint on convenient rock.

In America, however, the picture was quite different, and the first mountain selected for 'charging' was Mount Baldy in California, which rises over 10,000 feet. Here, with fine sunny weather for the whole of the climb, the job was done with no physical discomfort or danger attending. Mountain number two in America was another 10,000-foot peak in the Sierra range in California and its picture adorns the cover of *Cosmic Voice* for May 1960 above the ringing headline FIGHT YE THE EVIL. This time, while the ascent was no problem, the party found themselves scrambling anxiously down the slopes in pitch dark having been unexpectedly overtaken by sunset. Mount Adams, the next cosmic choice, was a mere 6,000 feet in height but the Masters had, somewhat unreasonably, decreed that it should be ascended in March and the party made understandably heavy going, falling now and again into snowdrifts and suffering from partial frostbite. Nothing daunted, in April the group, by now thoroughly kitted out with snowshoes, blue glasses and other professional equipment, set out up the snowy slopes of Castle Peak in Colorado, a height of over 14,000 feet. The December 1960 issue of *Cosmic Voice* gives a hair-raising account of what appears to have been perfectly genuine hardships, not to say real risk to life and limb, endured by the party on this trip. The group were assailed by alternating blizzards and brilliant sunshine which gave them both frostbite and severe sunburn, and experienced mountaineers might well decide that they were lucky to return from the climb alive. Later climbs in Australia and New Zealand, performed during more clement weather, and even the ascent of the 9,000-foot Madrigerfluh in Switzerland in 1961, must have seemed like picnic excursions. Any consternation felt at the Masters' selection of Mount Kilimanjaro (19,600 feet) for the final phase of Operation Starlight was swiftly dispelled when Aetherius advised them that, because of their splendid efforts on the previous twelve peaks, the charging of Africa's highest peak would graciously be performed from above by the Masters themselves.

The holy mountains are now, to members of the Aetherius Society, special pilgrimage points and it is believed that an ascent to the spot where their emblem is painted brings considerable spiritual benefit to the individual and also to mankind. Issues of *Cosmic Voice* and the newsletter give details of organized parties that make the pilgrimage from time to time, and also give dire warnings to lay enthusiasts against attempting the more formidable of the peaks in poor weather or without special equipment.

Operation Starlight having been completed, the Reverend Dr George King embarked upon its successor, Operation Bluewater. This, believe it or not, required the purchase of power boats and the shuttling of certain 'batteries' to and from the Californian coast and some points in the ocean. Issues of the magazine show King and disciples, with yachting caps and sunglasses, setting out on a nautical jaunt and one feels that if nothing else they had certainly earned it.

At the time of writing the Aetherius Society seems to be strongly entrenched as the primary religious organization weaving its philosophy out of the phenomena of UFOs. It is particularly strong in America with headquarters in Los Angeles. Here George King now resides, having long forsaken his bed-sitter in the far-off grime of North London. He moves around the world a bit, returning to Britain to straighten out the London branch when required and to visit Scotland where the Ben Macdhui range was recently declared a mystic mountain and an official abode of the 'White Brotherhood'. At its headquarters the Society holds regular meetings and distributes numerous books, magazines and tape recordings conveying the new gospel of the cosmic laws. In a recent meeting held in the Rembrandt Hotel in London, presided over by the Reverend Keith Robertson, 'Certificates of Merit' were formally presented to fifty-two members for their zeal in following the great teachings of the Cosmic Masters. Dr King, who was by then engaged in a later venture, 'Operation Sunbeam', was unavoidably absent.

Myths in the Skies

ONE OF THE first commentators of any calibre to realize the strong mystical and religious themes surging along besides the enormous public interest in UFOs was the psychologist and theoretician, Carl Gustav Jung. Jung, a potent intellectual figure even when an octogenarian, had championed lots of odd causes in his time. Perhaps the most famous was astrology which he took as providing evidence for his own theories of 'synchronicity'. This latter concept attempts to account for such dubious phenomena as telepathy, precognition, etc., as acausal but still *significant* events in the universe. Few people have managed to swallow his rather unclear arguments for the principle, but the fact that he was prepared to think in totally fresh terms when faced with an apparent conflict between philisophy and science reminds us that the great pioneer of psychoanalysis remained a force to be reckoned with throughout his life. It is no surprise therefore to find him turning a quizzical eye on the wave of UFO reports in the fifties.

The story of this interest he reveals in his controversial and significant book, *Flying Saucers; a Modern Myth of Things Seen in the Skies*, published in 1959 at one of the peaks of public interest in Ufology. It appears that Jung had been interviewed by the press in 1956 and had made statements indicating respect for the relatively large number of aeronautical experts who had indicated a belief in flying saucers—without however stating that he shared their views. The interview was later picked up by news agencies and metamorphosed, in the subtle way of the journalist, into implying that Jung himself was a believer. This made world news headlines, rather to the famous psychologist's chagrin, and he immediately issued a carefully worded press release to make his own position clear. To his surprise this made no kind of news anywhere, and Jung was forced to conclude that news confirming the existence of UFOs was welcome to press and public, while scepticism was undesirable. Why, he asks, should it be more desirable for saucers to exist than not?

Starting off with a hard look at the incredible physical feats of acceleration, change of course, overall maximum speed, which many UFOs are credited with, and their apparent lack of susceptibility to being caught by camera or radar, Jung adopts the premise that they are not physical in origin—that is to say they are not, collectively, aircraft, spaceships or weird interplanetary beings. Since they exist however, at the very least in the minds of the thousands of individuals who report them, then they have a psychic if not a physical reality and an examination of the reports of their sightings should reveal patterns in common with other major psychic manifestations. Not surprisingly for a man whose life has been devoted to a study of unconscious processes revealing themselves through dreams, Jung leans heavily on dream material which he suggests is increasingly filled with 'archetypal' UFO images. Artists, too, tap the unconscious and non-linguistic depths of the human personality and Jung finds many examples of UFO like objects featuring in modern abstract art—notably in works by Yves Tanguay, Jakoby and P. Birkhauser.

Flying saucers, the psychologist continues, are psychic projections or 'visionary rumours' which reflect a deep-seated air of disquiet amongst humanity. With the old Gods dying, if not dead, and the world menaced by threat of total destruction as never before in its history, men are turning to the skies to seek their redeemers there.

Flying Saucers; a Modern Myth is in its way a brilliant little book, foreshadowing the current developments in Ufology by almost a decade and revealing those flashes of insight which made Jung one of the great thinkers of this century. If today the dream accounts seem unconvincing, if the *post-hoc* analyses of the examples from abstract art seem lame, and the implicit suggestion that these psychic projections might ultimately come to have objective physical reality, quite unacceptable, this does not detract from the force of his main argument. If alive today, Jung would undoubtedly have watched with great interest the overt expression of religious belief to be found in the activities of the Aetherius Society and its numerous lesser brethren.

The Aetherians, as we have found, have acquired a complex set of beliefs, rituals, spiritual exercises and the like and have even woven some of the great religious figures of the past—Jesus, Buddha, St Peter, etc.—rather incongruously into a modern science fiction setting. It is certainly significant that the revelations of this cult are delivered through a single individual (George King has several times been declared by Aetherius to be his 'primary terrestrial channel') in a fashion very reminiscent of the messages that allegedly come from the personalities of the dead via Spiritualist mediums.

Spiritualism is a religion of minority standing which had its modern origins in an American cult and which has settled down as a specialist offshoot of Christianity in which survival after death is not just preached but allegedly *proved*. Although radical in a number of ways—for example most followers hold that Jesus was an exalted but not a divine being—its roots lie firmly in the nineteenth century and its mediums tend to relay prosaic, unimaginative information about a spirit world clearly modelled after Victorian ideals. A study of the nature of the information flowing from mediums today reveals a definite trend amongst some to incorporate or accommodate the data of Ufology. For example, the 'School of Universal Philosophy and Healing' run by the medium Mrs Gladys Spearman-Cook in London regularly delivers information, often unconsciously hilarious, about spaceships and their occupants. Hints of the coming 'Interplanetary Brotherhood', plus more specific information on flying saucers, have also come from the White Eagle Lodge, a well-organized Spiritualist group in Kensington. The late Lord Dowding was but one of a large number of Spiritualists who believed in flying saucers and at one time the movement's official organ, the *Psychic News*, devoted a good deal of space to reporting major saucer sightings, as the result of readers' interest.

In America, in particular, contacts with space beings (as opposed to the 'spirits of the departed') through mediums have been on the increase for some time and there is some suggestion, which Spiritualists are quick to challenge, that the actual location of the 'Summerland' as revealed by the nineteenth century mediums is not in some non-physical or extradimensional sphere, but on a separate planet either in this solar system or in some other galaxy.

In the first edition of *Flying Saucers Have Landed,* Desmond Leslie refers to the work of a 'Dr' Meade Layne of California who was experimenting in 'very advanced and mysterious fields of physics' and who believed that 'life on Venus takes place at a higher octave of matter than on Earth' —or in other words, in case one is not exactly clear what this means, at a 'higher vibrationary rate'. In a recent edition, Leslie evidently has examined this nonsense more closely and decided to delete it. Most of Meade Layne's data, it turns out, came not from physical experiments but from communications through a 'deep trance medium', one Mark Probert of San Diego. In his book, *The Coming of the Guardians,* Meade Layne spells out the role which the majority of saucer fans no doubt hope that the saucer's occupants will play. Most of Probert's communicators—including such distinguished figures as the late Thomas Edison and the mystic Lao-Tze—live on an etheric counterpart of earth from which they launch their etheric saucers. These are but the vanguards of large-scale landings to take place on earth at an unspecified time in the future. Their main concern is the evil trend of life on earth and our dangerous tampering with nuclear fission.

Probert's communicators are at pains to point out that man survivives death and that the astral worlds of the more orthodox Spiritualist mediums are interchangable with the 'ethereal' which they inhabit. It is all, it turns out, a matter of what we simple humans can accept without psychological collapse—i.e. the truth about flying saucers and even their existence could not safely have been given to people in Victorian times when aircraft of *any* kind would have been incomprehensible.

Closely paralleling Meade Layne's findings in ethos, though not in their method of delivery, are those that come from a Mr George Hunt Williamson of Prescott, Arizona. Williamson's major contribution to the tomes of alleged psychic communications from space beings is a curious volume, *The Saucers Speak*, in which he recounts in detail messages received in *morse code* by a radio operator, 'Mr R.', later revealed as one Lyman H. Streeter, a telegraphist for the Santa Fe Railroad. In his introduction to the book Williamson states confidently that the saucers have been surveying us for thousands of years and makes the obligatory dig at the American Government for prevaricating. When will the world's leaders wake up to the facts, he asks, concluding ominously, 'only time will tell, and there isn't too much of that left'.

The book itself contains material of such banality that it is hard to credit that it could be published as a work of purported fact. After a long opening account as to the circumstances by which he came to hear of the mysterious messages and why he is obliged to accept their authenticity, Williamson then reveals that some of the material came via 'automatic writing', some through a kind of home-made ouija board, and others yet through the tried and trusted method of the inverted tumbler.

For those readers who have not come into contact with this parlour game, it requires the distribution of the letters of the alphabet (together with one or two useful words, such as Yes, No, etc.) in a ring on a polished table, after which a tumbler or wine glass is upturned in the centre. Participants place a finger on the glass which will soon begin to move around the table, passing from letter to letter. There is no mystery in the fact that the sequences of letters frequently spell out coherent messages, as anyone who cares to try the experiment will find out. The glass moves with an ease on the polished surface which often surprises the novice, and most people soon find that they can easily exercise control over the glass without giving themselves away.

Whether the motive power in the case of the Williamson's experiment was spiritual or human is of course a matter for personal opinion, but the nature of the material itself does not leave one with the impression that the communicators were of particularly superior intelligence. One calling himself Nah-9 of the Solar X Group said that they had been observing earth for 75,000 years but were not interested in 'those of carnal mind'. Another, Kadar Lacu, announced himself as Head of Interplanetary Council-Circle and stated that in due course certain chosen ones would be removed from earth and only a few would be saved. 'Ankar-22' reported that the nuclear tests on earth had set off volcanic activity on Mars, and a being called Zrs, who hailed from Uranus, advised that earth had two moons, one which we never saw because of 'certain conditions'. . . . Other alleged space entities had names like

Zo, Regga, Actar (from Mercury) and Affa. Zo's wife, incidentally, was named Um.

In 'Cosmic Rays and a Baby Sun', the fantastic final chapter of the book, the author attempts to stitch together all the material which came through the various forms of mediumship and concludes that the earth's path in space is heading for a cosmically disturbed area, the effect of which would soon be manifested in strange weather, melting polar icecaps, earthquakes, etc. He declares that the governments of the world are aware of this and that the UFOs are here to awaken us not merely to the cosmic catastrophe towards which we are surely moving, but also to fulfil 'all ancient prophecy in that they remind us that "our salvation draweth nigh"'. The space visitors cannot themselves intervene to avert the catastrophe but they will assist the remnant who survive to return to the arms of the 'Interplanetary Brotherhood from which it fell countless generations ago'. The final sentence of the book is a biblical quotation, 'Watch, for no man knoweth the hour!'

A somewhat more sophisticated analysis of the link between UFOs and theological beliefs was given at the 1968 UFO convention, held in Cleveland, Ohio, by an Evangelical Minister, the Reverend Frank R. Basille, who said that there was no doubt in his mind that we were under surveillance. The space people were probably performing 'the will of God to raise us spiritually to stem the tide of evil'. There was a fair risk, however, that there might be both good and evil spacemen—an unfortunate complication if true, for one would never know whether the messages received were cunningly designed to mislead us or were genuine warnings from friendly aliens. The Reverend Basille added that the evil space-beings could collaborate with an evil group of humans with the eventual aim of forming an unholy alliance to take over the earth. If this were so, then we could expect some frightening things to happen before long. 'Evil spacemen are, I believe, one day going to pick a man to whom they will give tremendous power and who will prove that he is almost God-like by the miracles he will perform.' These would be supernatural powers which would parallel the biblical prophecies about anti-Christ. 'We are living in days of fulfilled prophecy', he concluded, but if we 'keep ourselves right then maybe we can keep the world right too.'

The cleric's amazing speech drew considerable applause, as had an immediately previous address by a Jewish theologian who claimed that he had had fifteen years' study in theology in seminaries and who held that the Book of Moses is an accurate account of an encounter between a small group of people living in the Middle East and a race of space beings.

Such revolutionary interpretations of biblical stories are, as we have already seen, not uncommon and for anyone not convinced of the conceptual link being forged between UFO phenomena and religious beliefs, the writings of the Englishman Brinsley le Poer Trench are recommended. Mr Trench —his most important book is probably *The Sky People*—holds (and quotes extensively from the Bible and other holy books to prove his point) that the Greek Gods Apollo, Hermes, Prometheus and others, as well as Egyptian deities such as Osiris, were all visitors from outer space. The author writes in a scholarly and literate style. Unfortunately this does not make it any more credible. The Garden of Eden, he discovered, was on Mars and was in fact a kind of open-air laboratory designed to allow a significant genetic experiment—the crossing of two species of man—to take place under controlled conditions. For various reasons this failed, the 'garden was shut down and its people turned out to fend for themselves'. The legend of the Flood is explained by the fact that the garden had been located by one of the polar icecaps which melted rather suddenly and drowned most of the inhabitants. One group alone, by dint of foresight and hard work, had taken the trouble to build a ship of refuge on to which, as the calamity approached, they duly climbed. Not for them, according to Trench, forty days of rain on a storm-tossed sea, for their lifeboat left the surface of Mars and headed for our own planet Earth. Noah's Ark, you see, was a spaceship.

The antiquity of flying saucer sightings can be attested in ways other than those of biblical reference. The most common of these is based on the marvellous principle of orthoteny, developed by the French mathematician, Aimé Michel, which consists of a careful analysis of the sites of all saucer sightings and their subsequent plotting on a large-scale map. When the points are plotted, Michel claims, statistical distributions build up which are not simply a function of population centres, etc., but which seem to imply that the spacecraft follow definite courses and tend to congregate in certain specific areas. Much has been made of orthoteny in recent years, thanks to the publication of Michel's book, *Flying Saucers and the Straight-line Mystery*—the straight lines in question being the supposed 'preferred pathways' chosen by the vehicles. The principle has a superficial curiosity value which, when backed by the author's unquestioned status as a mathematician, might reasonably be counted as a weapon in the Ufologist's armoury.

Unfortunately, mathematicians who have found time to look at the material of orthoteny are more likely to see it as a case of selective *post-hoc* analysis—the kind of exercise which used to lead people to say (not without some justification) that you can prove anything by statistics. The point is of course that the linear masses plotted by Michel and others look immediately impressive but they are open to at least two serious criticisms. (1) It is not at all clear what criteria are used in deciding whether to plot a UFO sighting or not. If this is at all selective then there is nothing surprising about the fact that some significant pattern appears to emerge—it is rather like pyramidology where, by dint of suitable filtering of measurements, the most amazing data can be produced. (2) The plotted points appear to be the positions of the *observers* rather than the UFOs themselves—an important distinction if the point being made is that the saucers are following rather precisely repetitive courses.

Although these criticisms have not gone unnoticed by the protagonists of orthoteny, the myth that saucers have and did, even way back in historical times, move around the world as though from checkpoint to checkpoint still survives. In England it is looked on with especial favour, and orthotenists have made good use of the country's magnificent one-inch ordnance survey maps to bolster their case. Opinion as to what are the significant reference points chosen by the saucer pilots in their restless scouring of the heavens varies, but for the argument about the antiquity of the space people's interest in earth to hold, it is universally agreed, they must be sites of historical importance—King Arthur's Castle, for example—or spectacular rock formations such as Glastonbury Tor. Hunting around on maps plotting saucer sighting points and joining them up in one or other of the myriad possible combinations will soon show the lines crossing historic buildings or prehistoric mounds—it would be very surprising indeed if it did not. And if a plotted line should just miss the White Horse of Uffington, Banbury Cross or some long forgotten Sussex burial site, well then the explanation must be of course that the observer was slightly incorrect in his original report and a little judicious correction will soon put matters right.

So keen in fact are many Ufologists in this curious variant of saucer lore that a little magazine, *The Ley Hunter,* is published giving up-to-the-minute details of the latest plottings, and exciting articles suggesting that these may be used to locate the Holy Grail (an old favourite of cultists) or unravel the mystery of Stonehenge. For those who feel they are getting left behind here, a ley is the special kind of line (most easily visible of course through the porthole of a speeding saucer) which you get if you join up prehistoric sites and you will not be surprised to learn that England is simply covered with them.

Some of the most important leys, incidentally, pass through (or near) the historic town of Warminster in Wiltshire, and for many people this has become the Mecca for saucer spotters in this country; UFOs appear, by all reports, with amazing regularity in this part of the world, and credit for drawing our attention to this phenomenon must largely go to a Mr Arthur Shuttlewood, whose book, *The Warminster Mystery* is a minor classic of its kind.

Arthur Shuttlewood, a good-natured, intelligent chap in his late forties, is a journalist on the local Warminster paper. As a reporter, of course, he was in an excellent position to document the amazing wave of UFO activity which started on Christmas Day 1964, and which has continued on and off ever since. Most of the activity seems to consist of lights in the skies, bangs, buzzing noises, etc., and these are particularly likely to be observed from the copse on Cradle Hill, a high point overlooking the town. Cradle Hill also happens to be close to the Army's training and firing ranges nearby and many Warminster inhabitants are inclined to think that the bangs, bumps and flashes come from such terrestrial nuisances as tanks and guns, but Shuttlewood points out that the noises frequently come from the 'opposite direction' to the Army ranges. Whichever viewpoint is correct, throughout 1965 literally hundreds of people in the town reported mysterious flying objects of one kind or another and public disquiet began to grow. The principal objectors seem to have been local tradesmen who complained that the publicity the huge wave of sightings was getting in the national press was frightening people away and acting therefore as a kind of anti-tourist attraction.

If there were any doubts about the pulling power of saucers, however, the local tradesmen must soon have had their minds put to rest. A public meeting called to air the matter was a complete sell-out. Over 350 people were turned away from the doors of the Town Hall which, bathed in the glare of TV lights, looked as though it was the focal point of some popular uprising. The weekend following the meeting a vast surge of curiosity-seekers descended on Warminster, raising its population momentarily from 10,000 to nearly 20,000, bleeding the souvenir shops dry and bringing to the point of collapse the town's modest catering establishments. Motorists and radiators fumed for hours in immense, static traffic jams, pubs ran dry of beer for the first time since World War II and the roads to Cradle Hill and Colloway Clump (the strategic spots for optimum UFO spotting) were black with inquisitive humanity. If ever testimony to the pulling power of saucers is needed, the account of the invasion of Warminster on August Bank Holiday 1965 may be offered up with confidence.

Once a 'hardened sceptic', Arthur Shuttlewood has now made so many sightings of UFOs over Warminster that he is quite convinced of their existence. The title of his second book *Warning From Flying Friends* gives some idea of the trend of his thinking at the moment. More than once he has been personally visited in his home by mysterious beings with unusual eyes, including one called himself Karne who said that the end of the world was due quite shortly. Mysterious telephone calls from individuals known as Selorik and Traellison, Queen of Aenstria, he thinks might have been hoaxes.

There is little point in plunging more deeply into the exotic details of the Warminster mystery, or for that matter any other of the many manifestations of the cult of Ufology that has spread across the world. Today it is the happy hunting ground of people from all walks of life—scientists, doctors, admirals, bishops, secretaries, soldiers, policemen, magistrates and hippies—no single group appears not to have representatives immersed in its mythology. The phenomena appear to be simple in essence, if complex in detail. Genuine unidentified flying objects prove to be not only attractive to the minds of a very sizeable slab of humanity but also, to many, *essential*. Thus despite all the denials of Air Force Generals and the tempered scepticism of specialist scientists, flying saucers and their superior occupants, whether sacred or profane, exist, have existed and probably always will exist. As someone else said in a slightly different context—'If UFOs did not exist it would have been necessary to invent them.'

PART III: BLACK BOXES

The Pioneers

THE DISCERNING READER will have noted an interesting common link between Scientology and at least one aspect of Ufology—a preoccupation with gadgetry of arguable practical value. The Scientologists have their E-meter which, as we have seen, plays a significant role in the training of auditors and the advancement of preclears up the many-runged ladder to the highest strata of the movement. Flying saucer fans, who are not one homogeneous group but rather a patchwork of humanity representing all shades and the colours of belief from the hard-headed to the simple-minded, favour various technical aids. These may be as straightforward as the camera or telescope, or as boldly off-beat as the spiritual energy radiator employed by members of the Aetherius Society during times of crisis. In most, if not all, cases the gadgetry serves as quasi-scientific equipment whose physical reality is unarguable but whose role is comprehensible and meaningful only to individuals embroiled in the cult itself. The E-meter, for example, is a piece of apparatus which may easily be described in the terminology of mechanics or electronics, but whose value in the role claimed for it might be a matter of scientific dispute. The same presumably is true of the spiritual energy radiator.

The enthusiasm for such devices is not hard to understand. To most people any bit of technical apparatus, provided that it has a wheel turning, a light flashing or a needle wagging, is immediately exciting and somehow convincing on its own. This is particularly true when, as with the average Scientologist or Aetherian, the individual himself has a limited scientific background. Then the mysterious apparatus acquires an aura of profundity which serves as the physical equivalent of the specialized jargon on which so many cults rely. The E-meter and its analogues are actually the cults' implicit obeisance to the machine age, an unconscious recognition that the icons of today must be cast in the image of the jet engine, the television set and the digital computer.

The examples given above are intended as technical aids and are treated as such by their operators. They are not—as the Food and Drug Administration found to its embarrassment in the case of the E-meter—sold or promoted as therapeutic devices. But, granting human beings' fatal fascination for mysterious gadgetry—anyone who doubts this has only to watch people at play with pinball machines—it will be no surprise that complicated and incomprehensible equipment has found its way into quasi-medical areas and has there formed strong platforms for a number of cult-like activities. The best example of these are the various devices which have lately acquired the generic term of 'Black Boxes'. They are important to this book because, while few actually have cults built around them, all have acquired cultish significance. They may exist as peripherals or technical aids—as with the E-meter—or they may have a more dominant role to play—as with the various radionic devices which we shall look at shortly. At heart however they are all really doing the same thing—seeking to demonstrate or prove the existence of some independent mental or psychic process, some *élan vital* or spiritual component in man. When a Scientologist, an Aetherian or a radionics expert twiddles knobs on his particular gadget he is on one plane performing a routine act of diagnosis, psychic defence or what have you, on yet another plane he is reminding himself and his colleagues of the most important single fact motivating all religious thought—man is both flesh *and* soul, the latter as real and measurable as the former. A close examination of the fascinating data offered up by Black Box protagonists of one kind or another will make the above argument only too clear. Occasionally the veneer of science is superficially convincing, but it is never necessary to scratch deep before the true nature of the material reveals itself.

In the language of electronic theory and related fields, a 'black box' is a hypothetical system whose internal logic is unknown and for which one can normally only specify the presence of inputs and outputs. For example, the brain may reasonably, if not very helpfully, be described as a black box, fed by the senses and able to *cause* events to occur on the outside world by speech, muscle activity, etc. The only thing that one can say about a black box is that it works—its mechanics remain unknown. To most people the average radio set falls into this category. It has switches which serve to determine the kind of noises it produces, and batteries to replenish from time to time. For the rest the owner is happy that it works along the lines of the claims made for it. This gentle naivety, which is not confined to relatively complex devices such as radio sets —the camera and the motor car engine are black boxes to vast slabs of humanity—puts very many people at the mercy of the mountebank, the quack and even the honestly misguided eccentric who claim to have developed revolutionary scientific inventions. The most elderly of these is probably the perpetual motion machine, a contrivance which mad scientists are continually requesting patents for, and more recently, but still quite venerable, the anti-gravity machine.

One of the earliest and most enduring examples of amazing gadgetry working wonders in the medico-psychological field was the wand used by Mesmer to manipulate the so-called animal magnetism. Mesmer and the ultimate muted triumph of hypnosis are great favourites of cultists, for they are the supreme case of an apparently mystical technique universally scorned by contemporary scientists which later was to prove its reality. Even today the theory of hypnosis is almost completely obscure and the steady improvement in anaesthesia has limited its use to peripheral areas. But it is still one of the major weapons in the armoury of the pseudo-scientist when defending his own particular obsession against orthodox hostility.

Mesmer's wand was no machine of course, and merely a hangover from medieval belief in wizardry and such. The first convincing black boxes did not appear, quite predictably, until people had become accustomed to the existence of genuine working mechanical or electronic devices whose overall effect they understood, but whose mode of operation might as well have been magic as anything else. The first man to realize the considerable potential in this field seems to have been a Dr Albert Abrams who manufactured and marketed black boxes of various kinds in California in the early part of this century, and died in 1923 a millionaire.

Unlike so many of the so-called doctors who peddle their wares in this territory, Abrams was the recipient of a genuine scientific and medical education. Somewhere along the line his brilliance began to show signs of diversion from the monotony of orthodox medicine, into methods of diagnosis and treatment which dismayed many of his friends and colleagues. At first these consisted merely of attempting to diagnose the condition of patients by tapping sharply on their abdomens and listening carefully to the resulting sounds. Different diseases and physical malfunctions would, he believed, produce unique and readily distinguishable noises when the abdomen was percussed.

Even today, doctors tend to tap here and there when examining patients, so at first Abrams's percussing attracted little comment. It was when he developed a machine to assist him with the diagnosis that eyebrows began to be raised. The 'Dynamizer', as it was called, was a box with a bird's nest of wires inside. One lead was connected to a battery, another was attached, by a metal clamp, to the forehead of a healthy human being. Once this weird circuit was hooked up, Abrams would then take a blood sample from the sick individual, placing it on blotting paper inside the box somewhere amongst the wires. Then, believe it or not, the doctor would start tapping the abdomen of the *healthy* person, and by duly considering the sounds made by the raps would diagnose the condition of the patient whose blood sample was in the apparatus. Those of a scientific bent will already have deduced that some kind of emission from the blood cells on the blotting paper was being detected and amplified by the black box and that the human was serving as a living loudspeaker. No reader of this book will be surprised to learn that what was emanating from the blood sample was described by Abrams as 'vibrations'—a word of great utility to cultists of all persuasions.

With this invention the great doctor was just flapping his wings, but when he discovered that he could pinpoint not only physical, but also psychological conditions by this means he really began to take off the deck. Before long another breakthrough occurred, when it was discovered that the dynamizer could also determine a person's religion—it was particularly hot at winkling out Theosophists and Seventh Day Adventists —to say nothing of their age and sex. For those for whom a blood sample was not readily available, the dynamizer and its various successors could produce accurate diagnoses from handwriting in lieu.

The next step was logical enough. If diseased bodies gave out specific, describable vibrations, should it not be possible, by devising a sufficiently versatile vibrator, to send therapeutic signals back into the unhealthy tissue and so correct matters, Dr Abrams felt that it most certainly should and built a machine known as an 'oscilloclast', which transmitted beneficient vibrations of all kinds, and which he kindly rented out in large numbers to the quack doctors with which America has been and, no doubt, always will be richly endowed.

Like many other cult leaders or fathers of eccentric scientific theories, Abrams had enthusiasm and personal magnetism to spare and, one supposes, an honest belief in his own genius. These qualities, which are formidable indeed when encountered, led many men to champion his cause. One of the most articulate of these was the prolific novelist, Upton Sinclair, who declared that Abrams had made 'the most revolutionary discovery of this or any other age'. In his long life Sinclair revealed himself as a sincere but gullible man whose tolerant attitude to the world and humanity rendered him almost incapable of believing that members of the species homo sapiens were guilty of telling lies. The outcome was that he successively championed in turn just about every barmy idea, political, religious or scientific, that swam into his ken. His enthusiasm for Abrams, his dynamizer, his oscilloclast and a later invention called the 'reflexophone' (which allowed one to conduct diagnosis at a distance) was no exception.

A contemporary drawing of the reflexophone in use reveals that it was about the size of a briefcase and, apart from jack points for input and output, was equipped with three or four dials and knobs. Simple-minded people looking at the drawing (which also shows a scientific-looking chap rapping someone's abdomen) might think that these knobs, etc., were connected in some logical way to a meaningful electrical current inside, but if so they would be wrong. In almost all medical black boxes, from Dr Abrams's original to its numerous successors, the wiring of the interior—if there is any at all—follows no kind of pattern to be found in any textbook of electronics. In many cases dials on the outside of the box, which are twiddled and set with great solemnity by the operator, may even be found not to be connected to anything at all inside! But before dismissing as lunacy the task of manipulating knobs and switches unconnected to anything but thin air, it is only fair to look at the theory which underlies this aspect of invention and discovery to see whether it helps explain the addiction of many thousands of apparently sane individuals to black box diagnosis and therapy. The most convenient and instructive case is the remarkable story of the late Mr George de la Warr whose laboratories at Oxford, and their sensational by-products, made newspaper headlines across the world in the 1950s.

George de la Warr was born in 1905 in the North of England and started his unusual career as an engineer, specializing in civil and building problems, and was for many years in the employ of the Oxford County Council as assistant to the county engineer. His resignation in 1953 was to allow him to devote his whole time to the study and development of black boxes, a topic for which he was already acquiring an international reputation.

Though of an orthodox engineering background, de la Warr was not totally without grounding in fields peripheral to science and medicine. His mother had been greatly interested in homœopathy, a borderline aspect of medicine which holds that disease may be treated by the administration (in minute doses) of drugs which would produce, in a healthy person, symptoms like those of the disease treated. This controversial theory attracted much attention in the nineteenth century, when it was a favourite with lay therapists, as it requires no academic or university training for it to be practised, but it has been fading out of fashion steadily in recent decades. De la Warr, it is claimed, found the theory of homœopathy, such as it is, to be 'so much rubbish', but he was nevertheless impressed by the fact that it seemed to work. Instead of adopting the view that homœopathic cures probably amounted to temporary symptomatic alleviation only, he came to the conclusion that they implied the existence of some kind of fundamental 'energy or life force' in all living things, from human tissue to the smallest virus, and that the presence of this energy ought to be detectable and measurable by scientific means.

This energy, by the way, was no simple variant of the

radiational spectrum known to science, but something which had only hitherto made its presence known in peculiar and unpredictable ways. For example, in the practice known as dowsing, a man (with the right kind of sensitivity) may detect the presence of underground water, minerals, etc., by watching the twists and jerks of a bent stick held in his hands. The water, it is believed, emits its own kind of energy radiation which, while not registerable on the most delicate of scientific instruments, can nevertheless be detected by the unique combination of the right kind of wood and the right kind of mind. A variation on this theme is the so-called science of radiesthesia, in which the divining rod or twig is replaced by a pendulum device, the pendulum swinging around in circles or ellipses when the substance to be detected is near. Diviners and radiesthetists are prone to fantastic claims in support of the power of their technique, including such unlikely matters as the sexing of newlaid eggs or the determination of some one's political affiliations with only a hair from his head to go on. Needless to say, few dowsers or radiesthetists care to submit their powers to the essentially simple scientific tests which could easily verify their reality, and those that have been tested have generally been the most ghastly flops. Nevertheless, the topic and its endless permutations exert a deep fascination for a sizeable section of humanity, and de la Warr was by no means the first or the last to paddle in these waters.

In 1943 (according to a lecture he delivered to the Oxford University Scientific Society some twenty years later) de la Warr and his wife made serious attempts at detecting 'life radiation' in a number of forms of plant life from seedlings to a fully developed larch tree. Showing his engineering bias, he spurned the unreliable foibles of the dowser's twig and erected a series of metal aerials—using his wife's hairpins in early improvisations. These experiments proved disappointing, for although he used aerials of a variety of lengths (the optimum lengths had been determined by prior experiments of a radiesthetic nature) when these were hooked up to an amplifier and thence to a cathode ray tube, no electrical signals were detected. De la Warr thus concluded either that any electrical signals given off by the plant were too weak to be recorded on his instruments, or that he was not dealing with electro-magnetic energy at all. He settled for the latter, apparently disregarding the third possibility—that the reason no signals were detected was because the plant was emitting none in the first place. These early experiments did yield something of interest, for it was found that when the miniature aerials were wired up to certain plants, there was a tendency for these to grow more rapidly or more sturdily than control plants not given the benefit of the radionic treatment. This unexpected result served to convince de la Warr that they were on the track of something big, and he began to wonder if the 'life radiation' he had discovered might not be put to some medical use. Perhaps it was behind the phenomena of Abrams's Box?

It will be remembered that Abrams's diagnosis relied on the skilled interpretation of the sounds made by percussing the chests of a healthy individual. The complete kit of his diagnostic device, therefore, included not only the dynamizer itself, with its wires and controls, but also one healthy adult human prepared to stand for hours on end, stripped to the waist and endure no end of rapping from the practitioner's busy fingers. It is a daunting thought and one which prompted de la Warr to simplify matters.

His first and major decision was to get rid of the human 'loudspeaker' and substitute a simple rubber pad which, it had been found, could also give significant information to the trained ear when rapped—always providing of course that a blood sample or some such was placed inside the diagnostic box. A later development did away with the rapping of the pad and substituted *rubbing* it with the fingertips.

Now when you slide a finger briskly across the surface of a small sheet or diaphragm of rubber it will normally move very easily, but with a hint of the potential friction which could build up if the pressure of the finger is increased. In fact, if one does press rather firmly as one rubs, then there comes a point where the finger is brought sharply to a stop as the frictional forces exceed those being applied by the lateral movement of the finger. The point at which this frictional buffer occurs may also be induced by other variables, such as changes in temperature, the addition or reduction of lubricants such as sweat, grease, etc. In black box theory this 'stick', as it is called, is of immense significance, for it denotes not only such mundane factors as the co-efficient of friction between fingertip and rubber pad, but also that the operator has detected a significant signal of some kind from the apparatus and its sample. With this apparatus all one now needed to set up in expert medical practice was the Delawarr apparatus, a few patients (or some part of them) and a muscular, durable finger.

The box de la Warr constructed consisted of a cabinet—black of course, and finished handsomely in leatherette, chrome and bakelite—a number of control knobs set out in rows, the rubber detector pad and a couple of containers for the blood sample or hair of the diseased person or animal. Inside the box there was nothing. No valves, condensers, diodes, relays—just ordinary air. How could such a simple contraption be used to diagnose illnesses which it might take the resources of a major medical establishment to pin down accurately? To understand this we will need to go into some technical details and anyone who finds himself baffled will have to go back a few pages and start again. I am happy to assure readers, however, that no profound knowledge of electronics is required to master the principles of the devices—in fact the more electronics one knows, the less comprehensible the whole affair will seem.

To begin with we must imagine the 'circuit diagram' of the system, which is given quite openly in a number of de la Warr's publications. From the rubber detector pad (it was set in a metal frame) a wire leads to the first of the knobs or dials and thence to all the others in series and finally to the specimen wells. Thus a connection capable of conducting electricity is made from the containers in which the diseased samples are kept, through the eight knobs, to the rubber stick pad and thence, one supposes, to the operator himself. Now the purpose of the knobs, which could be set in any one of ten discrete positions marked out something like a clock face, was to alter the effective length of the circuit from blood sample to detector pad.

The function of the dials was not to raise or lower volume, or to change frequency in any meaningful way, but merely to alter the *length* of the circuit, which in some uncertain way was supposed to make it capable of detecting the characteristic radiation which all living things emit and by which they can be identified. Of course the first step for the pioneer working in this field would be to compile a comprehensive list of the wavelengths of the most important and commonly occurring diseases. The principle adopted was a simple one, requiring only a blood sample from an infected human or animal whose disease had already been accurately diagnosed by orthodox methods. These would then be placed in the sample wells of the Delawarr apparatus (one being the positive pole and the other the negative) and all dials would be set to zero. The operator would then start rubbing away with his fingers at the detector pad. If he failed to get a 'stick' with the dials at zero he would then alter the first dial to one, rub away for a bit, turning up another and yet another notch if necessary, until he felt the characteristic stick, as his finger stopped on the rubber pad. He would then start all over again, but with dial number two, until he got a stick and so on until one had been achieved for each of the knobs that were to be used. For reasons which we won't bother to go into here, it would rarely be necessary to use all eight dials in tracking down the average complaint, but in sum it was generally found that a short number tended to denote a rather general type of complaint and a longer number a more specific aspect of one. For example, the *Guide to Clinical Condition*, which went along with every diagnostic black box sold, reveals that a 'rate' of 97964 denoted the presence of a 'virus', a rate of 07752 a 'bacterial condition' and one of 80810 a 'parasite'.

Reading the *Guide* is a peculiar business. The number 30528, for example, denotes a condition called 'mineral' (deficiencies of, one assumes) while 60404 implies the ominous-sounding 'secretion imbalance'. There are also some interesting discriminations which can only be counted as major contributions to medical diagnosis; 'toxins' rate a lowly 901, while 'poison' scores an impressive 700457. To confound the issue even further, we find that lower down the list, a 'toxic state' registers 90222. It is all very strange, and one turns with relief to such simple homely conditions as 907 (fracture), 1014 (contraction or spasms), and 80799 (bruise), all mere trifles to the skilled practitioner no doubt, unlike the dreaded 60682587 (pericardial effusion).

The Delawarr box, like many of its predecessors, was not limited to the diagnosis of physical malaise and, using a different combination of dials, the enthusiast could soon determine, with only a blood or hair sample, whether a man was in the grip of any one of a number of psychological conditions ranging from 'malice' (30341) and 'vanity' (50413) to 'thoughtfulness' (40421) and 'self-indulgence' (70442). It is only when we read that 40107 on the box denotes 'unrequited love' that we begin to wonder (as we did with some of the odder stuff from the pen of Hubbard) whether someone, somewhere isn't just conceivably pulling someone's leg.

De la Warr's next step was to move into the field of treatment, and special boxes were manufactured for this purpose. These were smaller than the diagnostic devices but equipped with a rather similar array of dials, none connected to any orthodox power source or transmitter. Treatment was simplicity itself. Having arrived at a diagnosis one then looked up the illness's 'Broadcast treatment rate' in a catalogue, set the dials on the treatment box and away one went. Away one went quite literally, for the box would go on merrily broadcasting twenty-four hours a day, whether anyone was near it or not. It was apparently even unnecessary to tell the person receiving the benefits of its healing rays that he was being so favoured. This fact is never better attested than in the case of the scores of animals which made wonderful recoveries from all manner of complaints as the result of long-distance radionic therapy. Most of these fortunate creatures were pet cats and dogs, but some larger specimens, such as cows, are stated to have shown improvements in health which proved a puzzle to veterinary science. All these developments paled into insignificance, however, at the next breakthrough in the Delawarr laboratories—the construction of a camera capable of photographing human 'thought forms'.

Thought photography, or 'thoughtography' as some addict with a tendency to whimsy once christened it, is not a completely new development in this field. The so-called science of spirit photography, by means of which the features of the departed, ringed with cotton wool, are caused to appear miraculously on film, dates back to the turn of the century. Spirit photography, an important branch of fraudulent mediumship at one time, relied heavily on the average person's more or less total ignorance of how a camera works. Even today when, thanks to the march of science, it is possible to bore friends silly with technically excellent colour slides of one's holiday in Cornwall or the Canary Islands, few amateur cameramen are aware how easy it is to contrive images on film without light passing through the lens in the traditional way. Apart from such obvious tricks as tampering with the negative in the development stage or allowing the light to enter the camera through one or other of its sides, it is not at all difficult to mark photographic film with radioactive energy. In this latter case the trickster would merely have to arrange for a small piece of radioactive material to be near the camera —he could, for example, conceal it in a finger ring—and real, if rather diffuse, images would appear on film which had never been exposed to ordinary light. These and many other tricks have been used and, no doubt, will be used again in the production of thoughtographs of one kind or another. And when deliberate trickery is not resorted to, carelessness, ignorance or simple human naivety will frequently produce peculiar effects which serve to bolster belief in the phenomena.

A recent and most interesting development in this area features the phenomena surrounding a hard-drinking, chain-smoking Chicago hotel porter named Ted Serios. Mr Serios, whose work has been pioneered and publicized by the American psychiatrist and parapsychologist, Dr Jules Eisenbud, claimed to be able to project images of his own thoughts on to photographic film. In a fantastic book, *The World of Ted Serios*, which has sold thousands of copies in all parts of the Western world, Eisenbud compares this talent to a thought-directed paint brush, a phrase whose meaning evaporates on closer inspection.

Serios's technique involves a polaroid camera (for rapid inspection of results), a few quarts of his favourite beer, Budweiser, and a tiny cardboard tube which he calls a 'gizmo'. When sufficiently lubricated by the Budweiser, Serios strides up and down in front of the camera and at some psychologically critical moment rams the gizmo up against the camera lens, at the same time crying 'Now' as a signal for someone to open the camera shutter. The polaroid print is then inspected and frequently reveals, to murmurs of amazement from the credulous bunch who tag around with Serios, a tiny image of some kind. This may vary considerably in quality and information content, being sometimes an amorphous, cloudy mass, sometimes clear miniature images of such exotic structures as the Taj Mahal or Westminster Abbey.

The natural reaction of critics is to suggest that the gizmo conceals a tiny focusing lens and photographic negative which induces an image by perfectly traditional means through the lens of the polaroid camera. Despite the fact that Serios has never successfully induced a thoughtograph under scientifically controlled conditions *without* placing the gizmo up against the polaroid lens, this latest example of thoughtography is still treated by an amazing number of people as one of the unexplained wonders of our time.

To return to the de la Warrs, they moved into radionic photography as the result of dramatic experiments conducted at their laboratories in 1950. The first public announcement of these was made at a conference on 'Radionics and Radiesthesia' held in London between 16th and 18th May 1950, the report of which was published in a two-hundred page proceedings later that year. This rare document merits the closest study as being a splendid example of the kind of eccentric pseudo-science which cultists thrive on. It also shows clear traces of the deep roots of mysticism and occultism which permeate so much of cultish thought. The titles of the addresses range from the borderline prosaic ('The Gravitational Wave') to the more explicitly cranky ('Research Work on the Human Electromagnetic Field'). Few of the papers bear anything other than a passing resemblance to scientific documents in the established sense, though it is evident that all the participants took everything with complete seriousness.

In the first paper, 'Vis Medicatrix Naturae', given by a medical man, Dr Aubrey Westlake, there is much talk of 'odic forces' which permeate the universe. These turn out to be just another name for the impulses detected by dowsers and, presumably, by Abrams and his successors, including the de la Warrs. Dr Westlake felt that they were the manifestation of something called 'odyle'. Odyle has remarkable properties for 'running water develops it while static water does not'. It also 'quickly penetrates and courses through everything' and flows in concentrated form from special sources such as friction, sound, electricity, light, and the moon. Substances can be charged with odyle, which itself may be negative, giving a sensation of coolness, and positive, which gives a sensation of warmth and discomfort. It is also luminous and since human beings are odyle containers they are luminous over their whole surface. Hence the so-called aura surrounding the physical body.

Some substances are better conductors of odyle than others, and since one of the best passports to health and happiness is the filling of the body with the right kind of odyle, some attention should of course be paid to the type of clothing one wears, lest odyle-insulating materials are unwittingly used. Asked during question time about the wearing of silk underwear (within the above context of course) Dr Westlake replied that it was 'good, as silk was a perfect conductor of odyle'.

All papers at the conference are united in showing a preoccupation with the notion of fundamental forces, undiscovered or ignored by science, and closely tied to the psychic powers of human beings. For example, Professor H. Larvaron of the University of Rennes, in his paper 'The Earth and its Effects on Life', spoke of the grave consequences of 'imbalance in cellular oscillation' caused by excessive cosmic and nuclear radiation and drew the conference's attention to his discovery of 'telluric radiation.' (i.e. emanating from the earth rather than from outer space). This was essential to the smooth operation of the vital field. Whereas excessive doses of cosmic radiation led to the death of the irradiated life-form, controlled over-exposure to telluric radiation has just the opposite effect, and Professor Larvaron, an agriculturist at heart, showed his audience photographs of large beets, potatoes and quite enormous melons fostered by this method.

Some additional measure of the intellectual and scientific level of the conference can be gauged when we read that in the discussion following the French sage's paper, the conversation rapidly swung round to radiesthesia in ancient Egypt. The ability to manipulate odic, radionic or telluric forces, it emerged, was very probably one of the secrets of Ancient Egypt, being of course essential to the construction of the pyramids. Nor did the discussion ignore the fascinating questions raised by the *shape* of the pyramids, one participant pointing out that the pyramid form brings about desiccation and mummification. Anyone sceptical of this could easily test it for himself, he added, for when an egg out of its shell on a saucer is left beneath a cardboard model of the Great Pyramid, the albumen hardens in less than a week, while another similar egg left in the air elsewhere remained liquid. As a tour-de-force this same participant later exhibited at the conference, eggs which had *actually been mummified under a cardboard model of the Great Pyramid.*

As we have said, it was to this unusual gathering that George de la Warr presented his paper, 'Aspects of radionic research; the manifestation of fundamental energy', in which the first details of his experiments in thought photography were leaked to the world. This paper, which declares that a New Era was about to dawn, is illustrated with a number of photographs of a splodgy kind, allegedly of blood spots and the force fields which surround them. These, it must be understood, were not taken by so simple an exercise as pointing a camera at the spots and opening and closing the shutter in the normal way. They were taken by enclosing both blood spot and photographic plate inside a black box, tuning its dials to match the disease from which the afflicted donor was suffering, and subsequently removing the plates for developing. The images, which de la Warr had little hesitation in identifying as the blood spots with their accompanying force fields, were then revealed, though the plates had never wittingly been exposed to light. Simple experimentation along these lines led him and his technical assistant, Corte, to the belief that just as particular illnesses, whether physical or psychological, had their own fundamental 'waveform', so they also had a characteristic visual pattern when photographed in this unusual fashion. In 1950 these experiments were in their early days and participants at the Radionics Conference had to rest content with Mr de la Warr's assurance that one could diagnose a person's physical or psychological condition from his blood spot photographically. Within months far greater marvels were revealed, including the perhaps predictable finding that to the de la Warr camera, the boundaries of space and time presented no obstacles. For example, on one occasion the former civil engineer sat down by the camera and 'thought' about his wedding day, an event which had occurred twenty-one years previously. Plates taken from the camera (which had also been provided with samples of his own and his wife's blood) revealed when developed a wedding group, thus implying that the camera was either taking a look back into the past or, more prosaically, was taking a picture of de la Warr's contemporary mental imagery. Either explanation might just as well be adopted. The range of images which subsequently began to turn up via the camera, if not planted there deliberately by normal methods, suggested that the traditional laws of physics and even of cosmology were being violated. Merely by thinking of, for example, a penknife, a succession of images showing objects very like a penknife could be produced. A thoughtograph taken of the blood spot of a cow, sick with some unspecified complaint, revealed something claimed to be the 'reticulum of its stomach with foreign bodies present'. Veterinary surgery of the cow, which had been twenty miles away from the camera when the picture was taken, disclosed a large stone and piece of wire in the stomach, the removal of which led to the animal's immediate recovery.

Even more sensational were thoughtographs of Oxford tap water (a few streaks of light coming from a single central nucleus and spa water (which looks quite different). When the water was blessed by the broad-minded rector of St Mary Magdalen Church, Oxford, the Reverend J. C. Stephenson, the resulting thoughtograph was miraculously changed, the tiny central nucleus now being overlaid by a large, amorphous splodge. On the other hand, water blessed by the Reverend P. W. Eardley of London, but following a 'fifteen minute service according to the Sarum rite', revealed the central nucleus again overlaid, but this time by a large, very well-formed white cross. Whether the sensational difference between the results of the blessing was a function of the power of the Sarum rite or of the relative holiness of the two clergymen is not recounted, but those of a popish disposition will be interested to know that Lourdes's water contains radiation 'much attenuated with several images superimposed'.

Despite all these sensations de la Warr's work was relatively unknown outside the fairly limited world of the cultists and the so-called 'borderland sciences' for it had failed to attract the attention of the press on any great scale. All this was to change with the publication in September 1956 of Langston Day's *New Worlds Beyond the Atom*. This book was written in collaboration with George de la Warr and set out to give a kind of potted history of the latter's researches between 1942 and 1956—the years of struggle so to speak. The blurb makes it clear where Mr Day stands on the matter. 'The discoveries [of de la Warr] are a step away from the gross materialism which still fetters thought towards a new standpoint bridging the world of matter and new worlds of subtle influences', and the story inside the covers is that of a man who has stumbled on one of the most important discoveries ever made, and who is meeting only deep-rooted prejudice and arrogance from scientists for his pains. The book includes a section on de la Warr's proposals for a more or less completely new science of physics, incorporating a Fundamental Ray, and outdating with one fell swoop the laboured theories of physicists from Newton to Einstein.

While most previous publications on this general topic had been purchased and read only by ardent fans of black boxes and were, as far as the general or scientific public was concerned, merely extras on the huge pile of the world's barmy literature, *New Worlds Beyond the Atom* received an unusually favourable reception. Hard-nosed scientific journals like *Nature*, for example, to say nothing of the *Bulletin of Atomic Physics*, passed it over with the bleakest of stares, but it nevertheless received enthusiastic reviews in the most unexpected quarters.

The most influential of all these was easily that written by the well-known medical popularizer, Dr Kenneth Walker, author of a number of paperbacks with such titles as *The Physiology of Sex, The Psychology of Sex*, etc., and a key figure in the intellectual occult underground. Kenneth Walker, a florid-looking individual with an impressive flock of white hair, was involved in just about every aspect of fringe psychic activity in the 1950s, and thanks to his book *Venture with Ideas*, published in 1951, was partly responsible for reviving public interest in the curious Russian mystic, Gurdjieff, about whom we shall hear more later. In the early fifties he had even shown a fleeting interest in L. Ron Hubbard and had gone so far as to recommend, in the high circulation weekly *Picture Post*, a brief course of Scientology for those unable to get joy out of standard psycholanalytic treatment. At this time the combination of Walker's lucid prose, his more than tolerant attitude to borderline medical and psychological theories, and his undoubtedly impressive medical and scientific background, made him a highly significant figure whose pronouncements were treated with considerable respect.

On de la Warr and his boxes, the famous surgeon waxed

most eloquent. Reviewing *New Worlds Beyond the Atom* he went so far as to say: 'Either de la Warr should be put in the scientific stocks and have things thrown at him or else he should be awarded a Fellowship of the Royal Society and a knighthood without delay.'

Following this and similar reviews by one or two lesser figures, the Oxford laboratories were besieged with inquiries for information and with orders for one or other of the marvellous boxes. All over the country, in London flats, in country cottages and even, very occasionally, in doctors' surgeries, radionic practitioners set up their equipment, enthusiastically diagnosing, treating and thoughtographing.

In Oxford all systems were at go. Diagnostic instruments were of course the most popular and literally hundreds were sold at £100 a head. Most practitioners would also decide to invest in a treatment box which at £50 each ought to be counted as cheap if the claims that were made for it were even fractionally correct. For the really ambitious the kit could be completed, at a cost of a further £1,400, by the purchase of the famous camera to produce distant photographic confirmation of the original diagnosis and even the success of the treatment. A handy vest-pocket version of the basic diagnosing instrument, only inches across and with tiny dials and a miniature rubber stick pad, even appeared. Some models went overseas to help boost Britain's export drive, but any contribution they might have made to the balance of payments was severely limited by the unreasonable attitude of foreign customs authorities. In 1952, for example, the Brisbane customs prohibited import of a diagnostic instrument and 'Colourscope Major' (a diversion of the Delawarr laboratories into 'colour therapy') together valued at £280, on the grounds that the 'claims made on behalf of the instruments were fantastic and untenable'. There was even a year's delay in shipping a Colourscope to a doctor in Ghana when the apparatus was impounded by mystified customs officials at Takoradi. It was later let in thanks to the good offices of a friendly Assistant Commissioner.

Apart from the sale of instruments, the de la Warrs were also in lucrative private practice, treating everything from broken legs to worms and with an estimated income in 1956 in excess of £5,000 per annum for treatment alone. Nor were the frontiers of research neglected. Experiments were carried out in such *outré* fields as the blessing of plants (blessed plants grew up to 50 per cent more rapidly than those unblessed), the preservation of milk and attempts to detect underground water in the desert near Kuwait. In 1957 a quarterly journal *Mind and Matter* made its appearance, the list of patrons on its title page including such notables as Dr Leslie Weatherhead, leader of the Methodist Church's brief revival in the fifties, the agriculturalist Lord Noel-Buxton, the novelist Barbara Cartland and, of course, the ubiquitous Kenneth Walker.

Mind and Matter, which came out spasmodically until the early sixties, is an incredible publication, its contents seesawing from topic to topic as the fickle winds of radionic fashion changed. Printed on high quality gloss paper and with an expensive multi-coloured cover the journal lived up to the promise expressed in its opening issue to 'bring something of interest to everybody'. The same issue included an article on *Mind and Matter* by de la Warr himself, illustrated by the now famous photograph of the blessed Oxford tap water, plus photographs of monster cabbages, lettuces and broad beans which had been subjected to radionic treatment. There was even an article on 'The Mother Instinct in Plants' by Mr J. I. Rodale from Harrisburg, Pennsylvania and a couple of quotations from Sir James Jeans and Albert Einstein thrown in for good measure. Subsequent issues included features on 'Do plants like music?', 'Miniaturized radionic instruments' and on attempts to control the movements of *paramecia aurelia* at a distance. Some conception of the amazing scope of radionics can be grasped when one finds in the issue dated December 1959 an article from South Africa claiming that by suitable use of a black box the runt can be eliminated from a litter of piglets, and a few pages later a letter from one of the cast of the Windsor Repertory Theatre thanking the de la Warrs for clearing up his wife's sinus trouble in time for a critical performance. 'She sailed through last night's performance without any strain on her throat at all', the grateful husband writes, adding that 'As this is the most exacting part she has had to play in twenty-five years on the stage, it was a remarkable tribute to the swift effectiveness of your treatment.'

Not everyone was so delighted with the efficacy of the various black boxes made and marketed by the Oxford pioneers. In due course the Delawarr laboratories found themselves sued in the High Court for 'misrepresentation by Miss Catherine Phillips of Dorset Square, Regents Park, London. This sensational case, which finally got under way on 20th June 1960 in the Queen's Bench Division before Mr Justice Arthurian Davies, lasted a full thirteen working days and is of considerable historical interest. It also represents a turning point in the history of radionics.

The main complaint made by Miss Phillips was that George de la Warr was 'an exponent of and practitioner in the pseudoscience of radionics and that in 1956 he fraudulently represented that there were associated substances, distinctive waves, vibrations or radiations capable of affecting a device of the defendant called a Delawarr diagnostic instrument'. The crux of all this of course lies in the word 'fraudulently'.

In view of the inherently implausible nature of the various and partially-baked theories behind the Delawarr apparatus, the plaintiff's case must have seemed stronger than it actually turned out to be. Unfortunately Miss Phillips's counsel relied on a string of eminent, establishment-type witnesses—surgeons, pathologists, physicists, photographers, etc.—to declare the equipment ridiculous and, in principle, unworkable. For his defence counsel de la Warr had perspicaciously chosen the brilliant and slightly eccentric Mr Christmas Humphreys, a man who had adopted the Buddhist religion and who was known to be tolerant and open-minded to what are generally called psychic matters. He merely decided to go one better. He called even more 'expert' witnesses on the defendant's side, including Air Marshal Sir Victor Goddard, former head of technical services of the RAF, the Reverend Dr Leslie Weatherhead, Minister of the City Temple, and our old friend Dr Kenneth Walker. All stated, in effect, that the de la Warrs' work involved *bona fide* scientific investigation, and it was ridiculous to call it fraudulent.

In a tolerant summing up, Mr Justice Davies suggested that the effectively nonsensical interior of the box was irrelevant to the case in question as no one had claimed that they knew how it worked, but merely that it did, on occasions, work. In an important caveat, however, he stated that he was certainly not emphasizing that the box *did* work, as this was still a 'very open question'. The camera and its peculiar photographs were even more open, and the judge went so far as to state that it seemed completely bogus. However, he was satisfied, and so found, that Mr de la Warr honestly believed in the camera no less than he did in the box. For these reasons there would be judgement for the defendant.

As George de la Warr and his family left the court, friends clapped and embraced them. It was in its way a triumph for the radionics case, a pronouncement from that most crucial seat of the establishment, the Law, that this kind of work and these kind of beliefs were 'all right'. To many it must have seemed as though radionics had moved from pseudo to genuine science, the culmination of all de la Warr and his associates had worked for in the past three decades. Alas, all was not so simple. Looked at in the coldest of lights, it was clear that while the judge had little doubt as to de la Warr's honesty, he had the gravest reservations as to the operation of the various boxes and even as to whether they worked at all—a judgement hardly likely to encourage financial or technical development in the Oxford Laboratories.

Worse for the de la Warrs was the grim fact that although they had won their case they were unable, owing to a technical anomaly, to get judgement for costs which, in their case, amounted to the awesome figure of £10,000. Announcing this news in the final issue of its glossy journal *Mind and Matter*, the editor stated that the next few years would be a period of retrenchment, and though the omens read well for the future, they might take some time to mature. On the back cover is reproduced a cartoon from the *Daily Express*, showing a doctor with his stethoscope up against a rather obvious Delawarr box—a tribute to the considerable public interest the case had engendered. It was the one note of levity in a justifiably heavy-hearted number.

On 2nd April 1969 de la Warr died at work in his bedroom. He had been suffering from asthma and angina for some time. Only at his death, it seems, did his closest associates learn how little money of the considerable sums the laboratory had earned in its golden days was left. The practice, invariably, had suffered and the spacious premises of Ranelagh Park had been first heavily mortgaged and subsequently sold to meet the remorseless flow of debts since the ironically successful case. In its heyday the laboratory had employed literally dozens of helpers; in 1969 they were reduced to a handful, including Mr Corte who, at the last count, was engaged in the construction of an 'eight channel multioscillator' for sonic therapy. Mrs de la Warr, who continues her radionics practice, does not disguise her belief that her husband was a misunderstood genius, born years before his time. She is equally confident that in due course his pioneering work will receive the recognition it deserves. On the desk in her study is a large framed photograph of de la Warr, revealing him to have been a handsome and intelligent-looking man. It is the same photograph used by *The Times* in the half-column obituary they devoted to him—an amount of space some deceased cabinet ministers might have envied.

More Mental Marvels

WITH THE DEATH of George de la Warr, the most interesting and potent protagonist of radionics moved off the stage, and it seems unlikely that the topic will rise to such public prominence again. In the mid-fifties the excitable science fiction magazine, *Analog*, which had given Hubbard his first proper exposure for Dianetics, ran a series of articles on something called the 'Hieronymous machine'. This device, if one can call it that, consisted of a kind of rudimentary circuit of about equivalent vagueness of the Delawarr or Abrams boxes, with few electric components and of course with no power supply. To call it a machine might be thought to be stretching the imagination a bit far, even for the anchorless minds of SF fans, for the system, in its simplest form, involved merely drawing a circuit of some kind on a sheet of paper and using this blueprint itself as the machine! John Campbell, editor of *Analog* (or *Astounding Science Fiction* as it was then called), spoke on the wonders of the device to an enthusiastic audience at the World Science Fiction Convention in London in 1957, backing up his talk with a practical demonstration of an instrument which had been made to the Hieronymus specification by a Mr Eric Jones of Cheltenham. Commenting on the conference, and on Campbell's talk in particular, the entertaining weekly paper, *Psychic News* via its science correspondent, Dr A. H. Janser, described so-called 'psionic' and radionic instruments as 'magic modernized', adding that 'the sooner this was recognized, the better'. It was a shrewd comment. The search for modern magic continues today with as much enthusiasm as ever before.

While on the subject of mysterious gadgetry and the iconography of modern cults, it is worth saying a word or two about that complicated tool of medicine, psychology and physiology, the electro-encephalograph. Like the psycho-galvanometer, which has had a limited role in psychological laboratories for a century or so and has metamorphosed into one of the most significant features of the *mythos* of Scientology, so the EEG has acquired, subsidiary to its medical role, a minor cultish significance. This has manifested itself particularly in one of the latest off-beat quasi-religious movements to flourish in the United States of America—the so-called Feedback Cult. The evolution of the ideas inherent in the Feedback Cult are interesting and particularly relevant to the theme of this book, but before they can be fully appreciated some background to the basis of electro-encephalography must be given.

Most biological systems rely on electrical energy for the transmission of neural information—vision, audition, touch and pain sensations, etc.—and it is possible to detect the presence of minute electrical currents, measured in microvolts, in all living nerve cells. The greatest concentration of neurons being in the brain, one might expect the richest source of electrical energy to be concentrated here as indeed it is, though the discovery of cerebral electric currents on a grand scale had to await the development of suitably sensitive recording apparatus. The first successful recording of 'brain waves' is generally accredited to the Frenchman Berger and the English physiologist Adrian. These pioneers, using electrodes attached to the outside of the scalp and linked to powerful amplifying equipment, found that the central nervous system was generating a relatively massive supply of electrical energy, but also that this was broken down into a number of distinct and characteristic waveforms whose frequency and amplitude seemed to bear some kind of relation to the mental state of the individual under study. In sleep, for example, waves of erratically high amplitude and relatively low frequency appeared, whereas during concentrated mental activity the waves flattened out and disappeared altogether—almost as though rhythmic neural pulsing had ceased. Most interesting of all, Adrian found that when people were in a relaxed, passive state of mind—halfway, if you like, between active attention and sleep—a striking and dominant rhythm, occurring at between 8 and 12 Hz and of very constant amplitude, appeared. This was christened the *alpha rhythm* and was soon taken by psychologists to be an indication of the brain in a 'relaxed' state, and for decades has been one of the primary props of the technique of electro-encephalography. While it has, for various reasons, not lived up to its early promise—the pioneers had all clearly hoped that whole regimes of brain waves reliably corresponding to specific psychological states would soon be found, which they have not—the EEG has turned out to be of value in determining the foci of cerebral tumours, epileptic lesions, etc.

In psychology, as opposed to medicine, it has turned out to be something of a disappointment. The polygraph or 'lie-detector' favoured by police forces in various parts of the world incorporates an EEG, along with an EKG (heart-rate detector), a plethysmograph (blood volume measurer) and even the GSR (psychogalvanometer), which forms the basis of the Hubbard E-meter, but few people, either police or criminals, take this too seriously today. As far as the public was concerned the EEG itself might easily have remained tucked away in the scientist's toybox were it not for the discovery, made more or less simultaneously by a number of scientists in different parts of the world, that individuals could, under certain circumstances, modify their brain waves at will.

There are a number of ways in which this control can be effected. In the simplest case, the alpha rhythm (reputedly only to be found when the individual is relaxed) may be induced simply by rolling one's eyes up in a rather extreme fashion, or alternatively by a conscious act of focusing and defocusing on some distant object in the visual field. One scientist employed by the US Air Force, Dr Edmund Dewan, even trained some of his subjects to switch their alpha rhythm on and off in morse code, arguing that this might conceivably be employed in an emergency by astronauts strapped up to EEG equipment whose normal radio channels had failed.

The initial bout of investigatory scientific work on control of the EEG, which began in the early sixties, soon petered out as the limitations of the method became obvious. However the field has remained enormously attractive to the speculative scientist and much unusual material has been written about it. Typical of such work is a publication, *The alpha rhythm; its meaning and applications*, by Dr Marjorie Kawin-Toomin, writing from the Toomin Laboratories in Los Angeles. In this privately published work, Dr Toomin points out that Western man is increasingly concerned with exploring, understanding and controlling his inner world. This is leading him into paths which unite the science of the West with the mysticism of the East—a common strand in modern cults which we shall be inspecting more closely in the next chapter. Man can, the doctor claims, control all aspects of his being particularly if he is allowed to observe his brain waves while attempting to effect this control. In other words he can learn to control his conscious cerebral state at will, provided that immediate feedback of what is happening to his brainwaves is given to him. This could be done, for example, by arranging for a light to switch on whenever alpha rhythm appeared on the EEG machine, or even for displaying the EEG recordings before the subject's very eyes. In her paper Dr Toomin waxes enthusiastic on the subjective benefits of being able to induce the alpha state at will. A man from India who has practised Raja Yoga for forty years reported that when his brain was generating alpha rhythm he had 'succeeded in stilling his mind' and had achieved a 'state of knowingness', whatever that might be. The study of yogis had indicated that these enlightened individuals' brains were particularly likely to flip into alpha rhythm.

Attempting to answer the question, What can be done with alpha control?, Dr Toomin states that first and foremost it can be looked upon as a new and perhaps hitherto undiscovered sensation of pleasure. 'With feedback', she says, 'individuals are able to discriminate the kind of thoughts, feelings and attitudes which represent an easy flowing with the environment and with their inner selves (the inner synchrony of the brain).' It is possible, she adds, to learn to function at this level more often, 'thus generally making life more *comfortable*'. Comfort and pleasure aside, Dr Toomin (who manufactures and sells an interesting device called the Toomin Alpha Pacer) suggests that alpha control has an exciting future for meditation and achieving altered states of consciousness. For quickly acquiring voluntary control of such states, she points out that there is much to commend the Toomin Alpha Pacer which not only gives visual feedback of the pattern of brain waves but also introduces audio feedback, a pleasant tone rising and falling in step with the EEG. Users of the Pacer have reported a marked feeling of well-being, to say nothing of a 'sense of one-ness with the universe and great joy as they moved into higher frequencies (up to 12 Hz)'.

The wonders of feedback control, particularly when coupled with the proper us of the Toomin Pacer, could even be an aid to psychotherapy. Not only would the therapist find the patient's ability to drive his own brain waves a significant index of progress, but he might also get useful information by examining his *own* brain waves while conducting a psychotherapeutic session. The image that is conjured up here of both patient and doctor with their heads wired to Toomin Alpha Pacers against a background of rising and falling auditory bleeps is a curious one, and reminds us of the strange directions which the super-technological Californian society takes.

Aroused by the message writ so bold by Dr Toomin and others, enthusiasm for learning to control one's own brain waves has leapt to a fad of major proportions in the USA. The craze has recently advanced to an extent which would be incredible unless matched up against the other data presented in this book which reveals beyond much question that modern religious strivings can only find satisfactory expression in creeds which embrace the terminology of fringe and pop-science. A quick glance at psychic and occult magazines shows feedback devices, similar no doubt in many ways to the Toomin Alpha Pacer, being marketed at prices ranging from 50 to 1,000 dollars. In essence these are no more than immensely simplified EEG machines, sensitive only to those frequencies in the range known as 'alpha' (8–14 Hz), and fine as long as all one wants is the crudest possible index of what is going on inside one's head.

As an aid to meditation, psychic ecstasy, 'knowingness' or even plain old-fashioned relaxation, the feedback cult is reputed to have no equals. No self-respecting yogi, swami, Zen Buddhist, transcendental mystic or bogus psychologist would, during the height of the cult, feel his equippage to be anywhere near complete without a simple EEG machine. Those with a mere pair of waggling pens, recording signals from the occiput at the back of the skull, of course, come at the bottom of the league. Optional extras such as audio tones will cost more, and flashing coloured lights in tune with the cerebral rhythms yet more again. Stories even circulate of feedback orgies, with whole groups of individuals of *both sexes*, linked to each other's alpha machines, enjoying the thrill and challenge of manipulating each others brain waves.[1] In fact, the latest trend is very definitely away from solitary exploration of the phenomena into real group activities organized within the framework of formalized religious organizations—Feedback Churches, no less, with such free-floating titles as The Church of the Sacred Alpha (Los Angeles), the Holy Feedback Church (San Diego), etc. At the time of writing an embryo Feedback Church was being formed in London, its advertisements, offering spiritual comfort and enlightenment for those who would know the one true Alpha, appearing in the raffish publications of the Underground Press. In America it is possible to be ordained as a Priest of a Feedback Church and acquire as a bonus the degree of Ph.D. or D.D. (Doctor of Divinity) without whose assistance many cultists—in particular cult leaders—evidently feel themselves naked in the Conference Rooms of the World.

Since the various feedback devices employed by Feedback Cultists are perfectly describable and sensible from the point of view of electronics, if of dubious psychological merit, it is perhaps a bit unfair to call them Black Boxes as such. It is clear, however, that to most of their users they are effectively as mysterious as Abrams's reflexophone or de la Warr's thoughtographic camera and thus, for all practical purposes, may be classified under this heading. Their role would seem to be to make the achievement of yogic or meditational states more credible and acceptable by adding a pinch of science to an otherwise mystical notion. Where ideas themselves may be hard to grasp or accept, there's nothing like a working box of tricks—never mind what it does—to add a bit of extra conviction.

So far the mini-EEG machines marketed in the interests or self-revelation, etc., seem to have escaped the heavy-handed assaults of one of America's many guardians of public man-

[1] The erotic, or at least emotional, possibilities of feedback devices, incidentally, have not gone unobserved by Dr Marjorie Kawin-Toomin, who reports that subjects in her laboratory have conducted experiments in attempting to measure their depth and quality of feeling for each other. One couple found that when they looked deeply into each other's eyes the 'amplitude of their alpha activity increased substantially'.

ners and morals, the Food and Drug Administration. The FDA, it will be recalled, takes an interest in Black Boxes of all kinds and has been putting the screws remorselessly on the Scientologists for their E-meter for over a decade (without, incidentally, getting very far). Presumably it finds feedback devices to be totally harmless, even in the hands of the bemused individuals likely to be interested in purchasing them. One particular box, and its creator, were not so fortunate and after attracting the FDA's attention were well and truly sat upon. The box in question was called an Orgone Accumulator, and refusal to obey an FDA order to cease distributing it led its creator, Dr Wilhelm Reich, to imprisonment, death and something pretty close to martyrdom.

The history of Reich and his remarkable studies about the nature of the Universe are highly relevant to the theme of this book, but they deserve a more lengthy treatment than we are able to accord them here. For those who require a full and frank discussion of Reich's work and his theories, the reader is referred to Martin Gardner's interesting *Fads and Fallacies*, or alternatively to Reich's own voluminous writings, which range in scope from *The Sources of Neurotic Anxiety* (published in 1926 in honour of Freud's birthday) through his well-known *Character Analysis*, *The Mass Psychology of Fascism* and *The Function of the Orgasm* to *Deadly Orgone Removal and Cloud-Busting* (1952), which was one of his last published works. The story in brief is that Reich, who was at one time a brilliant, if somewhat unorthodox, adherent of psychoanalytic theory, felt he had discovered one of the fundamental secrets of life—the existence of orgone energy. Orgone is an energy corresponding rather loosely to the elusive *élan vital* which has intrigued philosophers and mystics for centuries; its proper regulation in the body is essential to psychological and physiological well-being. The unimpeded flow of orgone energy in the body is necessary for gratifying sexual orgasm; the source of the energy is the sun. The Orgone Energy Accumulators, which Reich's American organisation manufactured in the 1940's and 50's, were relatively simple devices which were so constructed as to accumulate orgone energy from the atmosphere, subsequently releasing it to anyone requiring additional orgone. The patients merely had to sit in the special boxes or booths for a number of short treatments. These boxes are mentioned incidentally because they were at the root of Reich's investigation and, some say, persecution by the FDA, which in 1954 pronounced that there was no such energy as orgone and that the accumulators were worthless as therapeutic aids. Reich vigorously defended himself against the FDA in court, but was given a two-year prison sentence and fined $10,000. The Court, in an intolerant mood, also ordered his books to be destroyed and Reich died in the Federal Penitentiary in Lewisburg, Pennsylvania, on November 3, 1957. His tragic death lifted him briefly into the role of martyr, and American liberals, a distinct minority group at the time, rose to his defence, with prominent intellectuals, such as Norman Mailer, undergoing Reichian therapy as an experiment. In 1960 the United States boasted about a dozen qualified medical psychiatrists who practised Reichian therapy, but the movement inevitably suffered in the absence of the founder's dynamic and crusading personality. At the present time there is a distinct upsurge of interest in his ideas, and a curious and insightful East European movie, *WR, the Mysteries of the Organism*, which has achieved international release, has brought his unusual ideas to a new and wider public than they ever achieved in his lifetime.

This must complete our review of the mysterious and wonderful cultish devices which have sprung from the minds of some of the world's most *outré* and scatterbrained inventors. Before dismissing their efforts too lightly we should pause to recall that in all probability 95 per cent of inventions, and particularly those with a really original twist, seem *outré* at the outset—to all except their inventors. The creator of anything is a lonely individual who has only the fire of his own belief, and perhaps the psychological support of family and close friends, to warm him. If all inventors paused on the threshold of their work to pay attention to the sceptic, then the world would be a poorer place indeed. More to the point, the fascination that human beings show for hidden mysteries of the Black Box variety, whether at the creator or user level, clearly reflects the vital curiosity drive in man that makes him on the one hand twiddle knobs on the outside of an empty box and, on the other, train a radio telescope on the bleakest depths of outer space.

PART IV: THE MYSTIC EAST (OR THEREABOUTS)

Many Masters

THE CONCEPTUAL DIVISION of the world into two great slabs of humanity—East and West—has dominated the average individual's sociological outlook for centuries, and it shows little sign at present of being replaced by any more sophisticated notion. The idea seems to be particularly powerful within the context of religious belief, and there does seem to be a curious attraction to the notion that a spiritual frontier, drawn by God, passes somewhere down the middle of the Arabian desert. To the west of this line can be found those worshipping according to Christian or Christian-dominated ideas, while to the east, gazing inscrutably at various idols, are the followers of Buddha and Confucius. This frontier has frequently been battled over in mankind's history, as with the Christian Crusades against Islam, and even after literally centuries of intercommunication, some peaceful, some warlike, the Eastern and Western systems have shown little tendency to blur into one another. One might be inclined to mutter 'East is East and West is West' at this stage and leave it at that, were it not for the fact that recent years have seen an upsurge of interest in the theology of the Mystic East, mounting to fad proportions, in the affluent countries of Europe and America. Never has yoga been so popular, never the laws of Karma so earnestly taken into account; never has Indian and Chinese food been so acceptable to Western palates, nor the burning of incense (whether to disguise the pong of marijuana or not) so common in front rooms; never have saris, saffron monkish robes, shaven heads and ornate Eastern jewellery been so eagerly worn nor such words as vedanta, prana, mantra, Zen or Sutra so reverently incorporated into everyday speech. Since visitors to India, Japan and other parts East of Suez fail to report any corresponding upswing there in Christian or Judaic ideas, the exchange is apparently not reciprocal. No doubt the one-sided flow of ideas is due to the greater affluence of the West, greater opportunities for travel and the more effective communications media and, possibly, the relatively rapid collapse of Western orthodox religious beliefs. People today seem to be pillaging the East for spiritual support and iconography in the way that the conquering British collected material and artistic wealth from the Orient two centuries ago.

The basic attraction of religions with an Eastern ring can be explained on the basis of two principles: (1) that the strong 'mystical' current running through most Eastern religions with their implicit suggestion of heightened mental and physical powers strikes a fresh and welcome note with Western man; and (2) the logic, philosophy and terminology of Buddhism, Hinduism, Islam, etc., when translated into 'pop-European' language, are so vague and amorphous as to allow the average individual to read into them more or less whatever he likes. All the cults and other varieties of religious belief we cover in this book will be found to offer practical benefits to the adherent, either by promising enhanced mental or physical capabilities, the promise of eternal life or a significantly transformed state of existence or, at the very least, the privilege of being a member of some spiritually elite or informed group far beyond the common herd—as with the members of the Aetherius Society, constantly engaged in 'spiritual pushes' to save earth from marauding space fiends. It is lamentably obvious that for an enormous number of ordinary human beings, dissatisfied with life, with society or simply out of tune with the world as it is, the fruits offered above are much in demand.

One of the best known and westernized of all the major religious systems of the East is the practice of yoga—the very ancient Hindu system of mental and physical self-discipline which is first described in detail in the sacred text, the Bhagavad-Gita. An interesting feature common to most Eastern religions is their acceptance of the doctrine of reincarnation—the endless recycling of lives as the individual's spirit moves from body to body throughout eternity, subject to the remorseless Law of Karma. One says endless, but in fact it is possible to break out of the karmic circle by elevating oneself from the pigsty of life (as Hindu literature neatly describes terrestrial existence) and achieving true spiritual awareness. This awareness is best achieved by the multi-level discipline of yoga which necessitates performing certain psychic exercises coupled with complicated physical postures, some of which are rather peculiar.

There is little doubt that yogic practices, when taken to the level achieved by the Swamis or 'Masters', give evidence of quite remarkable control of bodily and, to a lesser extent, mental faculties. Postures may be held for literally hours on end, the individual may reduce his respiration to the minimum required for the maintenance of life, and even some degree of cardiac control may be demonstrated. At the 'mental' level evidence of especially abnormal powers is far less clear. Some conscious control of the electro-encephalogram or brain waves by yogis has been reported in scientific literature, but as we implied in the previous chapter this is not necessarily as marvellous as most people seem to think. On the other hand no serious evidence of telepathic powers—frequently claimed by disciples of yoga—has been reported from any psychological laboratories. Likewise claims that through yogic meditation one can gain great insights into the nature of the Universe and the mystery of life, etc., while very interesting no doubt for the yogis, have the regrettably subjective ring common to all revelatory tales. To the complaint that people who have great insights never seem to be able to pass them on to less favoured mortals, mystics traditionally reply that the only way to achieve the insight is to become involved in the system—advice which would be easy to follow if theirs was the only system on offer.

The lure of yoga remains, however, and is fostered by the fairly common type of tales of people who meet 136-year-old swamis in the foothills of the Himalayas. In the understandable absence of a birth certificate, most people are inclined to accept the swami's word for his great age, though it is probably just worth commenting at this point that Indians—in particular those fed on a diet of berries and asceticism—tend to age rather rapidly and your average sixty-year-old can easily pass for a sprightly centenarian if he chooses. Claims for significantly retarding the natural process of ageing are of course of immense interest to millions of individuals in affluent Western societies and these, coupled with the added yogic bonus of achieving mental relaxation, are no doubt behind the current boom in the practice of yoga in the USA. How many extra centenarians it will generate is very uncertain, but at its very worst the cult might do something to ease the minds and flatten the stomachs of millions of middle-class American women.

Yoga as practised in the West is more a bowdlerized version of an ancient religious ritual than a cult in its own right and has already been described in detail in hundreds of books of varying merit. Its present bias toward improving physique, rather than the psyche, would have been severely frowned upon by its original teachers who strongly disapproved of cultivating the body for its own sake. Nevertheless the idea, common to many Eastern religions, that perfect control of the body, its movements and functions, is a primary step in the direction of spiritual self-enlightenment is one which has attracted the interest of numerous occult and psychic teachers. Many of these seem to have made a conscious effort at forging a spiritual bridge between East and West, incorporating the best of the mystic East and grafting it on to the bleak remnants of Western religious philosophy. One of the first to don this particular mantle was the enigmatic, occasionally tedious but almost always amusing figure of George Ivanovich Gurdjieff, a fiercely moustached Russian-Greek who trod this earth between 1877 and 1949 in a quest for enlightenment which ended up leaving the human race, if anything, rather more confused than it had been prior to his arrival. Gurdjieff is still a major cult figure today, and we shall therefore spend a little time considering him and his contribution to the sum total of human knowledge and understanding.

The date of Gurdjieff's birth, of an Armenian mother and a Greek father in the Russian city of Alexandropol, is not really too certain for, as with most other matters of fact, Gurdjieff was a notorious romancer not to say downright liar. In the latter years of his life in particular he was particularly given to exaggerating his age, claiming he was ninety, for example, when his age was in fact closer to seventy. Other details of his early life are, like L. Ron Hubbard's, shrouded in obscurantism and questionable fantasy. He claims to have made extensive travels to practically every part of the world including, of course, that grand old standby of the professional occultist—Tibet. Some close acquaintances of Gurdjieff's were sometimes of the opinion that he had not ventured much into the Middle, let alone the Far East, and that such claims were to be taken as 'allegorical' or 'symbolic'. While on these rambles, phantom or otherwise, Gurdjieff is alleged either to have stumbled upon, or been handed on a plate, certain key insights into—need we say it?—the secret of the Universe. As the results of years of conversation with divers holy men (all centenarians no doubt) concerning the nature of this information, Gurdjieff decided to pass on his findings, suitably packaged, to the rest of humanity, and returned to Russia. Here in the city of Petrograd, seething at that time in the agonies of the First World War, he met Ouspensky, a teacher and mathematician of sorts, who had written books with such far-flung titles as *Superman, The Fourth Dimension* and *The Symbolism of the Tarot*. Gurdjieff's accounts of his trips to Tibet, etc., and of his companion adventurers, who called themselves The Seekers of Truth, struck a deep, solemn note in the mathematician's mystical soul, and before long the two men were holding forth on occult matters in general to the large population of floating intellectuals living in Petrograd at the time. As it happens, they picked rather an unfortunate time to spread the good news, for the average Russian in that dramatic decade was more concerned with such worldly matters as the disposal of a tyrannical monarchy than with Gurdjieff's mystical truths. Sensing this wind of change, Gurdjieff and Ouspensky moved away from the strife-ridden city in 1917 and took up residence in the Black Sea resort of Tuapse, where a small band of followers gathered around them. The Soviet revolution proceeding regardless, the two men finally gave Russia up as a bad job and departed independently for Istanbul. From here Ouspensky, thanks to an invitation from the right-wing proprietor of the *Daily Mail,* Lord Rothermere, moved on to London where he set up in the mystical lecture business on his own. Gurdjieff, after numerous adventures of doubtful authenticity, settled in France, forming an exclusive colony of disciples and general hangers-on at Fontainebleau near Paris. This was to be the parting of their ways in more than one respect, for despite the relative proximity of London and Paris, the two men were destined never to meet again and were soon to make it clear that a spiritual as well as a geographical gap had opened up between them.

Ouspensky, whom photographs reveal to be a chubby schoolmasterish figure, set up his court at 38 Warwick Gardens, where he gave a regular series of lectures to elderly audiences of mixed intellectual and creative calibre. These seem to have been largely made up of those floating, poorly-oriented intellectual souls that swell the occult underground in the capital cities of the west. Others, at least a substantial minority, were men and women of real creativity and talent—Aldous Huxley and Gerald Heard, for example, were frequent, if silent, visitors—curious and inquisitive about every branch of philosophy's proliferous tree.

The lectures, which Ouspensky delivered in a heavy, almost incomprehensible Russian accent, were by all accounts tough going and, if the versions that have subsequently appeared in print are anything to go on, reveal a notable lack of understanding of the simplest principles of human physiology and psychology. We will not attempt to summarize these here but the super-curious are invited to pit their wits against his two key books, *A New Model of the Universe* and *The Fourth Way*. These ponderous tomes, which have been treated with solemn reverence in occult and mystical circles, must be counted as amongst the most obscure and humourless works ever penned by man, and we will leave them with the comment that if they contain—as some of his followers believe—great insights into the mysteries of life, then the universe is a far, far duller place than most people believe it to be.

Life at Gurdjieff's bizarre establishment in Fontainebleau, by contrast, was anything but dull. Somehow the penniless Russian *émigré* had acquired the lease of a vast and elegant former priory set in rambling grounds. The dilapidated state of the property itself and the overgrown, brambly gardens posed no problem for, immediately the Community was established in 1922, members were set to work putting it into shape. Gurdjieff called it the Institute for the Harmonious Development of Man, and as one of his principal ideas was that humanity had become unbearably complacent and could only advance spiritually by having this smugness shattered, the numerous menial and back-breaking tasks around and about the estate were used as the essential first step in the 'de-smugging' programme. With the innate pleasure which Russians show in organizing large flocks of people to participate in manual labour, Gurdjieff soon had every visitor to the Priory, from the most wealthy, scatterbrained and bejewelled American widow to the most ardent and poverty-stricken poet with holes in his socks, working away like beavers washing dishes, scrubbing floors, painting walls and chopping wood. Gurdjieff himself, wearing a fez to denote his Turkish associations and chain-smoking black cigarettes, would circulate amongst the throng, encouraging, cursing or praising apparently at random. To those particularly in favour, he would distribute sweets from a paper bag.

A number of accounts have been handed down to us of the goings-on at this odd establishment, some very evocative since many of its members were people of considerable literary talent. Some stayed but briefly, brushing the presence of Gurdjieff from their minds with relative ease; the majority lingered and, apparently, even to this day find the man's extraordinary personality and opaque philosophy impossible to discard.

One of the best first-hand accounts of life at the priory comes from the pen of the remarkable writer, philosopher and mathematician, J. G. Bennett, whose autobiography *Witness* is commended as the story of a brilliant scientist's quest for a non-materialistic meaning for life. It also gives one a fascinating insight into the strange world of George Ivanovich Gurdjieff, and the numerous satellites of varying luminance that he gathered around him.

Bennett first met 'G' (as he was later to become known to his many adherents) in Istanbul in early 1920 and, while by no means an impressionable man, was immediately riveted by the other's extraordinary presence and persona. Like many others similarly smitten, Bennett made many attempts later to decide just what it was about the Russian that created such an overwhelming impression. Was it the long black moustaches, curled fiercely upward or the vast, dome-like shaven head? Perhaps it was the short, squat, gorilla-like figure? Or the one eye strikingly, but indescribably different from the other? Bennett cannot say. Most likely it was a combination of Gurdjieff's weird physical presence plus the special talent he displayed of uttering just about every remark he made, however commonplace, as though it was pregnant with great meaning and significance. Not an easy trick, and many politicians would give their back teeth to be in possession of its secret, but there are those who never have to learn it, and Gurdjieff was one of those fortunates.

It led of course to some peculiar experiences. People spending an evening in conversation with the mystic—particularly when caught up in the fairly hefty drinking bouts that he insisted in inflicting on his guests—would often leave feeling that they had been imparted with information of incomparable significance and magnitude. On attempting to relate the great news to friends the next day, or even trying to write it down, its significance and meaning would seem to have skittered away somewhere. Rather than believe that they had simply been caught up in a master psychological confidence trick, most fans of Gurdjieff's take the line that he subtly conveyed information of tremendous value in allegorical rather than factual form. Nobody could say *exactly* what had been said, but all agreed nevertheless that it was absolutely stunning.

Much the same impression is conveyed by his books—only two of any length have been published. The first of these, a long and undisciplined work with the characteristic title *All and Everything* and subtitled 'Beelzebub's Tales to his Grandson', makes infuriating reading. It is pure allegory, but the principal message seems to be that Man may believe himself to have free will, selfconsciousness and an immortal soul, but that these are not his as an innate right. The telling of this simple piece of philosophy takes up over a thousand pages of closely printed text, and if there is any deeper message hidden in the book than that, then no Gurdjieff disciple has ever been able to point it out to other mortals. It is possible, however, to get some idea of what he was apparently trying to say.

Gurdjieff, like so many other philosophers interested in the cosmological nature of the psyche, held that Man was capable of very marked evolution from his present state. Showing the occultist's traditional preoccupation with the magical number seven, he held that Man existed on one of seven evolutionary levels, and that his total psychological make-up could be divided into seven distinct centres. On the evolutionary ladder, the very lowest rung was labelled The Instinctive Motor Man. This did not mean simply someone who could drive a car particularly well, but rather a blind, instinctive creature tossed about through life at the whim of his animal desires and needs. Most people on earth, Gurdjieff let it be known, were Instinctive Motor Men and, what was worse, most of them seemed to like it that way. By suitable effort and self-awareness, or possibly a fortunate hereditary pattern, one might find oneself on Rung Two as The Emotional Man. This entity, while still a prey to animal desires, etc., was at least aware of these as motivating forces, and could manipulate them to some extent. At Rung Three was to be found Intellectual Man, a level at which reason, intellect, logic and pretty well all philosophical and scientific thought were the dominating force. Such individuals, though they might be enormously pleased with themselves and fancied they knew just about everything worth knowing, were in reality living in a fool's paradise and were scarcely more evolved than specimens of the doltish Motor Man. Gurdjieff himself thought least well of Intellectual Man and when faced with any kind of scientifically based argument would counter with 'Newton, he wrong', 'Mathematik, she is useless' or some equally plonking statement. Whether it was the bold conviction of his statements, the heavy Russian accent, or the menacing black moustaches and wrestler's shoulders that so effectively quashed further argument is hard to say, but many a world-renowned scientist and philosopher seems to have met his match most unexpectedly at the Château.

At Rung Four on the ladder (the first three rungs, in Gurdjieff's simple diagram, are effectively on the same level) we find Transitional Man. In simple terms this is man who, although not significantly changed from the rest of the herd, is at least conscious that he *wants* to change. This is the critical point in the whole Gurdjieffian philosophy. Man in his present form is asleep, unaware of his unproductive, meaningless state and untroubled by it. His self-consciousness and belief in his own personal identity is the biggest illusion of all. Descartes's dictum 'I think, therefore I am', could not be more wrong, for the notion of personal identity is the biggest mistake, the most seductive fantasy of all. Only by becoming aware of the illusory nature of self could one hope to move on up the ladder—whose first significant step was number four, Transitional Man. The remaining three rungs, which were theoretically open to all, were Integrated Man, when he acquires for the first time some *real* identity, Conscious Man, when he begins to acquire super-powers of a mental and physical kind, and finally Complete Man, where the individual has acquired 'everything that it is possible to' and is 'immortal within the limits of the solar system'.

And how could ordinary Intellectual, Emotional or even Instinctive Motor Man hope to ascend the golden ladder—so reminiscent, incidentally, of the ladder of progress in Scientology rising via Clear to Operating Thetan? Well, spending as much time as possible at the Institute for the Harmonious Development of Man and helping to finance it by handing Gurdjieff large numbers of francs was clearly one way. Another was the reading of Gurdjieff's works, of which *All and Everything* was the key one. Unlike the turgid and massively self-important works of Ouspensky, *All and Everything* does have the one, prime saving grace of humour. From page after page, the author's gross and rather bovine wit twinkles forth and, occasionally, there is more than the suggestion that he is enjoying an enormous joke—mainly at the reader's expense. This same touch of the charade, the hint of vast, if heavy-handed practical jokery, floats up from the accounts we have of life at the Château in Fontainebleau.

J. G. Bennett recalls that on his first visit a very large number of disciples were engaged in the conversion of a disused aircraft hangar within the grounds of the Château into a special hall for the practice of the peculiar dances or 'Exercises' which Gurdjieff liked his followers to indulge in. These took the form of a large group of people, up to fifty or even a hundred in total, performing in unison a series of body movements, lying somewhere between ballet and physical jerks. They had been dreamt up by Gurdjieff according to some oriental tradition, allegedly uncovered on his rambles to the East. Mostly they were fairly simple and straightforward, merely consisting of routine ballet practice movements—Gurdjieff liked to make it known that he had once managed a ballet troupe in Moscow. On occasions, however, they could get very complicated, and sometimes downright impossible, the members of the group desperately tying themselves into knots which would have dismayed professional contortionists. Now and again their eccentric ballet master would require that they held such extreme positions for many minutes on end, and it was not uncommon for individual members to collapse from exhaustion. Another favourite trick of Gurdjieff's was to command the whole troupe to rush full pelt from one side of the hangar to the other. In the middle of the rush he would cry out 'Stop', whereupon all would strive to hold precisely the position they were in at the command. Most, of course, merely toppled head over heels on the floor, gallantly coming to rest nevertheless still in running or leaping posture so the huge hall looked as though it was littered with the works of a lunatic sculptor. Gurdjieff, who supervised all this in a comfortable black leotard and furry hat, maintained that it was good not only for the physique, but also for the soul, and presumably the participants in the farce thought so too.

The exercises were supplemented by an assortment of weird tasks which Gurdjieff would occasionally demand unexpectedly of individuals. This might consist of learning by heart long lists of Tibetan words, or perhaps grubbing the roots of a giant tree with a tiny hand trowel. Occasionally his demands on the particularly credulous members of his group seem to suggest a streak of cruelty or contempt somewhat at odds with his interest in the harmonious development of Man. On one occasion J. G. Bennett recalls, Gurdjieff actually induced one particularly gullible woman to eat mustard with her ice cream, afterwards holding her up to ridicule before the group. It was not for nothing that over the door of his study the Russian had had emblazoned the aphorism, 'It is useless to pass through these doors unless you have well-developed critical faculties'. Admirers of Gurdjieff today like to maintain that his outrageous behaviour, his bullying, teasing and his extraordinary commands were all a test of the critical faculties of his disciples. This may be, but if so he was capable of taking things a bit far. There was, for example, more than one suicide at the Château, and other deaths too. The talented New Zealand writer Katherine Mansfield, a friend of D. H. Lawrence, became fascinated with Gurdjieff and joined him at Fontainebleau in 1923. Although ill with tuberculosis she was urged by Gurdjieff, who fancied himself as a medical and psychological expert, to ignore the disease and sleep in the loft above the cowshed. She did so and J. G. Bennett recalls that at the time of his arrival at the Château, the whole colony was agog with the wonderful cure that this treatment had effected in her. A week later she was dead, at the age of thirty-five. This setback failed to shatter Gurdjieff's image of himself as a wizard Mr Cureall, and until the end of his life he would solemnly prescribe herbal mixes and strange diets, hand round potent pain-killing drugs to all and sundry, and deliver lectures on the evils of penicillin, etc. A food faddist when the mood took him, the Institute's head provided a drab and generally inadequate diet for its toiling hordes. Survivors recall with particular vividness a horrible coffee—Gurdjieff's own invention—made from crushed acorns. Once a week, however, the menu would be enlivened with a vengeance and a feast would be held in the evening to which all were obliged to attend. At these sessions Gurdjieff, who was a great tippler, would call a long series of toasts to various kinds of 'Idiot', in which all, whether teetotallers or not, were obliged to participate. It was a great evening for those who liked alcohol, and a nightmare for those who didn't. The Russian's many biographers, great and small, have made numerous attempts at explaining the significance of the 'idiots' toast', and most have come to the conclusion that the not particularly ambiguous word had some symbolic significance. No one, it seems, has ever seriously contemplated the possibility that the idiots in question were those seated at the table, though one suspects that Gurdjieff, with fez awry and flushed, beaming face, had a pretty good idea of whom he was thinking as he raised his glass on high.

Another favourite diversion for the menagerie were long motor drives into the country. Gurdjieff loved the paraphernalia of the picnic and hours were spent loading up motor cars with hampers bulging with champagne, vodka, and caviar and dozens of enormous melons. At the appointed hour, or something approximating to it, a convoy of vehicles would set off for Vichy or wherever, Gurdjieff occupying the back seat of a huge open landau and smoking cigarettes through a long black holder. It must have been a weird sight. Occasionally, as the motorcade thundered through some decrepit village, Gurdjieff would order a halt, whereupon the group would decamp at a café for refreshment. Here numerous toasts would be proclaimed and Gurdjieff, whose pockets were always stuffed with thousand-franc notes (other people's of course), would amaze the local peasantry by buying drinks all round and playing a small, single-handed accordion. For most of these occasions a Russian chauffeur drove the Master's car, but Gurdjieff would occasionally be moved to take the wheel. This would strike terror into the heart of the company for he was an appalling driver, drunk or sober, and had had numerous spectacular car crashes from which he made miraculous escapes, though rendered black and blue for months afterwards. His death in 1949 seems to have been hastened by one such picnic crash.

The spell that this extraordinary individual seems to have held over people is really hard to fathom. His strongest adherents, there is no doubt, are those who met him personally, for there seems to have been an aura or presence about him which it is impossible to comprehend in the language of science and psychology. Most of the cult figures referred to in this book had this magnetism, and they seem to have shared it with less savoury figures, such as Hitler and Mussolini, who in their lives wielded immense personal power. Whatever this factor is, George Ivanovich Gurdjieff had it a-plenty, and when the day comes when some psychologist manages to identify it and tie it down, we shall all know a lot more about human nature than we do today.

Interest in Gurdjieff's ideas, and to a lesser extent in Ouspensky's, survives today in England and the USA. A Gurdjieff Foundation exists at 123 East 63rd Street, New York and there are also centres in Los Angeles and San Francisco. Much of the postwar revival of interest is due to books by some of his highly literate admirers, including Bennett, the surgeon Kenneth Walker (whom we met as supporter of de la Warr's Black Box) and the prolific Colin Wilson, whose books *The Outsider* and *Religion and the Rebel* heralded the resurgence of interest in mysticism on the part of the young. Nevertheless it is impossible not to feel that both the man and his philosophy, which he described as Esoteric Christianity, are rooted deeply in the politically unsettled years between World Wars I and II, when men whose faith in life and any purpose in it had been shattered by the 1914–18 holocaust. For them Gurdjieff had a message, perhaps a real one, that

Man's current state was indeed nonsensical and meaningless, but that he had within him the power for change.

Gurdjieff survived the war and the occupation of Paris somehow or other. The establishment at Fontainebleau had vanished and as he had never acquired a profession of any kind he might well have found it hard to keep body and soul together. Fortunately his verbal power stood him in good stead and he was able to borrow very considerable sums of money on the pretext that he was the heir to the Woolworth fortune. No one was more surprised than his creditors when, at the end of the war, former wealthy admirers flocked to Paris and settled his outstanding debts. Before long he was planning a trip to the States but an unfortunate incident with the French police, which had led him to a short spell in jail for currency offences, stood temporarily in his way. Suddenly he began to get old. The black moustaches turned snowy white and droopy and the powerful figure became hunched and tired A serious car smash in 1948 nearly finished him off and he became dropsical and suffering considerable pain died in the American Hospital on 29th October 1949. For a mystic he had always had a very high opinion of the technical achievement of the USA, and amongst his last words, as he gazed at the sophisticated equipment around him, were 'Bravo America'.

Divers Holy Monks

GURDJIEFF'S MIDDLE EASTERN associations, and his doubtful wanderings in Tibet and other mystic parts of the world, place him as an emissary of the Orient without much doubt. Furthermore, it is clear that the band of followers who helped sponsor his strange establishment at Fontainebleau, and those who continue to pay him tribute today, a quarter of a century after his death, see him as having offered some important slice of the Wisdom of the East to Western man. He was not the first of his kind, of course, but he was certainly one of the more successful. In the latter part of the nineteenth century two remarkable women, Mrs Annie Besant and the American, Madame Helena Blavatsky, decided that the continent of India would see the rebirth of religion as a dominant force in the life of Man, and set up the headquarters of their new movement, the Theosophical Society, in Madras. Madame Blavatsky, the queerest of the two on the whole, claimed that she had been inspired by Hidden Masters and Secret Brothers, etc., in the Himalayas and bolstered her claims with impressive demonstrations of psychic phenomena which included clairvoyant messages and the ringing of astral bells.

Theosophy—it literally means knowledge of God—was created by Westerners, largely for Westerners, but drew most strongly from the Vedic, Buddhist and Brahmanist literature. Although its founders made every effort to grant it Eastern authenticity—for example by living in India and siting its headquarters there—it has never been looked upon with much enthusiasm by genuine Orientals. It preaches a doctrine not significantly at odds with most other 'osophies' and 'ologies' of times both ancient and modern—that Man is capable of intuitive insight into the nature of God. The road to achieving this knowledge, incidentally, is through the theory and practice of yoga. Its aims were threefold: (1) to form a Universal Brotherhood of man with no racial barriers; (2) to further the study of comparative religion; and (3) to investigate the supposedly paranormal faculties of man such as telepathy and clairvoyance, which were believed in with great intensity in the nineteenth century.

In its early days, thanks partly to the magnetic and well-publicized figure of Madame Blavatsky, it attracted a good deal of attention from the intellectual middle and upper classes and drew into its ranks, if only briefly, a number of individuals of real creative ability such as the scientist and philosopher, Rudolf Steiner. The trouble with the Theosophical Society was that it was run by two very self-willed women and it nearly foundered in its early years in legal actions and wrangles over its leadership. These became particularly accute on the death of Madame Blavatsky in 1891, though Mrs Besant finally emerged triumphant. Just a year after she had been elected president she launched the Society on an unexpected course which caused a gigantic rift in the movement, from which it has never really recovered. This was the strange episode concerning the elevation of a young Brahmin child, Jiddu Krishnamurti, into the role of a new Messiah—a dramatic gesture which implied that Christ had returned to earth, but clothed in the body of an Indian child.

So enraged were Society members that Mrs Besant had dared to discover Christ's successor without their permission, that the movement broke apart. Amongst the most notable defectors was the interesting figure of Rudolf Steiner who departed for Europe and in 1912 set up his own occult movement, Anthroposophy. Steiner, who was enormously influenced by the writings of Goethe, caused a vast building of bizarre but powerful architectural merit, the Goethanum, to be erected in Switzerland and this is still the headquarters of his movement's activities. Anthroposophy has gradually emerged as the more significant philosophy of the two, and has attracted to its embraces a number of artists and poets of magnitude, including the stylish modern painter, Kandinsky. Though operating on vague and scatty ideas about the healing qualities of coloured rays of light, followers of Steiner have had notable successes in schools devoted to the care of backward or handicapped children. How much of this success is due to the 'colour therapy' and how much to the care and devotion with which the children are taught is a matter for argument, but it is enough to say that the results are beneficial and that is that.

But to return to the Theosophical Society, or the rump of it. Here the pathetic drama of Krishnamurti was acted out with great seriousness. Despite the protestations of the boy's father, who considered the deification of his son to be literally sacrilegious, and the mutterings of the press and orthodox religious bodies, Mrs Besant paraded the bewildered boy around the world, proclaiming him as the long-awaited second Messiah. What Krishnamurti thought of all this is really beyond speculation. It is doubtful if he believed in his supposedly divine origins for a moment, and where it was necessary for him to act as if he did, he probably played along to avoid hurting the feelings of Mrs Besant whom he recognized to be a kindly soul beneath her eccentric exterior. After twenty-nine years of growing frustation and embarrassment, however, Krishnamurti could take no more and in 1929, before a large audience in the USA, rocked the remnant of the Theosophical movement by renouncing his heavenly crown and declaring himself to be nothing more than a plain mortal. Annie Besant took the news badly, but soldiered on for a bit, dying in 1933 at the age of ninety-five, serene in the certainty of her own reincarnation. As for Krishnamurti, he was soon to find out that being a retired God is not the happiest, nor the most lucrative of existences, and in recent years he has roamed the world extensively, lecturing on mystical and occult topics.

One of the most recent invaders of the West to attract the public eye, and perhaps in world terms the most famous yet, is, of course, the Maharishi Yogi. This holy chap, who has shown himself to be amazingly at ease in the world of jumbo jets, television cameras and spun protein steaks, is considered to be of little consequence amongst connoisseurs of the occult, being largely a creation of those immensely potent figures, the Beatles. His fleeting rise to prominence, however, is a good indicator of the high esteem in which all yogis and Eastern Masters are held at this time. A more weighty and lasting incursion is that of the cult known as Subud, which we shall look at in rather more detail.

The man principally responsible for the introduction of Subud to England and America was the mathematician and author, J. G. Bennett, whom we have met already in his role as one of Gurdjieff's disciples. Bennett, whose life story is a tapestry of adventure, scientific discovery, philosophical speculation and a relentless search for spiritual enlightenment, makes no bones about his admiration for the complicated Russian, and since the latter's death had anxiously sought a worthy successor. In his various travels round the world he found himself continually bumping up against rumours that a major spiritual figure, of oriental origin, would shortly arise and make a stunning impact on the religious life of both East and West. Gurdjieff himself, when near the end of his life, had solemnly declared to Bennett, 'After I go another will come. You will not be left alone.' Bennett, who took the cheerfully open-minded view that one should never turn an interesting prophecy down flat, stored the information in his mind. A year later he heard for the first time of the Indonesian monk known as Pak Subuh, who was rumoured to be heading a big religious upsurge in the Far East and reputed to be exercising miraculous powers.

His first feelings, he recalls, were only of vague interest, suspecting that the new movement, Subud, was but another tiny diversionary scene in the world's immense religious cavalcade. Soon however he found himself being pressed by friends and acquaintances to look into it further. He also heard of the so-called *latihan*, a unique mystical experience, which was supposed to overtake followers of Subuh and adherents to his way of life. After conversations with friends who had undergone the latihan and been considerably impressed with the apparent change in their lives and personalities which had taken place, Bennett decided to investigate it for himself.

The idea of the latihan is similiar in principle to many other forms of spiritual or psychic conversion in as much as it relies on the individual making himself receptive to the metaphysical or divine forces of the Universe. Public conversions and testimonies of the kind popular with the fundamental sects are prosaic examples of this, while the phrase most commonly and aptly employed to sum the experience up is probably 'seeing the light'. The latihan, which must be undergone in the presence of and under the supervision of an adept (personally trained by Pak Subuh himself), begins prosaically enough with a period of silent meditation. In due course—minutes, hours or even days and weeks may elapse—the individual becomes conscious of a significant change in his personality which may involve an overwhelming feeling of calm and a great sense of insight or 'knowingness' as such things are frequently termed in the occult world. As with parallel occurrences in other areas of mysticism, the rosy glow of the happening (or 'opening' as it is referred to within Subud) lingers only briefly, and needs to be reinforced at intervals by other latihans. On occasions, as with a bad LSD trip, the individual may find the psychic blast of the latihan simply unmanageable, and adherents of Subud have a rich fund of stories of the screams and howls of the spiritually switched on. Bennett himself had a rib cracked by one energetic character who rampaged around the Subud headquarters like King Kong, smashing down doors and needing several men to cool him down. Fortunately such displays were the exception rather than the rule, and Bennett's own first latihan was a relatively gentlemanly occurrence merely providing him with a period of 'almost unbroken consciousness, free from all mental activity and yet intensely alive and blissful'.

It was largely on the basis of this experience, and reports of the impact that Pak Subuh was making in the Far East, that the mathematician made a momentous decision. This was to put aside the writing of his four-volume epic of cosmology, *The Dramatic Universe* (a work so abstruse and obscure that a reviewer of Volume I in the scientific journal, *Nature*, dubbed it as a horrible warning to scientists to keep away from fantastic speculations) and concentrate on studying and promoting the new religion. Bearing in mind the veiled references to a great successor that Gurdjieff had been making throughout his life, Bennett was convinced that Pak Subuh was the new Messiah. In March 1957, by his personal invitation, the Indonesian monk arrived in England and set up court at Coombe Springs, Bennett's big house near Kingston, Surrey. It was the first step in a sequence of events culminating in a gale of drama and sensation which were to flash Subud and its followers into the world's newspaper headlines.

The new Messiah, when he turned up, looked like a perfectly ordinary Indonesian monk, slight, bespectacled and gently-spoken. The evident contrast with Gurdjieff's dominant physical presence and personality nevertheless impressed Bennett. The monk's biographical details had the traditional vagueness of most Messiahs: born a sickly child in 1901 his name was changed on the advice of a passing beggar (such are the ways of the mysterious East) to Mohammed Subuh, whereupon his health miraculously improved.

So important and significant a figure amongst the numerous inquirers and devotees of the borderlands of science and religion was J. G. Bennett that the news of Pak Subuh's arrival spread rapidly across the world. Although he did everything to avoid the evolution of the kind of wild rumours which characteristically accompany major occult figures wherever they go, the psychic tom-toms were soon beating out a message of miracle cures and spiritual revelations taking place at the Kingston mansion. All might have been well had the rumours been confined to the rather private world of psychic enthusiasts, but Fleet Street quickly began to prick up its sensitive ears. The climax began when the beautiful actress Eva Bartok, whose tempestuous movie career had been spiked with scandal and personal tragedy, moved in on the Subud *ménage*.

For some time Miss Bartok, who was pregnant and psychologically distressed, had been seeking fodder for a spiritually bankrupt life in Gurdjieff's teachings. Her sudden departure from a film set in Hollywood to Coombe Springs caused a flutter in the press. On arrival she 'recognized' the mansion as a building she had seen once in a vision, and Pak Subuh himself made an immediate impression on her. Her sensational cure following the latihan, and the subsequent delivery of a normal healthy child despite her doctors' gloomy predictions, really blew the cork out of the bottle. Reporters descended upon the house in droves, interviewing all and sundry, and providing that aura of indecision and flap which is the hallmark of the living presence of the press. The newspaper publicity in turn bumped up the numbers of those interested in, or merely curious about, Subud and in one month in 1957 nearly five hundred newcomers were 'opened' by the latihan, many of whom behaved in a bizarre and unpredictable fashion as a consequence. One man was so overcome by it all that he lay down and died shortly afterwards, an event which Subuh himself correctly described as a warning. Curiously the man's post-mortem showed no obvious visible cause of death, with heart, lungs, brain, etc., quite sound. It was all very mysterious, and those involved can be forgiven for responding emotionally. In that heady summer it must have seemed to the followers of Subuh that world attention was focused on the Surrey mansion, in whose grounds a nine-sided building was being erected—its central axis pointing to Fontainebleau where Gurdjieff was buried. Bennett's book, *Witness*, includes a photograph of the great American architect Frank Lloyd Wright gazing quizzically at the structure which was known as the Djamichunatra—the peculiar name being taken from Chapter 46 of Gurdjieff's *All and Everything*.

Subuh himself seems to have been agreeable at first to wearing Gurdjieff's mantle, and on the ninth anniversary of the latter's death a great crowd gathered to hear some of his weird music played by a full orchestra to scoring and orchestration specially created by the talented conductor Basil Cameron. Bennett and his colleagues were by now absolutely convinced that Subud was set fair to conquer the spiritual world, and as if to ram the message home a new comet—the Arland-Rouland—obligingly made its appearance in the sky. What else could this signal mean but 'The coming of Subud in the West?' A lengthy world tour drawing frenzied press attention in New York, Honolulu, Sydney, Mexico and other major cities followed, culminating in a giant International Congress at Coombe Springs in 1959 with four hundred delegates attending from forty countries, testifying to the meteoric rise to prominence of the movement.

It was in fact the high water point of Subud and its modest and rather self-effacing leader or prophet. The monk, who had spent so much of his time denying that he was a Messiah began to show far less enthusiasm for his supporters than many of them would have liked, and the ill-knit organization soon began to suffer from internal bickerings and personality problems. Before 1960 was out, the press had lost interest (no bad thing no doubt), the camp-followers began to depart from Coombe Springs, and Pak Subuh left England for sunnier climes. At the present time Subud has settled down to being a minor splinter of the occult fringe, an Eastern-style religion with some support in the West, but only a pale glimmer of its former blazing noon. Links with the remnants of the Gurdjieffians (themselves a disconcertingly inharmonious group) are now almost non-existent. A few years ago there was a brief flap when a teacher sacked from the Architectural Association claimed that the organization was being run by Subud followers. The Association's principal at the time, John Lloyd, while admitting that he was himself a Subud fan, denied that the AA was at all influenced by his private beliefs and, quite justly, asked what all the fuss was about anyhow. This incident apart, Subud seems no longer to be news and a recent count of its world-wide support has come up with a figure of some 15,000 souls who have at one time or another been opened by the latihan. In world terms this is not a large figure, and serves to remind one that for a cult to be successful, headlines alone are not enough. As for Mr Bennett, whose roving mind and extraordinary personal zeal seems to have been largely responsible for launching the Indonesian mystic amongst us, he is now journeying down a more firmly-trodden path. In 1968 he came a convert to the Roman Catholic church.

Like so many of the intellectually-orientated cults of today, Subud appealed almost entirely to the spiritually disenchanted and well-educated middle class. A less intellectually demanding cult is that of Hare Krishna, whose more ardent followers promenade in picturesque fashion in London's West End. In part popularized again by two of the Beatles, George Harrison and Paul McCartney (two young men who wielded immense social power in their day), the movement was actually founded twenty-five years ago by the Calcutta mystic, Swami Prabhupad, and introduced to the West in 1965. Its basic theme is that the teachings of the great Krishna, who was responsible for bringing the Bhagavad-Gita to mankind, have become corrupted and ignored to the general detriment of human affairs. The first and most essential step in the revival of the world's fortunes is the restoration of an awareness of Krishna and his teachings—which are indeed admirable as they demand an end to all wars, a spread of universal love and ample food and drink for all. Those inspired by these goals make it their business to draw Krishna's name to the attention of the world by chanting 'Hare Krishna . . . Hare Krishna' over and over again in public places. Hence the interesting processions of saffron-robed youths and girls, the men with shaven heads, the women with beauty spots on their foreheads, marching up and down Oxford Street and Portobello Road ringing bells and chanting the magic words.

In fact psychologists know that when a word or brief phrase is repeated over and over again, it begins to change its characteristics in a peculiar way. This is not merely a matter of tongue-twisting (Hare Krishna soon becomes pretty muddled on repetition) for a word played repeatedly on a tape recorder will soon distort perceptually in the most strange way. The word kettle, for example, will soon be heard as petal, castle, rattle, etc. This phenomenon, which is an exceedingly striking one and which anyone can demonstrate to himself with a tape recorder and an endless loop of tape, has been the subject of much serious psychological experimentation and it is believed to say something about the nature of the auditory recognition process. It is very likely that this odd effect is behind the evolution of the mantra, a phrase or prayer which, repeated over and over again, is supposed to acquire a special kind of spiritual significance. The mantra of course was around long before experimental psychologists, but it is interesting that at the end of the Beatles' LP *Sergeant Pepper,* as the stylus cycles and recycles in the final grooves, a single phrase —'Fug you fugging superman'—can be heard over and over again. Thus was the mantra incorporated in the pop culture of the late sixties.

The Hare Krishna groups, many of whom are *émigré* Americans appalled at their country's war in Vietnam, caused a minor sensation on their first appearance in London streets in 1968 and 1969 and attracted a fairly considerable following. A 'Temple' appeared in a rambling Victorian house in Bury Place with lectures and chanting taking place on Monday, Wednesday and Friday evenings and, as a special treat, a Love Feast every Sunday. At one stage the movement appeared to be getting so successful that the length of the lines of chanters in Oxford Street and elsewhere began to constitute a traffic hazard. Also the noise of the mantra chanted by so many enthusiastic voices drew complaints from the public, and at this point the Metropolitan Police began to take an interest. Whether due to this attention or not, from that point on the numbers of robed and shaven-headed figures on the march began to decline. Actually, the most probable explanation is not police persecution, but that the movement suffers from a basic lack of stuffing and an insufficiently dynamic leader—the Swami Prabhupad is a benign and self-effacing septuagenarian. Despite its claim to thirty-five temples in various parts of the world, and its touchingly acceptable overall policies, the 1970s are not likely to see the movement sweep the world as its followers hope and believe, and it seems likely to drift into a gentle and generally unnoticed eclipse. Perhaps its converts, after their first flush of enthusiasm, become gradually aware that though the world does undoubtedly need changing, the endless repetition of 'Hare Krishna' is never really going to do much to set this change in motion.

Western interest in oriental religions, from the sublime to the ridiculous, is probably motivated by the hope that somewhere hidden amongst the mantras and the prayer wheels, lies a great truth which is missing in orthodox European religions. This is strikingly attested by the ease with which almost any tale of wonder, no matter how tall and fantastic, is eagerly accepted by the populace at large—in particular when it has an Eastern setting. The most illuminating example of this is the story of that holy guru, Mr T. (for Tuesday) Lobsang Rampa, clairvoyant, pilot, doctor and lama from Tibet, who is also known to certain people as Mr Cyril Hoskins, formerly of 'Rose Croft', Thames Ditton, Surrey. What possible link, you may well ask, could there be between a Tibetan lama and a Mr Hoskins from homely Thames Ditton? To get the amazing answer to this question it is necessary to unfold the story of the psychic doctor from Lhasa and how he came upon us.

The saga commenced in 1955 when a simply dressed individual presented himself with part of a manuscript at the offices of the highly respected publishers Messrs Secker & Warburg in 99 Great Russell Street, London W.1. Mr Frederick Warburg recalled the occasion very well, later describing his visitor as 'short, slim, dark hair cut into a tonsure, penetrating eyes, aquiline nose . . . a most unusual figure'. The individual's dramatically fluctuating physical appearance must have been at least one of his unusual features, for in contrast to Warburg's description, a BBC producer, Mr John

Irwin, who invited the mystery man to tea at about that time, remembers him as a portly figure, 'over six feet tall, bald and clean shaven'. To confound matters even further, a contemporary photograph of the man, who had introduced himself as Dr T. Lobsang Rampa, reveals him to be heavily bearded. At this late stage, alas, we shall probably never know exactly how Rampa looked in those days. Suffice to say that this tall, short, portly, slim, bald, dark-haired and clean-shaven chap with a beard stated that he was a Tibetan lama, medically qualified and now residing in England. The manuscript he was offering was his autobiography, an account of his amazing life and upbringing in the land on the 'Roof of the World'. To back up his claims to being a doctor of medicine, Rampa flourished a gaudy document allegedly issued by the University of Chungking. At the time the publisher thought it a bit strange that the document was written in English rather than Chinese, but managed to push such thoughts aside. When Rampa then seized Mr Warburg's hand and, inspecting the lines on it, correctly told him his age and also that he had recently been engaged in a big criminal case (again correct), all doubts were apparently dispelled and the publisher agreed to read the manuscript. With this the author, who indicated that he was also known as Dr Kuon, departed, evidently satisfied.

A reading of the manuscript, which arrived in a series of chunks via the literary agency, A. M. Heath & Co., convinced Secker & Warburg that they were on to something pretty interesting. The story was a fascinating one, written with a distinct literary style, and full of fascinating, not to say fabulous material. It reads like a cross between James Hilton's archetypal novel *Lost Horizon* and Alexandra David-Neel's travelogue *With Mystics and Magicians in Tibet*. Similarities to the style of the latter, incidentally, are occasionally remarkable.

According to the narrative, the young Rampa, born of wealthy Tibetan parents in Lhasa, was singled out by astrologers at the age of seven for incarceration in a lamasery, there to be trained as a priest-surgeon. A vivid account is given of the hardships of his long apprenticeship within the monastery, during which time the ability to survive extreme physical hardship and develop latent psychic powers was taught. The whole is richly backed by colourful details of the weird Tibetan terrain and the strange social life within the monastery itself. Much is written of the human personalities involved, ranging from Rampa's personal tutor and guide, the Lama Mingyar Dondrup, to the Dalai Lama himself, with whom Rampa became on better than nodding acquaintanceship. The atmosphere is packed with tiny, and superficially convincing, items of local detail—the dung fires sending blue smoke into the mountain air, the wooden bowls of tsampa (a kind of barley porridge which was the monks' staple diet), bumpy rides on yaks across bleak mountain tops, bowls of steaming buttered tea, etc., etc. There are also more fantastic episodes, such as terrifying rides in man-carrying kites ('he lost his hold and went tumbling end over end down the rocks five thousand feet below, his robe whipping and fluttering like a blood-red cloud'), the development of various supernormal powers ('levitation can be accomplished and sometimes is, solely for the technical exercise involved. It is a clumsy method of moving around . . . the real adept uses astral travelling'), spine-tingling encounters with the Abominable Snowman ('It was pointing a hand at me, and uttering a curious mewing noise like a kitten. The head seemed to have no frontal lobes, but sloped back almost directly from the very heavy brows . . .'), and so on.

By far the most sensational section, however, was the chapter which gave the book its name. When only eight years old, the apprentice lama states that he was submitted to a drastic brain operation to open the inner 'third eye'—seat of all psychic powers and the organ mediating clairvoyance and telepathy. The operation, which was conducted without anaesthesia, was performed by medically trained monks and it makes quite harrowing reading. An instrument made of shining steel with a rotating, sharply toothed end was pressed up against his forehead and slowly drilled in. A clean sliver of wood 'treated by fire and herbs' and very sharp, was then poked gently into the hole made by the drill and pressed slowly but firmly into the brain. 'Suddenly I felt a stinging, ticklish sensation apparently in the bridge of my nose', writes Rampa. 'It subsided, and I became aware of subtle scents that I could not identify.' This was followed by a blinding flash and a moment of searing pain. 'You are now one of us, Lobsang,' the Lama Mingyar Dondrup told him. 'For the rest of your life you will see people as they are and not as they pretend to be'. Gazing round Rampa was amazed to see that all the men present were surrounded by a luminous golden flame—the aura. The opening of the third eye had been effected.

Whether it was the opening of the third eye, the bit about astral travelling or the meeting with the Abominable Snowman (a particularly popular newspaper character in the 1950s) that made the publisher's breath catch is not known, but Warburg himself admits to being fascinated if very dubious. The details *seemed* authentic, but never having been to Tibet it was hard to say. For all anyone in the publishing office knew, there might be no such a meal as tsampa, buttered tea might have made the average monk gag, and in Tibet dung fires might have been thought positively improper. The only thing to do seemed to be to call in some experts.

The response from these gentlemen was curiously uncertain. Some damned it more or less out of hand, others thought it had the stamp of authenticity. Warburg sent for Rampa/Kuon and confronted him with the criticisms. Come clean, he told the enigmatic author, admit the book is fiction and we'll still publish it—as fiction rather than fact. The other stood fast, stoutly insisting that his story was one hundred per cent true. Warburg then submitted him to a simple test in basic Tibetan which Rampa failed miserably. When taxed with this lack of comprehension of his native tongue, he produced an ingenious and undoubtedly irrefutable explanation. When a prisoner of war with the Japanese (a new development) he was tortured for secret information about his country. Rather than be forced into betrayal he used some of his amazing psychic powers and put a hypnotic block on his knowledge of Tibetan, which he had of course been subsequently unable to remove. At this point, Warburg recalled, a violent spasm shook the monk and he 'clasped his hand to his head as if in agony'—warning, if ever one was needed, that the psychological effects of the Japanese torture had been grave indeed and that it would be unwise to question further. Now deeply suspicious he decided to reject the manuscript, but changed his mind once again on pondering the book's unquestionably fascinating material.

From a sales point of view the decision to go ahead with publication was one of the best things Secker & Warburg had ever done. *The Third Eye*, when it hit the bookshops in 1956, became a literary sensation. Sales were enormous and, perhaps surprisingly, reviewers were apparently able to take a charitable view of the book's bizarre story and occasional inconsistencies. *The Observer*, no scatter-brained Sunday rag, described it as 'an extraordinary and exciting book, and a disquieting one'. *The Times Literary Supplement*, normally the scourge of fringe and sub-standard works, went into raptures, declaring, '. . . it comes near to being a work of art . . . even those who exclaim "magic, moonshine or worse" are likely to be moved by the nobility of the ethical system which produces such beliefs and such men as the author'. Against such praise, the occasional highly critical review, such as the icy blast delivered in the *Daily Telegraph* by Dr D. L. Snellgrove of the London University School of Oriental and African Studies, could of course make little headway. Within a year *The Third Eye* was a best seller in twelve countries, netting its author some £20,000 in royalties.

Intriguing though the tales of man-carrying kites and encounters with the yeti were, there is little doubt that the real spice in the book was the account of the physical opening of the third eye. For centuries the idea that human beings have a latent psychic centre with a physical analogue somewhere in the brain has fascinated all the fans of the occult. Some reptiles do in fact have a third eye, or the evolutionary remains of one, in the frontal region of the brain and its function seems to be to detect low energy radiation in the heat spectrum. Man himself has one apparently functionless organ, the pineal gland in a frontal/central position, which Descartes thought must be the point of interaction between soul or mind and body. This is still often believed to be the psychic centre in the folklore of modern Spiritualism. The opening of Rampa's pineal eye, and its sensational consequences as personally testified by the author, himself a medically qualified doctor, had been given the seal of approval of a world-famous publisher. This seemed to imply a victory over materialism of a totally new kind, a dramatic new weapon in the armoury of the world of the psychic and the occult. No doubt it was for this reason that *The Observer* considered the book to be disquieting.

For a brief moment the prosaic, materialistic view of the

world flickered slightly, but it was to be a brief moment and no more. Had *The Third Eye* been less well written, less favourably reviewed, less popular and backed by some small crank publisher, things might have remained where they were with Rampa's story sliding gently into the mists of the psychic anecdote. But it was not to be. The book was too good, too clever to be ignored. Too good in fact to be true.

The trouble started when a vague and rather mysterious academic body, generally described in the press at the time as a 'team of Tibetan scholars', decided that the time was ripe to have a closer look at the now world-famous doctor from Lhasa, and to examine his credentials rigorously, third eye and all. Their first step was to hire a Liverpool private detective, one Clifford Burgess, to trot around in his tracks, and find out what was what. When did he arrive in this country for example from the Far East? What did the Tibetan authorities—admittedly rather difficult to get hold of face to face—know of him, and of such figures as the Lama Mingyar Dondrup? And what about Rampa's war record (he had claimed he was a pilot in the Chinese air force fighting the Japanese) and of course his alleged medical qualifications?

It wasn't long before the industrious Mr Burgess began to come up with some extraordinary facts. In the first place he found that Tuesday Lobsang Rampa came not from Tibet, but from rural Plympton in Devon, where he was born in 1911 with the very un-Eastern name of Cyril Henry Hoskins. Far from studying medicine and learning to be a lama during the formative years of his life, he was assisting with his father's plumbing business. This, incidentally, was the closest he ever got to any kind of basic anatomy, and was a chore which he was glad to abandon on his father's death in 1937. In 1938, just about the time when Rampa claimed that he had been training as a fighter pilot (a vivid account—full of aeronautical howlers—of how he taught himself to fly is given in his second book, *Doctor from Lhasa*), Mr Hoskins was taking a correspondence course in time-and-motion study with a firm in Weybridge, later joining that same concern as a correspondence clerk. An inquisitive journalist on the invaluable *Psychic News*, Mr John Pitt, supplemented the apocalyptic findings of the detective Burgess by tracking down individuals who knew and clearly recalled Hoskins in those pre-war years. A

Mrs Ablett, from Weybridge in Surrey, remembered him when he was taking the correspondence course, and stated that he was full of strange stories about China where he claimed he had been taken as a child. She stated that he had been very interested in occult matters, would cast horoscopes for all and sundry and was a generally good conversationalist, if a bit inclined to tell contradictory stories about his past.

In the course of browsing around Weybridge, Pitt was able to track down one or two other people who distinctly remembered Hoskins/Rampa. A Mr and Mrs Boxall, who lived on the same estate as he had, knew him well. 'He told me, in 1943 or 1944, that he had been a flying instructor in the Chinese air force', Boxall told Pitt. 'He said he had been badly smashed up in a plane crash when his parachute failed to open.' This no doubt accounted for Hoskins's tendency at the time to limp around on a walking stick. A rather similar picture came from a Mr Lorraine Sutton of East Molesey who met Hoskins in 1948, shortly after he had changed his name to Carl Kuon Suo. By that time the former Hoskins was describing himself as Dr Kuon and saying that he was born in Tibet—a fact which rather surprised Mr Sutton somewhat since 'The Doctor' both talked and looked remarkably like an Englishman.

One can imagine the smiles which wreathed the faces of the team of Tibetan scholars when their sponsored detective work paid off so handsomely. One can also imagine the consternation within the offices of Messrs Secker & Warburg. Frederick Warburg, in a lengthy statement to the press, expressed amazement at the turn-up of events, but pointed out that they had been in two minds about publication in the first place. To cover themselves they had written a foreword to the book, pointing out that it was hard to corroborate and had been submitted to 'nearly twenty readers, all persons of intelligence and experience' for assessment. Their comments had been contradictory, but that was to be expected. 'Was there any expert', the publisher asked, 'who had undergone the training of a Tibetan lama in its most developed forms? Was there anyone who had been brought up in a Tibetan family' and could confirm or deny the domestic details given? Apparently there was not, and Secker & Warburg decided to publish and be damned, adding that the proviso that 'the Author must bear—and willingly takes—a sole responsibility for the statements made in his book'. Even when faced with the new material on Hoskins's West Country, as opposed to Himalayan, background, Warburg appeared to be still partially unconvinced. His press statement concludes:

> But is the truth, the whole truth, out? How could the man alleged to be Cyril Henry Hoskins, known to me as Dr Kuon [*author's note:* that same tall, short, slim, portly, bald, dark-haired, clean-shaven man with a beard who entered their offices for the first time two years ago] write a book which has thrilled the world? Why did he choose this subject? How did he gain the material? From where comes his writing ability, his superb imaginative power? Did he believe his own fantasies? Was he, perhaps, the mouthpiece of a true Lama, as some have alleged? To these questions an answer must be found.

Most people would be inclined to agree with Mr Warburg that an answer to these questions was indeed required, and amongst the most enthusiastic seekers after truth were a team of newspaper reporters who soon tracked down Hoskins/Rampa to a hideaway home outside Dublin, discovering in the process the usual air of unreality and razzamatazz that reporters seem to find wherever they go. The 'plumber's son who posed as a Tibetan Lama' was apparently living in 'a cliff-top villa' where the door was guarded by a 'pretty society woman' whom Rampa had 'recruited as a disciple' and parted from her 'old Etonian husband'. The woman, needless to say, 'sobbed as she told her story', and the husband later 'shouted to callers to go away' from his 'luxury flat in Kensington'. The *soi-disant* lama himself was less communicative altogether, being 'ill, it is said, in bed'. It was, one suspects, a diplomatic illness, for when one reporter refused to be discouraged and hung around making a nuisance of himself, he was suddenly favoured with the personal appearance of Hoskins/Rampa, bald head, robes and all, who delivered upon his visitor a blood-curdling Eastern curse. The journalist, a hard-boiled type, was not impressed at the time. He changed his mind a few weeks later when he emerged as the sole survivor of a spectacular air crash, and now considers the curse to have been a particularly valuable one.

Naturally enough the Rampa flap died slowly down with no one really much the wiser. In due course a second book, *Doctor from Lhasa* (published this time by Souvenir Press), appeared which totally lacked the panache of the first book, and in no way helped to clear up the mystery of the author's true origins. Then, in 1960, came a third book—*The Rampa Story*—in which Rampa decided to tell all, and confirm rumours that had been circulating for some time. It turned out to be a wonderful story, and a most ingenious explanation for the confusions and inconsistencies of the past.

It appears that those people who claimed to have remembered Cyril Hoskins working for a correspondence college and pottering around in the western suburbs of London, while T. Lobsang Rampa was gallantly battling it out with the Japs in the skies of China, were not suffering from serious delusions. There really *was* a Mr Hoskins, with occult leanings, a passion for oriental matters and gravely dissatisfied with his lot on earth. He had even experimented in astral travel, without too much success, as a means of escaping from the environs of Weybridge and his boring existence in those parts. Unknown to the lowly plumber's son (the narrative reveals) he was being watched from afar by a *real* adept at astral travel. This was none other than the versatile Tuesday Lobsang Rampa, who really *had* been trained as a medical lama, *had* had his third eye opened, *was* a pilot in the Chinese air force, etc., etc. Rampa's interest in Hoskins was not entirely altruistic. What was really ticking around in his wily oriental mind was a staggering plan to take over the other's body—with the present occupier's permission of course. Rampa's own body, because of his general unselfishness and bravery in the war years, had got a bit battered about, and even the wonders of Tibetan super-surgery were unable to restore it to an acceptable condition. Such is the nature of psychic transplants, however—unlike the simple physical transplants of such trifles as heart, lung or kidney—that they must be performed with both donor and recipient alive and kicking. And, as we have said, there is the other matter of acquiring the donor's permission.

One night, in pursuit of his goal, Rampa made a psychic journey from Tibet to London and appeared before the astonished Hoskins who was at the time making a feeble attempt at astral travel himself. The Englishman soon cottoned on to what was happening and confided in Rampa that there was nothing he would like better than to 'find release'. Since the other planned to use his body in a good cause (something to do with saving Tibet from the Communists) he could hand over at any convenient time. After some friendly chat the two individuals left the astral plane to return to their respective bodies, one in Lhasa, the other snoozing away in bed in 'Rose Croft', Thames Ditton.

A month after their first meeting the amazing swop—later to be the cause of so much confusion in the world of publishing—took place. Hoskins of course only knew of the impending swop when conscious in the astral plane. His waking self remained oblivious and continued to drag his unwilling body around from employment exchange to employment exchange in the hope of finding a job commensurate with his largely unrecognized talents. He cannot therefore have been expecting anything significant when on 13th June 1949, while perched in a tree photographing an owl, a branch broke casting him to the ground head foremost. Rendered unconscious, Hoskins found himself floating above his body, though attached to it by a silver cord. The world of Thames Ditton appeared to be in suspended animation—he had time to note a horse-drawn baker's cart nearby, quite motionless, one of the horse's forelegs poised in mid air. Then, gliding across the garden in truly spiritual fashion (i.e. several inches off the ground), he saw the figure of Lobsang Rampa. After some discussion in which the astral Rampa told the astral Hoskins that as a reward for giving up his body he would have a sizable Kharmic debt eradicated, the lama severed Hoskins's astral cord and watched as the astral body of the former Devon plumber and correspondence course clerk floated off to God-knows-where. Rampa now severed his own lengthy cord (it stretched all the way back to Tibet), connected the loose end to the end poking out of the body of the recumbent Hoskins, and promptly took over. Thus were the anomalies in the Rampa/Hoskins story explained. In his new body Rampa found that he retained his own (i.e. Tibetan) memories and brain power but next to no knowledge of Hoskins's life and knowledge. It is doubtful if he was missing much, and apart from one or two moments of embarrassment, such as when he failed to recognize his (i.e.

Hoskins's) wife, he soon adjusted and before long was writing the book which was to create such a sensation.

It is clear that there are three separate and exclusive ways of approaching the Hoskins/Rampa saga:

(1) The story is true, or very nearly true, from beginning to end and the body of Hoskins is now occupied by the mind or spirit of a Tibetan lama;
(2) The story is lies, or mainly lies, and Hoskins's mind still inhabits Hoskins's body, the only significant change being a marked improvement in Hoskins's bank balance;
(3) Hoskins is a deluded, or mentally disturbed individual whose fantasies about Tibet, the lamas and their great psychic powers, have now assumed the dimension of reality—perhaps precipitated by falling from the tree while photographing the owl.

It is impossible and unnecessary to give specific guidance to the reader as to which of the above hypotheses should be adopted—so much will depend on one's natural bias and tolerance of the unusual. It is fair to say, however, that most uncommitted people will consider the first of the three interpretations to be improbable in the extreme. It is also fair to say that many thousands of people the world over—probably hundreds of thousands—take the amazing story of the Tibetan lama and the surgical operation to open his clairvoyant eye as gospel. More than a decade after the rumpus it is clear that, while the *exposé* of the book has been more or less totally forgotten, the theme and central images created in the narrative have remained vividly in people's minds.

Before closing this episode, it may be worth noting the subsequent history of Hoskins/Rampa, who has for some time resided in North America. He has been a fairly prolific writer, stretching the lama topic out pretty well on the whole, the three books we have already mentioned being followed by *The Cave of the Ancients* and *Living with the Lama*. There have also been two books with an academic rather than anecdotal flavour, *You-Forever* (a special course in psychic development and metaphysics) and *Wisdom of the Ancients*, which is 'A Book of Knowledge, with special sections on breathing-exercises and diet'. There is also a lesser-known, considerably less scholarly work called simply, *My Visit to Venus*, in which

Rampa describes the occasion when he was favoured with a trip in a flying saucer. It seems to have been a dull ride, if one may say so, as the company was limited to two partially articulate Venusians known as The Tall One and The Broad One respectively. On Venus, a multi-coloured planet with sky-scraper cities constructed after the fashion of 1950s science fiction, a visit was paid to the 'Hall of Knowledge' where the histories of Poseidon, Lemuria and Atlantis are thoroughly documented. The book closes with a clear warning that this was but the first of many trips, thus implying future volumes in store.

Advertisements regularly appearing in the magazine *Fate* give one an interesting glimpse into the lama's recent non-literary activities. 'Let Dr Rampa instruct you in the art of meditation', one reads, 'gain the inestimable benefits . . . Peace, Tranquillity, Inner Harmony, Knowledge . . . that can be yours so easily'. To assist the seeker in his quest for Peace, Tranquillity, etc., one is urged to buy one or more of the following aids: long-playing record on meditation, featuring the voice of Dr Rampa himself ($4.95); meditating figure ($5.00); a meditation robe (made personally for you; indicate small, medium, large—$25.00); Rampa meditation incense, tube of assorted ($3.00); incense burner ($1.00); and Lobsang Rampa original prayers, a set of two ($1.00). Two original prayers for a dollar sounds pretty reasonable, but an even better bargain would seem to be the COMPLETE HOME MEDITATION KIT (includes all of above in handy storage and carrying case) for just $37.50, or two dollars off list price. Lest the above advertisement should give readers the impression that the saintly Dr Rampa is seeking earthly profits from his spiritual gifts, one should point out that a foreword to *My Visit to Venus* makes it absolutely clear that all royalties from sales are to be donated to the Save a Cat League of 245 West 25th Street, New York City.

Yesterday and Tomorrow

THE INTRUSION OF flying saucers and Venusians into Dr Rampa's *Weltanschauung* serves to remind one that the catalogue of ideas employed by cultists of all persuasions is a relatively limited one, and it is hard not to keep returning to analogies with science fiction. The immense staying power of the myths of Atlantis and Lemuria is another example of this apparently unquenchable human appetite for fairy stories dressed up as fact, and true to expectations they feature in a number of quasi-religious settings. In fact in this concluding chapter we will take a brief look at the power of the myth within this context, and put forward the suggestion that the most recent wave of the occult revival appears to be drawing upon such myths for its raw material.

Up to the present point we have seen that the focal areas for cultish interest are largely concerned with significant modern concepts or technology—science fiction, psychoanalysis, space travel, electronics and mysterious gadgetry of one kind and another. Often one finds a curious mixture occurring, as when flying saucer believers use spiritualist-like mediums to gather information about life on other planets, or when a yogi recommends the use of an electro-encephalograph as an aid to meditation. Radionics devices have also been used to test the efficacy of blessing plants or animals, and really multi-purpose characters like Lobsang Rampa seem to be able to turn their hand to anything within the very broad spectrum of the mystical world. In the quest for enlightenment via the numerous Eastern religions, the tendency to incorporate 'modern' notions and attitudes is also strong, the prime example, one feels, being given in the work and philosophy of Gurdjieff, whose position seems to be that of a genuine halfway house between the East and the West. Subud too, offers a tempting amalgam of the ancient traditions of Buddhist thought and important elements of the West's great contribution, psychoanalysis.

But where will things go from here? While Scientology and the various other cults mentioned have had strong expansionist phases, and may grow yet bigger as Christianity's hold on twentieth-century mind continues to weaken, there is a definite tendency for adherents to work their way through and out of these movements' limited set of ideas. In Scientology even Clears defect, and larger numbers fall by the wayside at earlier stages. If this *is* due to the fact that the repertoire of good ideas which most modern cults contain is easily exhausted, then any really successful systems to replace the old religions must either offer more ideas (which could be asking a bit too much) or alternatively offer ideas which are richer, deeper or more enigmatic. The key here may lie in the word enigma, for the great religions of the past have always thrived on their mysteries and have weakened once they become pressurized, or feel obliged to unravel them. As an aside one might mention how curious it is that the Church of England, for example, seems so cluelessly unaware of this simple fact, and devotes its energies to such self-defeating tasks as the new translation of the Bible which has succeeded in robbing the work of its vast and potent imagery. True mystery, however, still remains in some of the great myths of mankind, and there is growing evidence that it is towards these myths that many spiritually disenchanted young people are turning. The immense staying power of these myths suggests that they touch deep chords in the human psyche, as Jung was constantly observing, and while it is not the purpose of this book to try to explain their power, it is interesting to relate it to some of the fringes of religious belief. The lost continent of Atlantis, long sunk beneath the waves of the Atlantic Ocean (at about the time of the great biblical flood as some historians would have it) is one of the most enticing current sources of myths. People with archaeological inclinations even spend a certain amount of time hunting around under the sea for traces of sunken land, now and again bringing up the odd bit of broken pot to wave around in triumph. Even without any pretensions to archaeology one can actually communicate with some of the most important inhabitants of Atlantis, now flourishing in the spirit world after their unfortunate drowning incident. The group which seems to be the most successful at establishing this contact (there are many people at the game) are the appropriately styled Atlanteans, a slightly more than minor religious cult who meet regularly in London, with a few branches in other parts of England. Keystone of the cult is a beautiful red-haired former actress, Jacqueline Murray, who is prone to pop into a trance from time to time to find herself under the control of a High Priestess of Atlantis, one Helio-Arconaphus.

The Society, which was formed in April 1957, believes that spirits from the planet Venus were once incarnated into the bodies of primitive earth people of the caveman type in order to give them a kind of evolutionary prod. The outcome was the great culture of Atlantis which they hold to be the forerunner of all modern civilizations. The Society swiftly achieved a remarkable following, its nightly meetings in Earls Court being packed to capacity. The bulk of its audience incidentally was made up of actors and actresses (some famous and successful, some just 'resting'), and others directly involved in the stage such as managers and agents. This glamorous following, presumably sponsored by Miss Murray's own background on the stage, together with the theatrical profession's own traditional obsession with superstition and the exotic fringes of the occult, itself engendered public and press interest in the cult and for a week or two the Atlanteans and their beautiful leader became nationally known figures. Famous stars such as the great sex symbol of British movies in the thirties, Chili Bouchier, testified to the deep spiritual comfort derived from Helio-Arcanophus's trance addresses, while lesser figures, fresh from brief appearances on television soap opera serials or the latest detergent commercial, waxed enthusiastic over the benefits achieved from Atlantean spiritual healing. Branches of the group sprang up in Croydon, Bristol, Bromley, Brighton and even Cheltenham. A monthly magazine *The Atlantean* appeared, initially built around transcriptions of Helio-Arcanophus's latest messages, but gradually adding articles on astrology, yoga, health foods, flying saucers, palmistry, the end of the world and other topics dear to the heart of today's occultist. The ethos of the magazine as a whole is curiously academic. The authors of the articles tend to sport letters after their name and deliver their pieces, whether they be on 'Red Indians—their cults and their beliefs' or 'Radiation—the psychic ramifications', in a totally dead-pan fashion. Helio-Arcanophus's own messages seem generally good-natured and harmless, though they tackle very profound subjects indeed such as the population explosion ('Is there an occult answer?') or Power Centres of the Psyche ('From whence and whom do they originate?'). There is even a kind of psychic agony column conducted with almost contemptuous ease by 'Merlin', who tackles problems which would send Mary Grant, Suzie Knickerbocker and others of their ilk into spiralling nervous breakdowns. Faced with such questions as 'Will spacemen landing on the moon go mad?' (Answer: They won't, but might get 'euphoric'), 'Why do you call the planet next to the sun, Orpheus, when everyone else calls it Vulcan?' (Answer: Everyone else doesn't call it Vulcan), or 'What astrological sign rules Switzerland?' (Answer: Virgo), Merlin passes with flying colours. Only when faced with 'When will Christ come again?' does he admit that 'This is indeed the 64,000 dollar question' and opts out lamely by saying that such plans are 'well guarded by the hierarchy'.

Another enduring myth of the West concerns the legend of the Holy Grail, a mysterious chalice which features strongly in Celtic and early Christian legend. The vessel is sometimes said to have been the one used by Joseph to gather the blood from Christ's wounds at his crucifixion, or more frequently that held by Jesus in the Last Supper when the powerful ritual of the Mass was first set in motion. Legends in various countries claim that the Grail was in due course abducted from the Holy Land, and the British version holds that it ended up in England where it was entrusted to the care of one or other mystical society. The Arthurian legend connected with the Grail is well known and we will not retell it here, but merely remark that at the time of writing this book, the chalice is featuring increasingly as a cult object amongst many young people. The vague associations of Arthur with Glastonbury Tor, the fabulously sited mountain in the West Country, and the so-called Chalice Well in the valley between the Tor and the smaller hill beside it have even made the place a kind of modern pilgrimage centre, and in 1971 tens of thousands gathered for a magical weekend featuring a mixture of rock music and incantations of the Hare Krishna variety. There were also, as the newspapers swiftly noted, a lot of pretty girls without any clothes on. Glastonbury, as we mentioned in Part II, has recently also acquired a reputation as being an important marker beacon for flying saucers, and the myth is compounded and muddled by another discovery—that the Tor is the centre of a vast zodiac, surrounded by ancient astrological signs marked out in the ground for miles around. These are easily spotted from a flying saucer, and may even be seen—assuming one has the right kind of eyesight—from a high flying aircraft.

Another interesting and on the whole youthful audience for mythology of one kind or another could be found amongst the readers of the magazine *Gandalf's Garden*. This appears to have folded, along with the Chelsea coffee bar and hippy commune from which it was published, quite recently but it is worth referring to as a good example of present cultish trends. It is also a particularly suitable point at which to end the book, for the good-natured outlook of the new wave of occultists, as exemplified by the readers of publications like *Gandalf's Garden*, is one of the more hopeful messages that we can find to spell out.

There can be few readers, incidentally, who fail to recognize the allusion in the magazine's title to the tedious wizard in J. R. R. Tolkien's saga *The Lord of the Rings*. This immense work, three volumes stuffed with the adventures of a group of semi-human hoofed creatures known as Hobbits who between them manage to save the world from the evil hegemony of a magician-dictator, has become one of the publishing bonanzas of the century. The travels of the Hobbits, who have names like Bilbo, Frodo, etc., across an imaginary land known as Middle Earth, and their encounters with trolls, werewolves and giant spiders, are recounted in immense detail, and stacked with cross-references, glossaries, maps, notes on dialect, genealogical tables of the reigning dwarf monarchs, regional folk songs, poetry, etc. The author, a distinguished academic and historian, tells his tale with panache, though racked with whimsy, and it is not hard to see its appeal to the schizophrenic latent within us all. This is the quirk that leads small boys to document train numbers and adults to collect stamps, butterflies or plot the tramway system of Amsterdam. No doubt Professor Tolkien had a shrewd idea of what a powerful obsessive spring his saga would tap in the minds of his readers, but it is doubtful if he could have foreseen the speed with which his entirely legendary figures would acquire a strange kind of reality, a weird sort of living presence which leads people to write 'Bilbo Baggins is a queer' or 'Frodo is alive and well and living in Argentina' on lavatory walls, and which gained for the wizard Gandalf a substantial number of write-in votes in the 1968 American presidential election. At one level such anthropomorphisms are funny, and at another they are sad, for it is surely an acrid comment on the world of the late twentieth century that so many of its inhabitants yearn for a universe populated by Hobbits, elves and gnomes in preference to that run by their fellow men. But perhaps what the world really does need is a bit of mystical shake-up, and electing a genuine wizard to the White House might sort things out in double-quick time. The readers of *Gandalf's Garden* would be the first to agree on this point, for their magazine described itself as 'the cry of the Now Generation seeking an Alternative to the destructive forces of today's world'. It was the 'magical garden of our inner worlds, overgrowing into the world of manifestation . . . a wellspring of love and anguish that those with searching thirsts may drink thereof'. The publication, as the above extracts imply, was written in a simple-minded, good-natured flowery style, and packed with articles allegedly reflecting the Mystical Scene. These included the obligatory features on Buddhism, the Swedenborg Society, Subud and (a particular favourite) Atlantis. There were also pieces on the allegorical significance of Tolkien's trilogy, an apologia for the failed black magician Aleister Crowley, and even a do-it-yourself brain surgery article in which the author gave handy tips on how to open the third eye (*à la* Lobsang Rampa) by physically trepanning a hole in one's cranium. This latter was counted as a bit much even by the broad-minded editors of the magazine who added a footnote to the piece sternly warning: 'We do not advise anyone to try trepanning themselves, since even a fractional miscalculation could cause death or insanity.' Readers were advised to try yoga instead for a less drastic permanent high.

The strongly pacifist tone, the open-minded interest in eroticism, the search for alternative socially acceptable drugs to alcohol and the moralistic trend towards vegetarianism were striking features of *Gandalf's Garden* and for this reason its social importance should not be underrated. Admittedly the explicitly underground publications such as *It, Oz* and *Ink* exhibit some of the above trends, but whereas the latter seem always to be viewing the world through clenched teeth, the *Garden* exuded an aura of tolerance and compassion which, even if naive, is both credible and commendable. Furthermore where *Gandalf's Garden*—significantly it called itself the 'Free Press of the Overground'—and equivalent specialist publications, from *Cosmic Voice* to *The Atlantean,* differs from the Underground publications, is in its over-riding emphasis on mysticism, the occult and the spiritual nature of Man. The Underground, both in its press and in the philosophy of its followers, is essentially pessimistic. Its anti-establishment views are based on the assumption that organized society and with it no doubt the whole world, is doomed to destruction. In its heart of hearts the Underground is nihilistic, believing that when the system collapses there can be nothing really to fill the void.

The message of *Gandalf's Garden,* and of virtually all the cults we have discussed in this book, is almost the opposite. Man, they proclaim, does have a future, and a future far better, far clearer than the one predicted by orthodox politicians, clergymen and technocrats. For some it is a future where the secrets of life energy—orgone—are harnessed and utilized in the general interests of mankind and the total orgiastic experience; for others it may lie in the coming of Christ anew (in a spaceship) attended by a host of saint-scientists to sort out our desperate problems; for others the future path lies through the evolution of the mind via such systems as Scientology and its various imitations; or perhaps it lies in the tapping of psychic power through partly understood technologies such as radionics. Yet again, it could be that the key to the future will come to us from the past, from those wise priests and sages who sank with Atlantis and whose wisdom yet can be passed on by a chosen few. The list is a long one, and only partly tackled in this book. Hopefully, however, the tackling has been comprehensive enough to make the point that the cults, while revealing themselves as insubstantial and occasionally eccentric to the point of being purely funny, nevertheless do their level best to fill a serious vacuum—a vacuum which man has created by his own diligence and scientific curiosity. The truth is that we have been too clever for our own good, and have let our technical mastery of science move far, far ahead of our philosophical and social expertise. With contemptuous ease Man has kicked away from under his feet the bases of his age-old truce with the unknown—the multiple belief systems which we know of as religion. Now that the truce has been broken, the glowing uncertainties of the Universe and the enigma of Man's existence and purpose are revealed only too clearly. It is little wonder that millions of uncertain souls, appalled by this, have striven to make peace again. Many have succeeded, but the terms of the truce have of course been changed. And that is what this book has been about.

Index